NATIVE MET HOW

Improving Posterity

Jay Miller, PhD

© 2019

THANKS

Abundant Thanks to Isabel Arcasa, Larry & Adeline Fredin family, Jerome Miller, Mary Marchand family, Sue Matt, CB Suszen Timentwa, Chillowhist Jim, Cecilia Juliann Timentwa, Leslie, Jim, Elaine Timentwa, TB & Pearl Charlie, Carolyn Schmekel, Patrick Twohy SJ, Mike Fitzpatrick SJ, Bruce Morrison, Crystal Miller, Guy Moura, Marilynn Moses, Barry George, Gary Mundinger, Richard Ries, Charles Monty Nelson, David Rice, Mark DeLeon, Melvin Lucei, Rex & Angela Buck, Bill & Susan Layman, Chuck Borg, Pam Amoss, Carl & Charlene Gustafson, Brian & Suzie Holmes, Fred van Ronk, Darby Stapp & Julie Longenecker, Robert Walls & Laura Dassow Walls, Jack & Deborah Fiander, Blue, Sherry, and Sanger Clark, John Adams & Mary Laya, Florence Hawley Ellis, Mary Elizabeth Smith, Cynthia Irwin-Williams, Carol Eastman, Viola Garfield, Erna Gunther, John & Luceen Dunn, Glenn & Dorothy Heck Williams, Andrew & Nancy Core, Roland Wildman, Marilyn Richen, Tammy Jackson, Ann Schuh, Bob & Chris Keyes-Back, Tom & Donna Steinburn, Ellen Lowe, Nancy Griffin, Laurel Sercombe, Bill Seaburg, Gary Lundell, and, especially, Monday Nite.

Vic Kucera mapped and questioned in many languages and formats, gracious and intrigued throughout. Kurt Reidinger heroically tackled proofing, researching, solving, fishing, and outreach with enthusiasm and aplomb.

Methow portraits by Frank Matura, courtesy Okanogan County Historical Society
Jim # 7329, CBST family # 6405.

To all, we lift our hands in thanks!

Native Met How pulls together past interviews and publications to provide a scholarly overview to aid future researchers, so a publication's original page numbers are shown within [square brackets], with added information set between {curved brackets} and all native words in *italics*. Less reliable linguistic *spellings start with *, ?? are unknowns, ~ indicates alikeness synonyms.

Contents

Contents

Contents

Contents

Contents

Maps:...

          Methow v
          MidColumbia 31
          Plateau Tribes 109
          Place Names 145

Photos:..

          CB Suszen Timentwa, Chillowist Jim 6
          Norman Lerman 60   team 66
          CB Suszen Timentwa, Chillowist Jim, Moses 92

Figures:..

          disk 104
          Rock Drawings 127
          Methow Alphabet 141
          Schematic 159

    #1-131 footnotes

Map

Methow Drainage Now

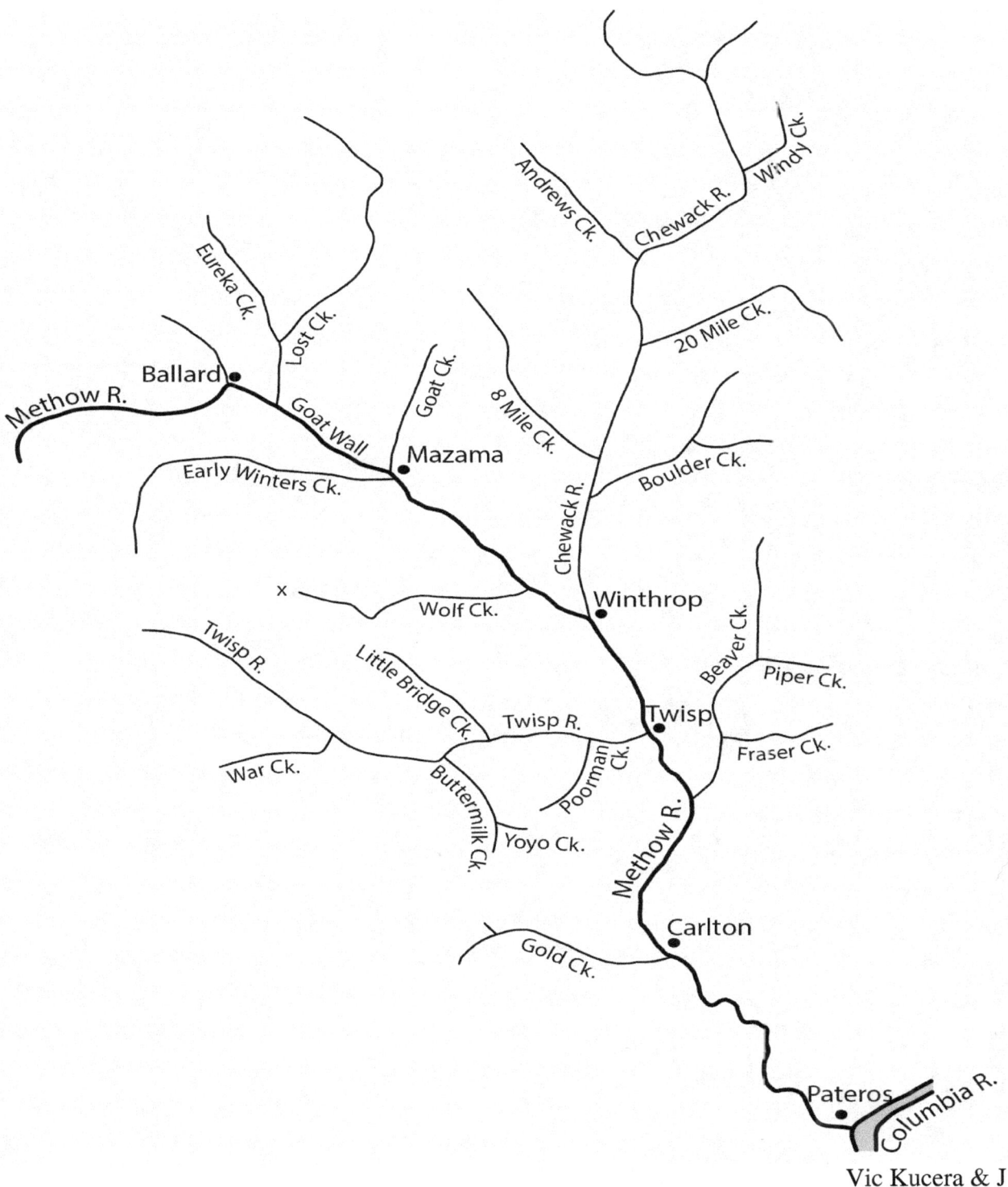

Vic Kucera & J

Cf Maps on pages 31, 109, 145

MET HOW[1]

Natives ~ Spirits ~ Abodes

A gift overdue, we herein review a century of place-based ethnography focused on the Methow peoples living on a major river flowing into the middle Columbia River of the Plateau area of Native North America. Known among scholars for its strong, creative, literate leaders and complex linguistic history, popular understanding has been slow to develop, opposed by some self-serving hostile locals denying any native presence, historical trauma, and holocaust.

Once noted for farming and locale, today the Methow Valley is a popular resort area, where many Seattle families have second homes. In summer, they drive east across the spectacular North Cascades Highway (SR 20) until it is closed by deep winter snows, so families drive east then north along the banks of the Columbia River. Further to the east, today's native Methows live on homesteads and trust lands under the jurisdiction of the Colville Reservation.

In this book, after addressing the river directly, we meet these lands via stories, as is proper; before expanding overviews of Methow lifeways outward to encompass the entire Plateau; finally turning to classic research concerns for the area, a necessity because Methows have rarely been considered in their own Methowcentric terms, but instead been subsumed among neighboring Psk^waws, Wentatchi, Okanogan, Colvilles, or Plateau Salish.

Watershed

The Methow (/mɛt.haʊ/ River, 70 miles long, flows into the Columbia River in northern central Washington state, with a watershed of 1,890 square miles (4,900 km^2) and a population today of 5,000 people. Its basin abounds in relatively pristine habitats as it mostly drains remote national forests, particularly the Pasayten Wilderness. Earlier settler economy based on farming, mining, and orchards has shifted to recreation and tourism, especially international winter sports. Indeed, near its headwater streams, Cathedral Creek approaches British Columbia, Canada.

This river is named "after" the native tribe, now among the Confederated Tribes of the Colville Reservation, and refers to "sunflower (seeds)". Its other name more common among Salishan tribes refers to its choice bitterroots. In 1841, US officials named it "Barrier River". In 1853 George Gibbs called the river Methow or Barrier.

Its tributaries include Twisp River, Cedar Creek, and Early Winters Creek, flowing from high mountains such as Golden Horn, Tower, Cutthroat Peak, Snagtooth Ridge, Kangaroo Ridge, Early Winter Spires, and includes Methow Pass, Twisp Pass, and the route of State Route 20 ~ North Cascades Highway. The Pacific Crest Trail traces the upper reach of the Methow River, after it turns east into the Methow Valley near Mazama, with tributary streams at Robinson Creek and Lost River. In the Methow Valley, between Mazama and Winthrop, are Early Winters Creek, Cedar Creek, Goat Creek, and Wolf Creek. The Chewack River enters at Winthrop,

---

[1] The title *Native Met How* conveys how it is usually said in English (without a TH sound), and in Salishan as *mitxaw*, derived from the word root $mk^w\mathʔ$ = balsamroots, locally called sunflowers, akin to a word root for snow = $mk^{'w}$ since they bloom as winter leaves and spring arrives. *Improving Posterity* reflects its long gestation and far future hopes.

draining most of the Pasayten. Along the lower 50 miles between Winthrop and Pateros, the river drops 1800 feet, squeezing from two miles wide through a narrow canyon. Twisp River joins from the west draining elevations south of Washington Pass and the eastern slopes of Sawtooth Ridge, with some of Washington's highest peaks, such as Star and Mt Bigelow. Downriver from Twisp, the Methow flows past Carlton to its mouth at Pateros, where it enters Lake Pateros, the impounded Columbia River behind Wells Dam[2], which flooded out Indian homesteads, farms, and orchards.

When David Thompson came down the Columbia in 1811, he noted a healthy fishery at the Methow, but early development and a 1915-29 power dam at Pateros blocked most runs. Hatcheries faltered at Twisp (1899) for coho silver salmon, moving down to Pateros (1915) to gain sport fish broodstock ahead of irrigation ditches (though native weirs were also blamed), and at Winthrop for sockeye (1945-57) to mitigate Grand Coulee Dam. Species now preserved at UW in the Burke Museum Fish Collection, formerly in School of Fisheries, include Methow-collected western brook lamprey (1931), Twisp River juvenile coho (1937), and Spectacle Lake sockeye salmon (1920). Bull trout (*Salvelinus confluentus*) native to Lake Chelan were last seen 16 July 1957 when two were collected for Oregon State University Museum. Once confused with Dolly Varden, they *are* a distinct species. The Grand Coulee Fish Maintenance Project (GCFMP) of 1939 redirected spawning into tributaries below the new dam, which damaged much of their past quantity and ended the great fishery at Kettle Falls.

The natives living in the valley for thousands of years are collectively known as Methows, from a native term. Along with closely related tribes throughout the region, they spoke a language of the Interior Salishan linguistic family, but provided a transition between the two neighboring dialect chains spoken along the upper Columbia River.

To the south ~ downriver ~ lower were the Chelan, Entiat, Psk^{w}aws (~ Wenatchi), and Snkyuse (~ Moses Columbians) whose dialect featured the "a" (ay) vowel. To the north ~ upriver ~ upper (and east) were the Okanogan, Nespelem, Sanpoil, Colvile {spelled with 2 Ls}, and Arrow Lakes, where the corresponding vowel was "i" (ee). Today these tribes are components of the nearby Colville {spelled with 3 Ls} Reservation.

Given the extent and isolation of the Methow drainage, they long remained distinct from either chain, elder TB Charlie suggested that aboriginal Methow was the parent or core group,

---

[2] AZ Wells bought 150 acres in 1910 of Moses Allotment 20 with the remaining 300 acres farmed by heirs Jerome and Henry Miller until flooded out by the "Wells" dam; the brothers were forced off the allotment in the 1960s and merely compensated for grazing land instead of the valuable fields and orchards actually there (Borg 2015).

AZ (Alfred Zebulon) Wells (1869-1950) was born in Missouri, grew up in South Dakota, and married Emogene Slick in 1896. They settled in Wenatchee in 1902, where he formed Wells and Morris Co with his nephew, Al Morris, until 1914, then ran Wells and Wade Hardware and Fruit Company until 1937. Active in the Wenatchee Commercial Club, he helped raise funds for the Columbia River Bridge, created the AZ Wells Foundation for nonprofit community causes, and is still honored in the Spirit of AZ Wells annual award from Central Washington Hospital Foundation, In 1919, The Wells bought the landmark Cobblestone Castle, renaming it Wells House, lived there for 30 years, then donated it to become Wenatchee Junior College. Wells died in Florida at the beginning of their around the world trip, and his wife died at 98 in 1973.

distinguished by the use of another vowel in place of Columbian "ay" and Okanogan "ee." Presumably, this aboriginal dialect became extinct after many epidemics decimated Methows.

Examining native place names in the Methow, Dale Kinkade[3] suggested a shift such that that they were originally closer to the downriver dialects, they later spoke using upriver forms. Indeed, a winter town on the Okanogan at Malott = *ləplup* ("dry, dry"), on the Chillowist = *səlax^w i'st* trail to the Methow, suggests how this shift intensified.[4] Methows also desired to maintain their own independence from the growing Columbian confederacy of horse herders under Split Sun who hunted bison on the northern Plains of Montana, on Blackfeet lands.

Met how Vow

Almost forty years may seem too long a delay to fulfill a promise, but life and lures have a way of getting in the way of vows taken in earnest at a moment of youthful resolve. Yet hindsight and experience have their advantages, as well as benefits. Since my 1980s editing of Mourning Dove's writings, I have sustained a slow and steady interest in the Plateau, demonstrated by a chapter on Colville tribes for the Smithsonian, but had not pulled together materials focused on the Methow itself, volunteered by elders concerned with leaving a record.

Our initial contacts were serendipitous and propitious, with elders asking for help with their own laborious efforts, propelled by fading memories of native life in the Methow. Once set aside as their own "Moses" reservation, its continuing rural isolation surrounded by protected federal lands has encouraged native use, at least seasonally. Settlers tolerated their return to fish, hunt, and berry; but never learned their names or families. There was enough for all. Today, however, some old timers in the valley deny natives were ever there, ignorant of the forced exit which drove Methows from their own homeland on to the Colville reservation.

The precipitating motivation was 14-15 June 1979 hearings were held at the Colville Agency on joint Senate Resolution 102, The Native American Right to Religious Freedom Act, passed by Congress on 11 August 1978. Many Colville religious leaders used this occasion to express their sense of resentment over past injustices, but also as a forum for their relief that their native religions were now legally protected.

Methows also had a family precedent in that the father of the key elder had worked with a graduate student in the 1950s when the GI Bill and post-war enthusiasm led returned soldiers into careers of scholarship. Designated a "lone arrow" as a child, one with curious interest and keen memories to absorb tribal lore, he was ready to review and share his knowledge, bolstered by support from other elders of his tribe and generation, especially a respected woman neighbor.

Unaware at the time, my edits and rewrites of his material prepared me, a decade later, to take on the voluminous manuscript pages typed, fortunately, by the native woman whose pen name was Mourning Dove. There again, I had the help of earnest elders, especially a brother, Charlie Quintasket, who read through her stories while they were in draft, and a classmate, Isable

---

[3] Dale Kinkade, On the Identification of the Methows, detailed in our last chapter on Research. Not all Methows moved to Colville. The Sam family split between Colville and Yakama, where they gained treaty rights once denied to Colvilles because Gov Isaac Stevens never came back as promised and instead fought Yakamas in the Treaty War of the mid 1850s.

[4] The Loup Loup {'dry dry'} Highway 20 paved over this Chillowist trail from Malott into the Methow. Behind the JR campground, a marshy love medicine (hellebore) grew.

Arcasa, who was then about to celebrate her 100th birthday.

Patience reigned rather than reasonable procedures. Determination conflicted with my advice and suggestions. Knowledge had to be written down, even when basic schooling was inadequate for the task. My repeated offer to provide tape recorders and then transcribe the narrative led nowhere. Granddaughters typed drafts verbatim, sometimes compounding text obscurities until we met and verbally reviewed the text and intended message.

The solution became to take the typescript, review it with the elder, in his own words, and then to rework it into something approaching standard written English, often shortening its length. This was not because of rhetorical repetitions, everything expectably done five times by Colville narrators, so classic in native texts, but because the narrative became much more grammatical and straight forward. Circuitous narrative was squeezed into linear sequence, albeit embracing the treachery inherent in any written expression.

Particularly compelling, throughout this process, was the grand sweep of the project, no less than an overview of the Methow world, its significant places, and fates of its spirits. Stories read in obscure reports now jumped off the page infused with life. Therefore, we begin with crucial place-based stories which inform present conditions, actions, and events. Some repetition has been inevitable, reinforcing understanding by widely expanding perspectives and contexts.

Methows in Person

JT[5] was famous for her native-tan gloves, preferred by local farmers during hay bailing. Her home included a creek that flowed beside an old wringer washing machine where she soaked deerhides in liquefying deer brains, using ages-old tanning techniques. As she always said, each deer includes the exact amount of tanning materials in its own brain for its own hide. Placing the brains and hides together in the tub had the advantage of using the wringer above to restore the fluid in the tub while the hide itself was wrung out. Then it was stretched out to dry in preparation for cutting out patterns to sew up, especially gloves. Since these were mostly work gloves, decoration was minimal, maybe a few colored lines of sewing machine stitches. They felt velvety soft and smelled slightly smoky, but were tough and ready for hard work. In time bailing wire cut into them and they had to be replaced, but, in general, they proved the value of brain tanning on hides. In addition, families fed on venison.

JT kept house for two sons, who ran their small ranch in the hills. On the flats, near the entrance to their road was the cemetery of graves relocated from famous Fort Okanogan when its sites were flooded behind a dam across the Columbia River.

She was firm in her convictions, traditional as much as possible. On one memorable occasion, I dropped by to chat and was told she was down the road at the clinic in a local town and her family was apprehensive for the doctor and nurse. I drove to the clinic, where a visibly relieved staff took me into room where she was waiting and resistant. I immediately became identified as her nephew and was allowed to stay as a young Anglo doctor and nurse made their checks and measurements. Defensive and unsure what they were doing, she was not entirely cooperative. She was in a gown and hints of her undergarments showed they were repurposed cotton flour sacks, in pioneer style. Afterwards, I drove her home, since her family had taken her

---

[5] Initials replace names as safeguard, since Mourning Dove continues to draw embarrassing visitors to Colville. The rez will know who these elders were, and that suffices for now.

down and went home to wait for a call to pick her up. Her sons welcomed her home and thanked me, while she whispered to them "he saw nothing" in defensive modesty. On other occasions, such clinic visits ended less calmly, which is why the family took her down and waited. Ambulances seemed to be for hospitals and emergencies.

TB lived on a family homestead, also near a local cemetery. His household was much more fluid and dynamic, with many children coming and going. A Shaker altar just inside the front door indicated the family's faith affiliation, especially through his Yakama wife. The household blended families from several marriages, and disruptions due to various chemical dependencies held in check by Shaker services.

As elder of the family, TB cleared out a space for us to work on the kitchen table, around the corner from the flow of constant traffic. Our constant tussle was invariably between literate and oral traditions, with TB insisting on writing out his topic, with interference from native language, and my suggesting that he tape what he wanted to write so it could be transcribed and edited for clarity. During the ensuing discussions, I better understood what he was trying to write and so could recompose his texts. On at least one occasion, not trusting myself to transcribe his esoteric Salish vocabulary, we sat with the maven Salish linguist who wrote down the words as TB said them.

Many of the Salish, especially the men, went by nicknames bestowed by some event in their lives. TB went by initials in lieu of his full name Theuphile, given by the local Jesuit during the week long encampment at St Mary's Mission, now Pascal Sherman School, outside Omak. In addition to processions, devotional services, feasts, and sermons, the priest was fond of providing names, often derived from Latin, to attendees. If someone already had a personal name, he might decide they needed a middle one. Usually these names soon had native or Red English pronunciations that obscured their original forms. In other cases, such as TB, they resorted to initials.

SM, confirmed Catholic, taught instructional and catechism classes for Omak students in the public schools. She may have also taught at Pascal Sherman nearby. As a girl she went with her family on horseback into the Methow, mostly to pick berries to dry and store, and may not have been aware of men hunting game, which seems likely. They did bring along store bought staples like flour, sugar, coffee, and salt in huge pack baskets, hand made and cherished for their durability, attached on either side of a horse. On the return, these were refilled with dried berries, and other products such as weaving bark and roots.

Two other figures loomed large in our project, only occasionally by name. These were leaders of a prior generation who were generous with their knowledge and skill. Both left details in other records, especially a two month field school.

A key Colville Okanogan leader of the early 1900s was CB Suszen Timentwa, who served as an outstanding source for this 1930 field school among the southern Okanogan under the auspices of the Santa Fe Laboratory of Anthropology. For project director, Leslie Spier (1938: 4), he was "an intelligent person with mystical tendencies; prone to formalize everything into a cosmic scheme centering around his religious ideas." All in all, of course, this is the hallmark of an effective native leader.

Later, he became a founder of the Indian Shaker Church at Mallott and a forceful advocate for the traditionalists, spearheading opposition to the Indian Reorganization Act of

1934. In a letter, Christine Quintasket ~ Mourning Dove said CB was writing a Bible, probably an Okanogan account of creation (see below). His family gained prominence in 1813 when an ancestress named Sally married Alexander Ross (1904), the fur trader at Fort Okanogan who later became prominent in the Red River Settlement (modern Winnipeg). "Suszen" was derived from a baby name, while CB remained unexplained until a kinswoman remarked it stood for "cow boy" because he was proud of his bronco riding.

Among their short biographies of the fieldschool's teachers, Leslie Spier (1938: 4-5) wrote:

Suszen Timentwa, 46 years old, present chief of the Kartar band, was born at Okanogan town. Ancestry is a mixture of Moses-Columbia and Kartar on his mother's side for several generations, father was Chelan. Intelligent person with mystical tendencies, prone to formalise a cosmic scheme centering on religious ideas.

More will be said of the field school later under Researches because it set a base line for academic study. A key informative source was:

Chilowhist Jim {*Lakakin*} was born at Entiat about sixty-five years ago. He came to Malott as a boy of eight or younger. His mother lived at Malott, his father at Entiat. He has been on the Methow River a great deal and still goes there often. {Jim and his wife Susanne had a dozen children, many of whom did not live; their daughter Lucy Sheolum[6] Jim married CB Suszen.}

Okanogan County Histl. Soc., Okanogan, Wash.
Fig. 7. Chilliwhist Jim, a Methow shaman. He wears beaded leggings, moccasins, and belt; his cloth shirt is decorated with fur strips. His feather headdress was a sign of his spiritual power. Photograph by Frank Matsura, 1903–1913.

Because our own focus is the native Methow, these elders provide experiences which were very much place based. The Goat Wall figured in many of their accounts as a landmark. Only when we visited it did I learn of the "modern" development that banished its ancient resident spirit. Indeed, I came to know the Methow through stories, epics of creation and geography, instead of geology and linear written history.

We are about to challenge the adage "You can't step into the same river twice," by repeatedly reviewing what seems to be much of the same terrain, but actually is an increasingly wider, better reconnaissance, with greater depth, insight, and understanding. Our initial guides are native stories and world epics, fifty years apart, set in local places, and typically illustrating what *not* to do with vivid negative examples, especially when Coyote is concerned. Outcomes and consequences are permanent, preparing the way for humans "coming soon", who here descend not from apes but rather from a special protoBeaver.

Though these stories seem to be randomly told, they do have an internal logic of chronology. There is a God, there is a need to populate space, animals are named, Coyote needs and gets special consideration, and Coyote makes the world ready for humans, who are sliced from a mythic Beaver, except for a particularly fierce tribe reconstituted from his blood.

---

[6] Her second name evokes that of the powerful Methow shaman *syolem* mentioned in our place name section.

Fifty years separate these versions, but those of 1930 clearly inform those of 1980, with more spiritual abstractions in the former than the concreteness of the latter. The *Law* of the earlier is objectified as the all important *"pole"* of the later. Such rods pervade all religious contexts, including the special stick prepared immediately after a vision to hold up a specific emblem of its success.

Origin of People[7]
1930

In the beginning, as in the Bible, God created the world, and created animals. He made laws for the animals. He said, "I'm going to leave. In one year, I will come back. I will give you a law if you will all not think in your own thinking for only yourselves. I've given you laws for one year; I'm going to make a human next time I come. If all you creatures think in your own thinking, you are going to be lost."

The creatures scattered and learned from God. The scattered creatures knew what each other thought. Finally the creatures knew that it is time to meet God again. The creatures said, "We know enough from God, but tomorrow there will be a person-to-be [human] in charge of us." Finally in the evening, the one we call Coyote thought a while, "I am smarter than all the other creatures. Whoever gets the first name of the creatures, he will be the leader of all; he who gets the last name will be worthless. That is the law God gave and left for one year."

Finally it is the evening before the meeting and Coyote thinks, "I am the smartest creature. I am going to run and get the first name." He had forgotten the law and was thinking with his own mind. He thinks, "I won't sleep tonight. I will be ready to run in the early morning and be the first man to get a name."

At midnight, he was sleepy. He walked around, and about morning he was awfully sleepy. He was thinking wrong and was going to lose the person. Coyote had learned that when his eyes closed, he would sleep. He thought, "How can I keep my eyes open all the time?" He put little sticks across his eyes to keep them open all the time. He did that and thought, "Now I can sit by a tree, I can't sleep because my eyes are open. I will be first to meet God."

Towards morning, he went to sleep with his eyes open. About noon, he awakened. He felt the sun and was blind from the sun in his open eyes. About nine in the morning, the creatures had met. God named them all. Then, God said, "That is all of you creatures?" "No," they said, "one is not here." "There is one name left. When he comes that is his name."

Blue Jay said, "I don't like my name. I want to be Eagle." Meadow Lark said, "I don't like my name. I want to be Grouse." God said, "No, it is already done."

Coyote woke up and could, not see anything. His eyes were dry. He crawled around a while. He heard a noise and thought, it was water. He thought he would wet his eyes. He crawled there, washed his eyes, and saw again. He looked up. It was afternoon. He thought,

---

[7] Told by Suszen Timentwa to Lucy Velpha W Walters (later Deacon). The name of recorder herein follows the name of the narrator. Walters, from Nebraska, disappears from academic records after she was dropped from UW Anthropology without explanation. In the 1930 US census she is in the Spier Gunther home, probably helping to care for their two young sons. See p161 Appendix A; cf Internet Archive *The Sinkaietk or Southern Okanogan*.

"Now I will be a worthless creature." He started running to the meeting place. God knew about it. When he got there, he saw all the creatures sitting in a circle and he saw God too. He said, "Have you named all these creatures?" God said, "Yes, I named then all. There is one name left. That is yours now."

Coyote said "What is the name?" God said, "It is Coyote (*snk'əl'íp*)." Coyote said, "I don't like that name Coyote myself." He looked at Grizzly Bear. "What is the name of this big creature?" God said, "That is Grizzly Bear." Coyote said, "Well, let's change names with him. He is big. I'm too small. Let me have the Grizzly Bear name." God said, "No, it is too late now. I named them. You are Coyote." He looked, again. "What is this big creature's name?" God said, "That is Cougar." "Well, let me be Cougar, and him Coyote." God said, "No, it is too late. I named them already." He looked at Wolf. "What is the name of this big creature?" God said, "That is Wolf." "Let's trade names with him." God said, "No, it is too late. I named them once. You know I'm God. I do things once. That is all. I am the only one to create. Once is all. There is no change. All you creatures know, last year I gave you the law not to think your own thoughts until I gave you a person [human] to be in charge of you. But today you missed that law. You lost the person today. Now you will be without a leader for years and years. You must take care of yourselves,"

God took an object from under his blanket on the right side. He said, "I gave you laws last year, and now three of you missed that law: Blue Jay, Meadow Lark, and Coyote missed it. Now you lost the person. He isn't going to be made today. I'm going to put it in water to be washed for years to get it clean. You creatures made it dirty with your own thinking." He put it in water. It swam and God named the person Beaver.

God said, "You missed that law and lost the person. I have hidden it in the water to [198] be wished for the future. There are two laws yet; you missed the first today. I'm going to explain. If one of you keeps smart and strong, he will get the beaver from the water and scatter it over all the land. He will come up and be a person. I'm giving all my power to one of you who will be good from now on. That is all. I'm going back. Remember this. Divide the beaver in twelve pieces. It is flesh. Scatter it in a certain country and give it your own breath, because I have given all my breath and power to you. Wake him up and give him half of your power and tell him what to do. That is all. There are three laws. There is another yet."

The creatures scattered, and they could not meet again until they took the beaver from the water. Coyote watched Grizzly Bear and went around in another direction. He met Grizzly and asked three times to trade names with him. Grizzly got angry and tried to kill Coyote. God came and said, "Go Grizzly, I want to talk to Coyote."

Grizzly walked away. God said, "You think you are smart, Coyote. You lost the person yesterday. I know. You know. I am God. I said, "The last name will be worthless." That is not so. I turn the law over. You are to be head of all the creatures. I will tell you the laws, Coyote. You are a power just like me now. From now, all creatures will become bad. They will fight and eat each other. You have to work from today until I meet you in this land toward the east. When you have finished, we will meet. If you tell the truth, then you can make the person. If you've done wrong, someone else can make the person instead of you."

God took the little book. "I give you this, I am thinking for you in your heart. Just think when you don't know and you will find out. That is my power. I will get you help to watch you from today. Fox (*x̱ʷ ʕʷílx̱ʷ*) is the witness. When you die, Fox will wake you up. That is all."

They all go. Later Coyote hears that others are doing wrong. He dies in one place two or three times. Fox wakes him up. People do wrong everywhere. The mountains swallowed the creatures; the wind blew them away. Coyote rescued the creatures. He stopped everything in the world: sun, moon, wind, rivers, mountains, whenever they did wrong. North Wind kills many in the winter. Coyote said, "You can only kill those who make fun of you."

Coyote kept everything peaceful. Coyote finally knew that he had finished his work. He knew that it was time to meet God again at a certain time and place. He thought, "God won't know what I have been doing. I think I am stronger than he." Coyote is wrong again. He went towards the east. He thought, "I'm going to say to God, "Hallo, youngest brother."

God knows his thoughts. Coyote thought, [198b] "I will see God today at nine in the morning." He sees God standing there. Coyote said, "Hello, my youngest brother. I haven't seen you for a long time. I'm glad to meet you again." God said, "I'm not youngest brother. I'm God." Coyote said, "Your name is God, but you are my youngest brother."

God said, "No, I'm not youngest brother. You know I am God." They said this three times. Then Coyote said, "When our old folks lived over there, I carried you around because you were small and I am oldest. You don't know."

God took out two white eagle feathers and handed them to Coyote. God said, "If what you say is true, you can move that hill over there." Coyote said, "You, little feathers, make mountains move over here." [Narrator stood and depicted Coyote holding feathers in outstretched hands and moving them to right.] The hills moved. Coyote said, "See, I am the oldest brother. You are the youngest." God said, "You have got to move it three times. That is the law." Coyote could not move them the second time and he knew that he had lost the humans again. He was scared and did not know what to say. God said, "I am God. I gave you all my power to do things easy. This is the second time you have missed the laws and lost the humans. Other creatures will make it now. I'm going to give you a place to stay. Let the other smart creatures make humans. You can go to the ocean. I'm going to give you a place to stay all the time." Coyote was scared and thought he would drown. He said, "Not everybody can walk on water." God said, "Go or that is the end of you today."

Three times Coyote steps on the water and shows he will not drown in the waves. He thinks that only he can walk on water; smart, strong, and knows everything. He believes he can not die. He went way out in the ocean without seeing land. Finally he saw God standing there. All the creatures knew that Coyote was going to meet God this day. All had power from God and all could listen. All knew that Coyote had lost the person a second time.

Coyote was not on the land now. God said, "This is going to be your house, your place; right here." Coyote saw a house, well fixed like a king's palace, with a sidewalk all around it. He went in. In the west side hung a black suit of clothes; toward the east hung a suit all white. God said, "Coyote, wear this black for so many months. It is going to be cold and wintry. Then take it off and wear white clothes. That will be summer and everything will grow. In the morning, you can eat. You wish and you will see whatever you want. You can eat it all till I see you again. Now I am going to give you my power not to get old. You will think it is only a minute before we meet. There will be humans on the land where you used to be. You decided the laws and you lost. Laws will be different now." God established his home far from the water. All the creatures on land could hear and knew [199] about Coyote. Coyote stayed there.

After that, the four wolf brothers were the smartest creatures. Youngest Brother was the smartest. The oldest brother was worthless. Finally God made Youngest Brother get Beaver from the water. One morning the oldest brother said to Youngest Brother, "I want you to kill the beaver. I want his tooth for a knife." The other brothers said, "No, the beaver is big and strong."

Youngest Brother said to his brothers, "You can make spears; a four prong spear for the oldest, then a three prong spear, a two prong spear, and a one prong spear for me. I will try my best so that we kill the beaver." All the creatures knew where the beaver was, under the water and under Moses Mountain. Under the lake at Nespelem was the beaver. Little ones swam around, making a home for the head beaver.

While the brothers were preparing the spears, the two brothers were afraid that they would lose their youngest brother. All the creatures were afraid that he would fail in catching the beaver, "the to-be-person".

At dusk, they tore down the dam and all the little beavers ran out. Then the big beavers ran out. The big wolf said, "Watch out! There are the ones." Near midnight, they started to come out; it sounded like thunder. Big Brother said, "Let's quit and not try to kill them." Youngest Brother said, "No, this is my business." The three brothers fell down. There was lightning. Youngest Brother took, the four prong spear end struck with it; it shattered; the three prong spear broke; the two prong broke. He took his own one prong spear and struck: it did not break. He followed the beaver down the Columbia River. He said to his brothers, "You go to Moses Mountain, and in three days if you see a trough at *Skutene* hill (near White Bluffs), I will come there with the beaver. If not, I am dead."

The beaver went down the river. The three brothers stayed there three days until they saw the trough at *Skutene*. The two brothers said, "He is alive." The oldest began to cry, " I think that hill is open." The two said, to make fun of him, "Keep quiet, it isn't so." He cried again. They told him, "Yes." They go to Nespelem Creek and level a place where they are going to meet. All the creatures came back to this place.

Wolf comes carrying the beaver. He said, "I'm going to tell a story before I cut this beaver. It takes me down the Columbia. The big mountains say, 'Hold on to me. You are going to get killed.' A plant and another plant said, 'Hold on to me.' I tried to bold on to everything. It did not help me. First I held a handful of the plants as we went by and stopped the beaver a little; then I took an armful and pretty nearly stopped the beaver; finally I held on to everything and stopped the beaver." Finally Wolf saw the plants. He threw the hops over the earth and the horse tails [*Equisetum*] in the earth. The beaver died. He put hops on the beaver. He said, "I paid the beaver the plants to save my life."

He butchered the beaver. He said to the creatures, "You know God said to cut the beaver into twelve pieces." He cut the pieces but could make only eleven. He had missed one. But it was not his fault; that belonged to God. "Fox, you are a good runner; Humming Bird, you can go fast, and you, Horse Fly, you take this piece over to that place. When you get there breath to wake it up." The three took it and gave it breath so Beaver pieces became persons. Wolf said, "Horse Fly, if the person should have blood poison, put in your nose and, draw it all out."

They scattered the parts everywhere. There is the Methow tribe; it was the heart. The Nez Perce are the liver, which was black. The Blackfoot people had no person, because there were only eleven pieces. All the creatures said, "There have to be twelve tribes." Wolf said, "That is not our business. Maybe God thinks we will use the blood for another tribe. Take the blood to the Blackfoot land and wake it up there. They look for blood always." They took the blood there and woke it up. That is why Blackfoot fought from that time.

When they woke each up, they told the humans, "Here are roots; salmon to spear; berries to pick. This is food." They told them how to eat. Finally the creatures said, "Some human should go to Lake Chelan, in the middle you will see pictures on the rock. You look and see how you should do." God had put the pictures there. From then until now, people go there and look at pictures of salmon traps and bow and arrows. People make these just like the pictures. People still learn from the rock. (The pictures are red.)

Contest of the Winds[8]

The North Wind [201] was one of four brothers; the South Wind was one of four brothers. The world was divided, one half ice, the other half summer. The North Wind had a house in the ice and the South Wind had a house in the summer. These houses were one hundred yards apart. The north Wind and his brothers always went north from there to kill people, to freeze them. (There were "laws" then, but no people.)

The North Wind thought, "We're going to gamble with the South Wind. Let's have a wrestling match with South Wind."

South Wind had a [male] relation, Crane, and another, sta'ɬmtqʷᵉ (an insect like a grasshopper [female] which lives near water). South Wind's youngest brother was married to a woman way down south. North Wind had only one relation, Sk!ōkōmīn'a (a small black bird living near the river).

Next morning, North wind decided, "We don't have to tell them. We'll do this." Early in the morning at sunrise, North Wind's oldest brother went out and hollered, "Weeeeeewah." South Wind knew. "He wants me to gamble." He said, "All right. When?" North Wind said, "In just a little while. Get ready. We'll go down river to the slippery ice to wrestle." South Wind said, "All right."

North Wind wanted to kill South Wind so he could take the whole world. He wanted to kill all the humans when they came.

In a little while, all went down to the ice: the four South Wind brothers, Crane, and Insect. The youngest brother's wife stayed home because she was going to have a baby, North Wind said, "Well, we oldest brothers will wrestle today. We will bet that if you win, there will be no more north time [winter]; if we win, no more summer. It will be cold whenever we want." South Wind said, "All right."

Now they started wrestling. In two or three rounds, South Wind fell down on that slick ice and smashed all to pieces: he was dead. Then the three brothers went back.

Next morning at sunrise, North Wind went out and cried, "*Weeeeeewah.*" He was ready to gamble again. South Wind said," All right. We will get ready." They all went down to the ice at the same place. They [202] wrestled, again; the South Wind's second brother against the North Wind's oldest brother. In two or three rounds, South Wind fell down, smashed all to pieces, and died. Now there were just two South Wind brothers left, for two were dead already.

Next morning at sunrise, North Wind hollered, "*Weeeeeewah.*" South Wind said, "All right. We will get ready." They went to the wrestling place and wrestled. South Wind fell down, smashed all to pieces, and died. Just the youngest South Wind brother, who was married, was left now.

In the evening, the youngest South Wind brother decided he was going to die the next day and he knew his wife was going to have a baby. He made a small bow and arrow, tied them together, and hung them way up in the house. He made a camas digging stick and hung it on the other side of the house. He said to Crane and Insect, "Tomorrow I'm going to die. She can stay with you. If the baby is a boy, you make him strong and bring him back here to wrestle. If it's a

---

[8] CB Suszen Timentwa to Lucy Velpha W Walters.

girl, you don't have to come back here to wrestle against North Wind." He said to Crane and Insect, "Watch this bow and arrow and the stick. When the baby is born, if it is a girl, the stick will drop and you will know it is a girl. If the bow and arrow drop, you will know it's a boy." Crane and Insect said, "All right. We will watch that." South Wind said, "Tomorrow, I have to die. My wife shall go where she belongs way down south."

Next morning; at the same time, North Wind hollered, "*Weaeeeewah.*" South Wind answered, "All right. I will get ready." They all went to the wrestling place on that slick ice. In two or three rounds, South Wind fell down, smashed all to pieces, and died. There were no more South Winds.

The same evening his wife went where she belonged in the south. Crane and Insect stayed there where they belonged; just the two. The same day it became cold where they were, where it used to be summer. The cold kept moving far to the south. Crane and Insect stayed there in that house.

Whenever North Wind's relative, Sk!ōkōmīn'a evacuated he had nothing to clean himself with, so he went to Crane and Insect. Sk!ōkōmīn'a took Insect's head to clean himself. Crane sat with his legs stretched out before him and S!ōkōmīn'a cleaned himself on Crane's legs.

It was cold. All the creatures, frozen and hungry, called a meeting. "Let's make laws." They had to get some power to make warmth in the winter. All the creatures said, "All right. What shall we do?" They decided for a while. "Let's sing a song for summer. We will get something to eat." First one creature sang and all followed him; singing for it to get warm, for the snow to go away, and for something edible to grow. North Wind was glad because all the creatures were scared. They sang over night, or [202b] maybe a few hours, and it did not get warmer. The first creature stopped. Others tried. No one could make it warmer, except Duck who, with his wife, makes a hole in the ice. Others said to him, "Duck, you had better come out here. You just sit there, always warm."

Next day, Duck sang, "*xat xat tum tum map'm, xant sant tum tom map'm.*" All the creatures were angry and said, "Shut up. You can't make spring." He sang, "*xat xat tum tom map'm.*" in a little while, the sunshine came and melted the ice where he was singing. The others could not believe it, but they all sang his song, "*xRnt xRnt tum tom ma'pem.*" Soon they see the ice where they are, melted; it is warmer. They all believe and sing his song to help him get more power in his song. The next morning, there is no ice on the hillside. They all went to get something to eat. All believe in Duck and his wife; that they can make the power for spring.

Nine months after the contest when the South Wind had died. Crane is lying about; just sitting in one place, hungry, cold and weak, and unable to work. Insect brings in food and wood for the fire. Finally in the morning, Crane sees the bow and arrow fall down. He said, "*kooRət, kooRət, kooRət.* The bow and arrow drop now," Insect quickly ran into the house and said, "Maybe, you touched it and made it drop down." Crane said, "No, I was sitting right here. It dropped down. We have a boy now," Both said. "We have a nephew now."

North Wind heard the loud shout. He sent Sk!ōkōmīn'a to find out about it. He said, "What were you hollering loud for?" Crane said, "Oh, I'm cold and hungry." Insect said the same thing. They did not tell about the boy way down south.

Well, that woman had a baby boy. She put him in cold water every little while to make him strong. In a few years, he was a grown man and strong. He swam in cold water every little while to make himself stronger. His mother told him, "North Wind killed your father wrestling."

After a while he said, "I'm strong enough now. I think I will go up there to wrestle with North Wind. I think I am a strong man now. I can't do any more now." He asked his mother.

She said, "All right, Let's go." They went north to meet the North Wind brothers and Crane and Insect at his father's place. All the creatures knew he was coming but their power blinded North Wind, so he did not know.

He got there late in the evening. Nobody knew him when he got there. He saw his aunt and uncle there looking awfully poor, Crane's legs were dirty. He asked, "What is wrong with your legs? They look as though somebody has been sitting there." Crane said, "That is Sk!ōkōmīn'a. He does that."

Young South Wind ground some obsidian and put it on Crane's legs and on Insect's [205a] head. Young South Wind hid himself in the house then. Early in the morning, Sk!ōkōmīn'a came there to clean himself. Sk!ōkōmīn'a cleaned himself on Insect's head. It cut him; made him bleed. He said, "Oh, why don't you wash your head?" She said, "I haven't got time. It's cold." Sk!ōkōmīn'a jumped on Crane's legs and it was worse. Sk!ōkōmīn'a ran home, crying loud. North Wind said, "What is the matter with you?" "Oh, I got hurt. Look here. I'm bleeding all over." The North Wind brothers told him, "We told you not to go there and do that all the time. They have power. Now they have caught you. Now you are bleeding all over."

They did not know Young South Wind was there, but all the creatures knew. They were all against the North Wind because he was chief and made cold. All the creatures knew that they had a boy to help them. If he won, everything would be all right; if he should lose, there would be no springtime, but cold forever.

Early in the morning South Wind Boy got up. He said to Insect, "You'd better boil some dried salmon head. Keep it hot all the time. When Sk!ōkōmīn'a gets cold water to pour under my feet to make it slippery so I will fall down; when he calls, 'Insect, you go ahead; Pour first, don't heed him. Just keep your soup there."

Crane went out and called, "*Weeeewah*." North Wind said, "He wants to gamble now. All right. We will get ready. We will be at the wrestling place." Crane said, "We will be there." North Wind thinks that Crane wants to wrestle. [Much laughter from Indian audience]

They all went down. Crane said, " Sk!ōkōmīn'a, you must get water to pour under the wrestlers to make it slippery." North Wind said, "We will get ready for the soup [?]."

They go to the place. North Wind saw this well-built boy, with muscles all over his body. Oldest North Wind was scared a bit. They wrestled. North Wind did his best, but for a while he could not do anything. Then North wind slipped to his knees and almost fell, but South Wind Boy did not, Sk!ōkōmīn'a was scared and poured the water to make it slippery. Then Insect poured the soup so that South Wind Boy could stand up. Oldest North Wind fell down, smashed all to pieces, and died. That same day, it got warmer; ice melted in places. Only one North Wind brother was dead, but it was warmer. It was going to be spring pretty soon.

Crane and Insect had much to eat because South Wind Boy brought plenty to them. Next morning Crane called, "*Weeeeewah*. Get ready." North Wind was crying. He knew they were all going to die, but he said, "All right." He could not give up now.

They went down to the wrestling place again. Sk!ōkōmīn'a was scared and poured the cold water first; then Insect poured the soup. South Wind Boy knocked down the second North Wind brother: smashed him all to pieces, and died. It was getting warmer. Snow melted on the hill side.

Next morning, Crane hollered, "*Weeeeewah*, get ready." North Wind said, "All right, we're ready."

They all went down to the wrestling place with its slippery ice to wrestle. South Wind Boy was strong. North Wind almost fell "down. Sk!ōkōmīn'a got scared and poured water at

13

South Wind Boy's feet. Insect poured the soup. South Wind Boy knocked down North Wind, smashed him to pieces, and he died. There was one more North Wind brother yet. It became warmer: more snow melted on the side hills. All the creatures went there looking for something to eat. All were wishing for South Wind Boy to win because his father and father's brothers were all killed the year before. All were against the North Wind brothers.

Early next morning, Crane hollered, "*Weeeewah*, North Wind, Get ready at the wrestling place." North Wind said, "All right. We will be there." They wrestled for a long time. Youngest Brother North Wind was strong; both were about the same. Sometimes one almost fell down, then the other. Sk!ōkōmīn'a told Insect, "Go ahead, Pour your salmon head soup first." "No, you go ahead. Your uncle almost fell down then." They talked a long time. Finally Sk!ōkōmīn'a got scared and threw the water. Insect poured the soup. North Wind fell down, smashed to pieces, and died. That was the end of him; there were no more North Winds.

South Wind Boy took his club to kill Sk!ōkōmīn'a too. Sk!ōkōmīn'a ran on the ice: he knew how. Pretty soon the ice cracked. He fell in and did, not come up. South Wind Boy said, "That's all right. You follow the cold places now. You will be in the cold, all the time from now on. If you get in warm places, you will get sick. You will always be in the cold forever."

Coning back to the wrestling place, he said, "All you North Wind brothers are dead now, but I don't kill you forever. When people come, they have to have winter. You shall bring the winter, but not too cold. I will bring the summer and warmth. You don't have to kill all the people. You can freeze those people that make fun of you. You must not kill people who know the laws and don't make fun of you."

Now spring began. In a few weeks lots of green things came up; the salmon ran, and everything came. Then certain cold months came for the North wind. That was the beginning: so it has always been till now.

[That is why some persons get power from South Wind. Some creature tells a man, "I know South Wind, if you wish power from South Wind, I will tell you how to make snow go away." In the same way other people get power from North Wind if they want cold.]

Mountain Goat Girls[9]

(People say, "Look. Here are deer bones. How can they come to life again?" Here is a story about a real Indian in Canada.)

One time there was a good hunter who killed lots of deer, maybe one or two for each person. All by himself, he could help all the people in only a few days. When he hunted, many people followed him. The stronger women followed him with the men. One day he killed four for his people; the next he killed for himself. All followed him in the summer.

One day he saw two mountain goats a little way from the dead deer. The hunter followed the goats. He went over the hill, following their tracks. He saw a little lake with good water. He saw two pretty women swimming, but no mountain goats. They stood off there and called, "Come on. After swimming, then we will go." He thought, "They don't know me." He sat down and waited. They came out of the water and put on two mountain goat hides lying there. Then

---

[9] Told by CB Suszen Timentwa to Lucy Velpha W Walters. Cross-species perspectives and empathy are underscored by stories like this one, along with sanctioned hunting rules and taboos specific to tribes and locales.

they were mountain goats again. He tried not to follow, but his feet went right along. Finally on a mountain between two other big mountains, the man saw a lot of ice where he could not go.

The two goats told him to close his eyes and hold onto them, and not to open his eyes. He did that and went a little way. He could not feel the ice so he opened his eyes. Then he slipped down, clear to the bottom. They said, "Now, don't open your eyes again. You might get hurt." He closed his eyes and it was just like walking on a level place. Finally they told him to open his eyes and he looked back. They had come straight up, perhaps six miles. [240b]

He went a little way and saw a door with ladders sticking out. He went in and saw many people. He saw an old man there who said, "Hello, my son-in-law." The old man said to the other women there, "You'd better cook something to eat for your husband." The man thought, "Why, he is going to give me all his women for my wives." They gave him a good bed with goat skins to rest on. When he lay down, the two pretty women took off their hides and became women again. All the other were goats when dressed, but people when they took off their hides.

In the evening, everybody lay down to sleep. One women slept on each side of him. He attempted to copulate with them, but they said, "Not now. When the time comes, all these women will be your wives." Next day, he was sorry and thought about it. The old man said, "Why is your husband sorry?" The women said, "He wants to copulate when it isn't our time." Old man reminded, "Every year, there is just one time for our people to raise children."

Next day, the old man sent the boys down to the river to see about the salmon. They said, "The salmon stay still. They spawn now." Every day they went hunting, and the man went along. The old man told him, "When you kill deer, don't throw away anything; neither the intestines nor anything." The man obeyed four times, then he thought he would find out.

Eight boys went hunting with him one day. He killed three deer and only five boys came back in the evening. He thought perhaps the boys had turned into deer. The next time he went hunting, he jumped quick and cut off the tongue of one deer and hid it. When they got to the house with the deer, they ate it all. The old man sent the boys to throw the bones in the lake, and all the deer came to life again. They returned to the house. One boy was sick and spit blood all the time. Other boys said, "Our partner is sick; His tongue is gone." Then the man knew. The boys would go hunting with him in the morning; they turned into deer and were killed, eaten, their bones put in the lake, and they were revived again. So the man gave the tongue to the old man, who put the tongue in the boy's mouth and it was all right. The man believed now. He knew. When deer bones are put in the lake, they come alive again.

In the morning, the old man sent the boys down to a certain Indian who was hunting. "You help this man, who wants something to eat. But there is one man there who makes fun of us. Don't go near him." All the deer put on their skins and went down. All the Indians, except the man who mocked them, killed deer. Some of the boys came back very soon. Others were kept a long time. [241]

When the deer came back, some said, "That man fed me well: camas, berries and everything." (When Indians put camas and berries by the deer when he is brought into the house, they are feeding him.)

The old man sent the boys down to see about the salmon again. When they came back, they said, "The salmon are spawning now." The old man said, "All you girls go to the lake and swim. When you come back, all you boys go and swim. Tomorrow is your time. Go and have a good time." The two women told the man, "See, you were in a hurry some time ago."

All went swimming, and after breakfast all put on clothes and became deer. The old man reached out and gave the man a thick goat hide to wear. He said, "Wear that so your friends can't hook you with their horns and hurt you." It was so heavy that he could only walk while everybody else ran and played as they chose. Towards evening, the others came back and left him. He tried to get near the does but could not. He went back and took off his skin. Everybody was laughing and playing. He thought, "Because I am a man, I can't do anything."

The old man said, "Maybe someone did wrong to this man and he is sorry." They all said, "No, we didn't do wrong. But he is too slow." The old man said, "That is my fault. I gave him a heavy skin so he would not be hurt. Tomorrow I will give him a lighter one to be fast."

Next day the old man gave him a lighter skin. He went out, trotted and ran, and caught up to the other deer. He was bigger than all the other bucks, so soon he was alone with the does and had all of the women all day. Now the man remembered that he had a little girl and a little boy with his own people whom he had left. He went with the does for nearly a month. When a doe felt that she was going to have little ones, she did not play any more. Finally just a few does went out. Finally there were no more. So the man learned to be like deer, and to have intercourse with women only once a year. He stayed three years and learned from them.

The man's people had followed him when he left that first day. They had found his tracks between the two deer tracks going up the ice mountain. They knew that the deer had taken him away, that he was not dead. So the people used their power to find if he were dead or alive. Then they knew that he was living with the deer. They made power to make him think, "Let me go back to my people."

Finally after three years, he thought, "I have a boy and a girl. I am lonesome. I must go back." He told the old man, who said, "All right. That is your affair; but any time you want to come back here, this is your home too." [241b]

When the man came back to his people, he told them all about everything. And he did not know how many of the young deer were his children.

The old man had given him shoes to wear over the ice. Finally he came close to the camp. He became afraid of the camp odors; just as a deer would. For four days, he tried to go into camp, but was always scared and ran back into the brush. Finally, the people saw him and went there, and saw the tracks. They said, "Maybe he is scared, just like a deer. All of you who have power come and try to catch this man who is coming back."

They all came together and lined up on two sides of the brush where he came out. They said, "When he comes, surround him." All the men and women did this. The others said, "We have to get some certain roots and weeds to put medicine on him when we get him."

They caught him. He was just like a deer, running around. He died, just like a deer; scared. They took him to camp quickly and washed him with roots. He woke up and was sick for quite a while. So they made him tame again.

Frog & Turtle Race[10]

One time Frog had a long tail and Turtle had none. Frog ran races and always won because he could jump. Turtle had three brothers. He dreamed that they could beat Frog. He said to his brothers, "Get up. I had a dream that we would win from Frog."

They went to a camp where Frog was with all the people he had beaten. Turtle sent his

---

[10] Told by CB Suszen Timentwa to Lucy Velpha W Walters. Small details, often based in species characteristics, are "Just So" stories to explain behaviors today.

three brothers to station themselves at intervals along the race track. Turtle bet his life against Frog's tail. Frog knew that Turtle could not run. He said, "All right, and you can free the creatures if you win."

They started. Frog ran fast and saw Turtle way behind him. Turtle stopped and hid himself. He called, "*Whooooo*." His first brother got up and began running. Frog looked ahead and saw him. He ran fast and passed him. Turtle called, "*Whooooo*," and hid himself. The next brother got up and ran. Frog saw him ahead and ran fast and passed him. Turtle hid and called "*Whoooo*." So the brother at the turning point started to run back. Frog ran fast around the mark and came back. He passed Turtle. Turtle called, "*Whoooo*," and hid. The third brother got up end ran. Frog ran fast and passed him. Turtle called, "*Whoooo*," and hid. The second brother got up and ran. Frog ran fast and passed him. Turtle called, "*Whoooo*," and hid. The oldest brother, hidden close to the finishing line, got up and ran. Frog ran fast but he lost. [Suszen represented the hiding turtles with his right index finger, and the sprinting Frog with his left index finger.]

Frog sat down to hide his tail, but Turtle said, "Well, I want my tail now." Frog sat there a long time, so Turtle pushed his head down and pulled all of Frog's tail off. Frog has only half a backbone now.

Coda

These epics and stories reside with family elders, who often are unnamed. To be more respectful of their contributions before and after 1900, Methows were guided by beloved parents, grandparents, relatives, leaders, chiefs, and Indian doctors. Important teachers were Dr Siyolem, whose English name was Patcheese, born in 1884 and died 16 May 1929 at 125 years of age; Harriet Swimptkin, sister of Siyolem, born in 1836 and died 10 February 1940 at 104; Michel Charley ~ *skwahemqn*, born 1859 and died 4 October 1963 at 104; Susette Kapoosal ~ *selmatkw*, born in 1832; Mrs Lucy Loya, died 8 March 1935; Mrs Sallie Michel ~ *s'ayxwal'qs*, died 14 March 1943; Chief Charles Swimptkin ~ *paqliwa* of the Okanogan tribe; Chief CB Suszen Timentwa ~ *kinnemil'xw* of Okanogan and Moses tribes; Sam Miller ~ *yexwa'skuerit*, and his son, Jerome; and Chillowist Jim of the Entiat and Moses tribes. Their legacy passed to elders alive later in the past century, with shifts in details and morals of some stories.

Creation ~ Name Day
1980

God (*k*^{w}*əlnčtn*, Quill-in-chut-in) stood in the Universe, as though He were in orbit, until He decided to create a planet (**tmx*^{w}*ula'x*^{w} ~ *mlk'ula'x*^{w}) covered by an ocean. Next, He formed an Eagle (**mlknups* ~ *mlqnups*) to fly eastward until He suspended it in flight, creating South America from the right wing and North America from the left one. According to His original plan, God would have created people (**skilx*^{w} ~ *sqilx*^{w}) to inhabit this land, but on the spur of the moment, He rather chose to cover North America with a white cloth so as to indicate that it was pure and innocent. He left this first continent and directed his attentions elsewhere.

Eventually, he returned to North America a second time, deciding to create all kinds of animals there though they were still without names. When He had made all of the animals species, those of dry land, underwater, and air; He told them all of a special meeting to be held the next morning. He said, "I am going to give each of you a name tomorrow morning. I will stick this pole in the ground and the first animal to arrive will receive the first name on my list, becoming the leader of all animals since that name will be placed on top of the pole."

God stuck a long straight pole in the ground and disappeared into thin air. The animals were much impressed, so they began to drift away in order to plan their activities for an early arrival on the next day. Two very close friends left together, but each of them had different personalities. One was an ambitious schemer, always [2] determined to win by hook or by crook. For all of his drive and determination, he was also stupid. Eventually, this one would become known as Coyote (snk'əl'ip). His friend would become known as Fox ($\underline{x}^{w}\Omega^{w}ilx^{w}$).

The friends parted, with the ambitious one saying he would be the first one to arrive at the meeting place for Naming Day and thereby become the leader of all the animals. He considered several plans before he decided that it would be best to stay awake all night in order to be the first one there when daylight came. He sat waiting for the dawn but about midnight, he became drowsy, then very sleepy. Then he got the bright idea to prop his eyes open so he could not go to sleep. He got up to gather some small sticks and selected two of the right size to hold up his .eye lids. He sat with his eyes propped to await the day. Time passed but this devious one fell asleep. Finally, he was awakened by terrible pains in both his eyes. He rubbed them but that only made the pain worse. He realized that he was blind. He considered this until he thought that if he could find some water and rinse out his eyes, the pain and blindness would go away. He rose and headed in the direction where he thought the meeting was to be held. Walking was difficult because he stumbled over everything in his path, rocks, bushes, trees, and so forth. Finally, he heard the sound of running water quite close. He was happy then and struggled toward the stream. He washed his face and eyes, but did no good. His eyes were so dehydrated that he remained totally blind. Undaunted, he continued on toward the meeting place, always he fell, stumbled, and struggled. As he encountered each obstacle, he would ask its name. For example, when he fell over a bush, he would ask it to identify itself. It would say, "I am a serviceberry bush." He continued on until he heard [3] some girls laughing nearby. He called to the girls, saying he had something to show them. They girls laughed and asked what he had. He said, "Come closer" as he started to stare upwards into the sky. Then he said, "I want to show you girls a little dipper." The girls laughed even louder, saying "there can't be a little dipper in the sky because it is daylight." The blind one said "I can prove to you there is a little dipper in the sky but you must come over closer to me so you can see it best." One of the girls moved very close to the man. He sensed her body, reached out to grab her, and dug out her eyes to place them in his own eye sockets. But the girl's eyes were very small, so he could only see dimly. However, it was better than being blind. To replace the girl's eyes, he found two red mountain berries and placed them in her sockets. The girl could see again. Ever afterward, she and her descendents, the catbirds, have had tiny red eyes.

The trickster traveled on with this dim eyesight, but at least he could avoid tripping over things. He moved steadily along until he reached the ridge of a little canyon where he heard a voice on the other side. It was a voice calling loud and clearly for double daylight (*lep leep xobe heep). He crept over the hill and crawled close to the ground using whatever cover was available to shield him. He watched as Blue Grouse ($x^{w}a'x^{w}a'yu\dot{t}$) would take out his beautiful big eyes, toss them high in the air, call for double daylight, and have his eyeballs automatically pop back into their sockets. The Blue Grouse was very proud that he had invented this game for himself. The traveler wanted these big eyes very much. So he planned his movements such that he could creep closer each time the eyes were in the air. With care and patience, in addition to the fact that Blue Grouse was [4] so proud of himself that he was off his guard, the schemer moved in so close that he successfully grabbed the eyes. Blue Grouse called for "double daylight" but nothing happened so he called again, and again trying different combinations of loudness, softness, highness, and lowness. Nothing worked. The big beautiful eyes were excellent, so the traveler walked over to a nearby thicket and selected two huckleberries. They were big and nicely filled Blue Grouse's eye sockets. Blue Grouse was told, "Hereafter these will be your permanent eyes. If someone later kills you and eats you eyes they will taste like huckleberries. Never play your game again, or you may never be able to keep these eyes."

With his excellent eyesight, the traveler went straight to the meeting place. He got there and walked right up to God, saying, "I am here to claim the most important name." God said, "I have only one name left, the last one on the list; since you are the last one to arrive it will be yours." "What name is that?" asked the last one to arrive. "Coyote (snk'əl'ip) will be your name from now on," God said. The other animals had received their names long before; many had left the area but a few had lingered. Coyote looked around,' sizing each of'-.them up as a prospect for a name trade. He pointed to one big animal and asked what name it had received. God said "His name is Grizzly (kilawna). Coyote said "Since he is such a big animal, he should really have a prominent name like mine, Big Coyote. Why don't you just give him the name of Coyote and call me by the little tiny name of Grizzly Bear?" God said, "Each name was fixed by the time each animal arrived here this morning. Grizzly Bear got his name according to proper procedure, it belongs to him permanently. There will be no trading of names, ever." Then God faded into thin air. All of the animals likewise [5] scattered into different directions, according to their personal choices. Coyote followed Grizzly Bear, looking for an opportunity to convince him to exchange names. Finally, in the dense bushes of the deep forest, Coyote found his chance. He stepped in front of Grizzly, saying "Your name actually means little tiny grizzly bear, but mine is Big Coyote. My name better fits your size so how about trading names?" Grizzly by now was fed up with Coyote and knew him to be a pest, so he thought that this was the ideal time to kill Coyote. As he prepared to lunge at defenseless Coyote, God suddenly appeared between them and told Grizzly to go away. God turned to Coyote and said than He now was going to pass on more information that went with the permanent name of Coyote. God said, "This is your final advice and instruction. I have decided to make you the leader of all the animals in North America. I am giving you a Special Supreme Power to aid you in your work, to make you win against heavy odds, and to help you benefit humans. You will not always be successful; sometimes you will win, others you will lose. You will become leader when I take the pole I set in the ground yesterday and turn it upside down. Since you were the very last at the bottom of the pole, now you will be the topmost. The majority of animals on this continent are monsters. Your job will be to neutralize, not to kill them, so that the future people will be able to survive when they get here."

Coyote interrupted to ask a question. "Where is this Special Supreme Power that you have vested in me?" God took his right hand and placed over His heart to indicate that the power resided right there. God charged Coyote to cover the entire continent, reducing all monsters to safe size, and establishing rules to be followed by the first people to arrive. [6]

God explained to Coyote that when he had set the rules and reduced the monster animals to manageable size, then he was to travel to the East until he met God again. God disappeared into thin air, leaving Coyote entirely on his own.

Unbeknownst to Coyote, God materialized before Fox shortly afterward. God told Fox, "I am giving you a special job with a Special Reserve Supreme Power. Your job will be to revive Coyote whenever you find him dead. No matter how badly deteriorated he is, even if there are only bones, or some bits of hair, all you need do is step over him and he will return to life. Coyote will be known for his stupidity sometimes and he will not be able to revive himself, so unknown to him, I give you this power to keep Coyote on his task." Fox accepted the power and continued on his way.

Coyote traveled about setting the world straight, neutralizing the monsters, and setting the rules that the future people would use to cope with this world. When he met the first monster, he was very uncertain until he remembered that God had given him the Supreme Power. He recalled the gesture made by God to locate the power and decided the power resided in his gut. He called forth this power by squatting down and relieving himself. He stood up and looked down on the waste produced, saying "My little sisters, will you help me or not?" They made very many excuses why they could not help him. Coyote got mad and said, "All right then, I will call rain clouds to wash you away or I'll call the sun to dry you up." The sisters became frightened, agreeing to help him as soon as they knew what he wanted. Coyote asked them how much power they had to help him with. They said that they had unlimited power. "We can do anything you want from changing forms to [7] giving advice or knowing just how to defeat an enemy. Coyote now understood the nature of his power. Whenever he was in a quandary, he would call upon his sisters to help him before they returned into his insides.

Coyote traveled from one end of the continent to the other. Along the way, he kept his friend Fox very busy for Coyote died many, many times. After each and every one of these thousands of deaths, Fox would find Coyote and step over whatever remained. Coyote would return to life and scold Fox for interrupting his nap. Then Fox would explain how and why Coyote had been killed that time before Coyote left to continue his task.

Eventually Coyote found himself in the far west and as he turned to face the east he felt that his job was completed. Everything was in order. Coyote was proud and content as he began traveling toward the sunrise. Everything was set so he traveled safely without any need to watch out for monsters or otherwise be on the alert. He went for months, then years. He came to a beautiful mountain range, taking a route through a wide green valley that rose gradually into high mountains. A green path led him to a green saddle-like summit from which he had an extensive view in all directions. Suddenly, God stood in front of him to ask "Have you finished all the work I entrusted to you?" Coyote replied "Yes, little brother, I did my job. The future is now safe." God only said, "I am the older brother, what do you mean calling me a younger brother'." Coyote corrected Him, but God said "All right if you really are older, take these two feathers and use them to wedge that mountain directly across from here and to move it to the left. If you can do this, then you truly are older." Coyote took the feathers without hesitation and wedged the mountain, saying "Mountain, [8] I am moving you to the left." The mountain moved to the left. Coyote became arrogant, saying "Now do you believe that I am oldest and you are youngest?" God said, "Before I am convinced, you must move the mountain back to its original location." Coyote thought that would be a snap, so he took the two feathers, wedged the mountain, and said "Mountain, move back to where you came from." The two feathers moved, but the mountain did not. Coyote thought he probably had not held the feathers correctly so he adjusted his hold several times but to no avail. Then God said, "Now you will know that I am the eldest brother. You could not move the mountain back because I moved it the first time. Now I will move the mountain without the feathers. Mountain, move back to your original place," and it went back.

God now said to Coyote, "Your job here on *skil'x^wulax^w* is over so I will now give you new directions for you to travel directly east from now on until we meet again." God disappeared and Coyote moved onward toward the sunrise. He went for days, months, years until he came to the ocean. He debated whether he should wait for God there, but then he recalled that God had told him to keep traveling east until they met. Coyote stepped out onto the ocean and it held him so after he had gotten over his Initial fright, he began to trot along the surface of the ocean. He briefly thought that it would be great if Grizzly and the other monsters he had defeated could see him running on the ocean splashing up water as though it was the shoreline. He went for days, months, and years on the ocean until God suddenly appeared to him, also standing on the ocean. God told Coyote that this was the place where he would live until the end of the world or humans were in temporary need. God made a house for Coyote [9] entirely out of glass, where Coyote would always stay although the time passes very quickly for him there. He never gets restless, but sometimes God calls him back to North America when things get out of hand and Coyote is needed to return them to normal. Coyote still lives on the ocean in his glass house. He can be seen with powerful binoculars and spy glasses walking around inside the house. Sometimes an ocean-going ship will approach his home, but then Coyote disappears into the sky and only his reflection can be seen. He is very much alone and keeps it that way. When the world ends, he will once again return as a person.

Methow at Heart

For Salish speaking tribes of eastern Washington, creation involved the first beings called Animal People, who interacted with features of the planets, ocean, mountains, rivers, lakes, cliffs, trees, and bushes. All of their activities paid heed to the prediction that human beings would eventually be created so this world had to be made ready for them.

Methow territory was marked by the main river stem that drains into the Columbia at Pateros, Washington. Starting upstream, this river system includes six main streams, with names written linguistically using International Phonetic Alphabet (IPA), in variation with impressionistic versions given as spelled by elders (in parentheses, eg, txjcaco for tx^{w}əcp) handicapped by the very limited options for letters in the English alphabet.

1. The main channel of the Methow ~ nmətx̱wit^w (nmikxawatkw)
2. The Twisp ~ tx^{w}əcp (*txjcaco)
3. Early Winters ~ nx̱əlwitn (nxelwiltn)
4. Lost River ~ šyapustn, šyapusən (sya'pustn)
5. Chewack ~ cwax (cxwax)
6. Gold ~ npəspisa'stm, npəspisa'stn (npəspisa'stm)

The drainage also includes sixteen smaller creeks feeding the six branches draining into the Columbia (*senseloxwi'itkwux).

The boundaries of the Methow territory include the area south of Osoyoos Lake, across the Canadian border, then west and south along the ridge of the Cascades to a camp in the Gilbert range, where it turns southeast along the ridges of the Okanogan National Forest; at the furthest south, it is two miles north of Wells Dam,[11] turning north along the bank of the Columbia and then [2] to the northeast, upstream along the Okanogan River to Osoyoos Lake.

---

[11] Named for the drowned community of Azwell, its backwaters of Lake Pateros flooded out native homesteads, including the native Miller orchard and ranch, as noted # 2.

After thousands of years, this region was prepared for the arrival of humans. The Animal People came to an end, scattering over the earth to become the ancestors of modern day species. Just before this change, the supreme chief (*elnix'əm~ ylmix^{w}m) called the Animal People together for their last instructions. The principals and procedures were set now so that humans could gain spiritual power (*sumix*) from these first beings. The only way that humans could survive in the new world was with the help of these powers. The chief had various of these instructions painted on a rock at Lake Chelan and the routes, trails, hunting, and digging areas that were to be, all over North America.

At the moment of the World Change, all of spirits moved to dwellings along lakes, rivers, creeks, swamps, mountains, cliffs, and prairies, where they will live forever. Some of them turned into species of birds, salmon, insects, mammals, and many others. These volunteered to do this, deciding to help humans by providing food, clothing, blankets, weapons, spears, baskets, and other items.

When humans did arrive, they learned to satisfy their needs by reading the painted signs and by the inspiration of *san's paxpaxt* (*txet'n tsutn), who guided them away from roots and berries that were poison. This satisfied the first goal of humans, to care for themselves. Their second goal was to be presentable to the spirits. It was met by the sacred sweat lodge, used by men and women, old and young. With this preparation, [3] they moved to goal three, the identification of the sites for getting spiritual power. The landscape was already filled with a bounty of roots, berries, nuts, medicine plants, fish, game, and other foods. Mountains, hills, valleys, rivers, and lakes have also hosted the spirits, since the time of the universal change (*ska'tul). At the last council, the Animal People made this sacrifice to help the coming generations of humans. Since then, they have been silent dwellers of this sacred continent. Those who have been ritually prepared can seek them out and learn survival skills from them.

The supreme chief vested universal knowledge in *san's paxpaxt*[12] (*txetn tsutn), who was to transfer it to the first human ancestor to settle in the Methow valley. This enabled our first parent to face the challenges of the new world and survive.

This power was transferred by three beings:

< Hummingbird ~ x̱^{w}namx̱^{w}nam > < Horsefly ~ *kuket'als > < Fox ~ x̱^{wҁw}ilx^w >

The original humans were created from the slices cut from a giant spirit Beaver, when placed on the ground, one slice became a human man and another a human female. One of these three fleet ~ fastest beings blew breath onto the creations and they came to life. They were fully adult, known as (*stl'sqelu) and as Indians (*sklux — cu'wilx). The helper instructed them very briefly on how to get food and water. Then he left. Later, they read the signs painted around them and received visions. One of the three helpers brought the heart (*spus'us*) of the sacrificed Beaver to the center of the valley, creating the Methow tribes (*cu'xilx). When the couple "woke up" [4] ~ came alive ~ gained consciousness, they heard "Here are roots, salmon to spear, berries to pick. These are food. You have to gather, prepare, and cook them in various ways. Also, go to Lake Chelan and look at the pictures on a rock in the middle. Look and see how you should do. God put them there to help you."

Though the first Methow had the bodies of adults, their knowledge was like that of a

---

[12] From French for 'holy spirit'.

child. Their instructions were brief and so they had to learn a great deal from their new land. They had lots of time to do this since they lived to be 800 to 1000 years old. They learned from the painted signs, from visions, from ancient knowledge (*mipnomt*), and from spirit partners (*slaxt-sumix*). They built up a long tradition about the variety of foods, equipment, dwellings, hunting techniques, fisheries, and the preparation of meals, clothing, and tools. This was the result of a hard struggle.

All of the first humans knew about the supreme chief and about the continents of North and South America. They all spoke one language and shared the same legends (*tcptikʷl*). The slices of the Beaver sacrificed at the last council of the Animal People were used to create 12 tribes living in 12 regions with 12 dialects.

After the change, the Methow tribes (*mitxwiw*) were at the center of all of them, living in Methow territory (*mitxwiw tmxul'xw*) along the Methow River in *metxwitkʷ*). They assembled ancient learning (*sm'imy'*) for 500 years. Their hard work was all uphill, but it was worth it. They gained appreciation of the sweat lodge, food cycle, hunting rules, and the manufacture of [5] weirs at proper locations. Individuals, families, communities, and tribes learned the locations where spirits lived. They learned the commandments (*sk̓(ə)tc̓ar̓ar̓* ~ *skc̓ar̓r̓ipla?*) that applied to the respect and use of the land, as instituted by the supreme chief and Coyote (*snk'l'ip*).

The Methow became famous for their stamina and dedication. A hunter could walk for miles over difficult terrain of mountains and valleys. He could easily carry home a 4-point buck, casually swung over his back. Women could go far for berries and roots, bringing back large, full baskets. Each took along a small basket for steady picking and bigger ones for storage. The camps sites were established and ideally located. Only the aged elders stayed in the winter villages when everyone else went to the seasonal camps. A few young married couples also stayed to help the older generation. Young girls from 12 to 15 served as messengers, running between village and camps to carry messages. Their elders loaned them some of their power so they could travel 20-50 miles in a day.

Eventually, a serious conflict broke out among the Methow. All of the tribes were gathered together, along with all of the important men and women. A mountain bird (*kokquee*) flew over the assembly and made a pretty noise "*xla-la-la-la-la-la*". It was the first time people had heard it and so they all stopped to listen. A lesser chief asked, "How do you suppose that bird makes its pretty noise?"

One of the great chiefs answered that it came from the *wing*, but another of the highest chiefs argued that it came from the *mouth*. People took sides and debated the relative merits of *Wing* verses *Mouth*. Tempers grew heated, but the sides could not [6] declare war because they were closely related. Finally, people were asked to choose sides. A chief said, "I am going to stand here and all of you who believe like me that the noise comes from the Wing, line up behind me. Those who think it is the Mouth, line up over there." The head chief said, "It is a free choice, act in the way you think best." When all had taken sides, they were divided exactly in half. They split up, each of the highest chiefs and their followers bid farewell. These were sad goodbyes. One chief led the way north and the other half stayed in the Methow valley.

In the north, these other tribes developed. The northern Okanogan, the Similkameen, the Inkamip, the Thompson (*nekwetəmxu*) and the Shuswap. The Thompson were noted for being spiritually powerful. They became enemies of the southern Okanogans, as did the Shuswap.

The problematic bird still flies. In 1934, Charley hunters were at their traditional camp on Leecher Mountain. When they paused at noon for a lunch of camas and dried serviceberries, this bird *Kokauee*, flew overhead, making the pretty noise of "*xla-la-la-la-la*". Michel thought that the noise came from its wing, and mused that possibly a spirit (**txet'n tsutn*) may have directed the bird to fly over the ancient assembly so that the vast regions to the north would become occupied by humans. As a Methow leader who stayed in the valley, it seems that it was the Wing faction who remained behind when the Mouth one moved away.

Another split occurred among the Methow in the mid-1800s, but this was did not involve conflict. The chief and several [7] families were living in their winter lodges. Spring came with its wild celery and other roots. This group went out to gather fresh greens and begin to store food for the next winter. They became so fond of travelling that they just kept moving on. They explored new territories, going south along the Cascade range, and learning from painted panels ~ signs ~ messages that they found along the way.

In a similar way, over time, small groups of people have scattered all over. From Vantage on the Columbia northward, these became the tribes known as the Moses, Wenatchee, Entiat, Chelan, southern Okanogan, Nespelem, Keller (Sanpoil), and Lakes. The Spokan were to the south. All of them share varieties of Salish called *nxum'tsin*, *celx'tsin*, and *spoka'inx^w*. During the 1000 years since the death of the first parents, only language changed. The means of acquiring powers and the raising of children are the same among all these tribes.

The original tribe was the Methow. Members who voluntarily wandered off founded the other tribes, at first, a chief and his followers went north into Canada, becoming the Okanogan. After they had been apart for a time, their language began to change.

An especially attentive child, a lone arrow, was selected for special training by elders. Naturally interested in history, these elders had never been to book-learning school and did not know English. They used Chinook Jargon {Chinuk Wawa} to speak with white settlers, to trade, and to make store purchases. Methows met to hold root and berry feasts, to give names, to clean cemeteries once a year, and to celebrate winter dances. Elders stressed that the oldest people were closest to the [8] facts and should be most respected. There is wisdom in this because memorized traditions are kept intact, not changed, amended, or modified.

Sun & Moon[13]

Coyote was living in a medium size lodge with his family and his faithful original wife, Mole. He had three boys, ranging in age from one year to five or six. There were three of them. While they were living there, they were struck by hard luck, so food was hard to get. Coyote had never been a hunter so he didn't even try any harder and they were starving, really desperately starving.

Coyote went and got a three foot branch from a service berry bush and carved a point at both ends, scraping off all the bark. When this was done, he called over his oldest son and said "You sure smell. You must have dirtied your rear. Stoop over so I can see your back end." He pushed the boy over and rammed the stick up until it came out of the top of his head.

There was a small fire burning and he set the stick up to roast his boy, like a salmon. When he was cooked, they all ate and that was how they got by that lean time. They had to eat their own child, oldest to youngest, each in turn, until Coyote and Mole ate them all.

---

[13] This version relies on TBC and other elders. Ending in the sky, the downriver trek of the boys also provides a time frame for the Ribbon Cliffs landmark.

Then he left his wife, and started traveling. Then he got to feeling hurt, feeling really bad and aching about his lost children. So he started crying pretty loud, continuously, as he walked until he came to a cliff (like the one down near this house). An echo started coming back to him. When he was crying, he could hear himself bouncing off the cliff. Pretty soon, Coyote got very mad at this. He tried to tell the echo to shut up and not to repeat the same words back at him. Of course, being Coyote, he said a few bad things, mostly about a too dirty rear end. But the echo repeated this back to him, and he couldn't figure out what was happening. So he called upon his sisters to come out of his insides and give him advice about what to do. The little sisters, of course, declined to help him because afterwards he would just say that he really knew what to do all along, just like always before and after this. Finally, as his constant threat, Coyote called upon Rain – to wash them away, and Sun – to dry them out into powder to blow away – before the sisters agreed to help. They told him "You gather some wood with lots of pitch, and build a fire right down at the base of the cliff. Make it a real hot fire close to the bottom of the cliff. When it gets extremely hot, the solid wall of the cliff will break apart and you'll hear a baby crying. That baby will be newly created so check to see if it is a boy or a girl. If it is a girl, destroy it and build another fire. Continue doing the same." Eventually, the cliff broke off many times until finally the baby was a little boy called *stk^watl. Coyote took care of that little boy as his son until it grew up.

About the same time, a beautiful woman was out digging roots. She grabbed a root and, as she was pealing it noticed how it resembled a man's member. It looked just like one and her mind fixated on that thought until she decided to use the root for sex while she hid herself.

Soon she was pregnant and gave birth to a baby boy during the same time Coyote was fracturing the cliff to get the other baby boy. Both boys grew up to be teenagers before they met and started to go around together, becoming close friends ~ chums. They were old enough to travel and to make a living by themselves.

They heard everyone was having a meeting somewhere in the south. The chief and the council were in charge of selecting who would be the Sun and the Moon because they had thought that they should have light in the sky. All animals tried it out, but none worked out. Long-legged crane tried but at noon his feet were still coming up from the east so he was eliminated. Coyote arrived and he tried, but he kept reporting what he saw from the sky, gossiping all over about misdeeds such as a man getting into trouble with somebody else's wife and many other embarrassments. Of course, they kicked Coyote out and he left.

As Coyote was coming back up the Columbia River, he heard about this monster Dog that was living at Ribbon Cliff near Entiat. It swallowed whole whatever came downriver. Coyote thought to challenge this Dog, so he went to get a giant pine tree with long limbs to choke that Dog when it swallowed the log. He dragged the tree to the shore, climbed on, and floated down the Columbia towards the cliff. The Dog was blind so he had Sparrow Hawk as watchman, eyes for him. Whenever he saw people coming, Hawk[14] would sing his own name "ch ch", and Dog would always ask "What did you say?" Hawk replied, "People are coming from such-and-such a direction." Then Dog would suck in his breath and swallow the people. When Coyote came down riding on the big tree, Dog, alerted by the Hawk, swallowed Coyote.

Meanwhile, those two chums had grown up to be strong men, probably in their 20s, and

---

[14] Hawk is *ciqwwya'* < *cqw5* 'digger, snake eater, hawk' (Mattina 1987: 10), with the first sound "*ts*" not "*ch*".

decided to go down to the meeting to try their luck. On the way, they too heard about this monster Dog and decided to detour there by canoe, staying out of Hawk's view until they could land on the back side of the mountain. Climbing up right behind him, they sneaked to within 20-30 feet of him. Hawk now saw them and just started to sing when these chums made a motion for him to stop and he did. Puzzled, Dog asked "What did you see?" Hawk said he had just dozed off and started to dream.

The boys motioned for the bird to follow them over the hill, where they said to the bird "We're going to make a real pretty bird out of you. When we finish with you, then you will be able to travel on your own." Then Sparrow Hawk was made pretty, just as they are now. With Hawk happy, gone, and silent; they took big sticks and whipped Dog until he started bawling like any dog does. He was bleeding and running around on that cliff, leaving behind those red bands that provide the name for Ribbon Cliffs.

Everyone who had been swallowed came out Dog's rear end, most of them alive and well. Ant was the last out, squeeze around the middle by the closing anus. Then the men issued a commandment that Dog would become a young pup thereafter and live in the cliff. If humans camp there, and a close member of their family is going to die, the Pup will cry out. Because of this, today, people are reluctant to stop or camp there.

The boys continued down to the big meeting. A plump, short lady there fell in very much in love with the two men at first sight. Using her power to make rain, she urged the men into her home. All the lodges were miserable inside because the downpour kept dense smoke from leaving. The men kept moving around, visiting all of the lodges, looking for a place to sleep, every one was very smoky. Finally, they noticed one clean lodge with smoke rising up perfectly. Walking in, they found the plump lady, who said "You can stay here." She was especially looking at the boy born from the root. She got more bold and asked "Where do you want me to fix _our_ bed?" He took exception to this, and he pulled out his eye lid, saying, "Fix it right here on my cheek." Equally mad, the woman jumped on to his face. She was Frog. He was making fun of her, so she jumped right on his face to spite him forever.

Though they tried to get her off, she was there to stay, "just like a woman". This Root-boy thought to be the Sun, but, with a Frog on his face, he told Cliff-boy to go first and so he became the Sun. and that is how the Sun was created by Coyote's boy. Man and Frog became the Moon, and at the full you can see Frog right on his face.

A good storyteller, at the very end, should look up into the sky, strongly exhale, and say, "Tomorrow will cloud up and shower before Sun comes out bright."

How Beaver Stole Fire[15]

In the early days of the animal people there was no fire on the earth. The people ate their food raw or cooked it by the heat of the sun. They had no fire in their teepees.

"There is fire up in the sky," Eagle said one day. "Let us go up to the sky and get it." So the animal people had a big gathering they came from all over the country, "We must have a war dance before we go," Someone said. "Someone sing a song that we can dance to." So different

---

[15] Relying on Clara Moore's wire recording (June 1950) as told by her Sanpoil great uncle. The "Little Fellow" shooting arrows is variously Woodpecker ~ Sapsucker ~ Wren. Beaver's heroics in gaining fire fits with his equally cosmic role in the creation of tribes.

ones would sing. "Oh that is not good enough," Someone said, "We can't dance to that." Magpie sang his song, it wasn't good enough. Crow sang his song, that wasn't good enough. They couldn't dance to that. Wolf sang his song but it wasn't good enough. Then the people called on Grizzly Bear to sing his song. "Oh that is ugly!. We can't dance to that!" The people kept on singing until it was Coyote's turn to sing his song. It was a good song but the people didn't like it. It's good enough," they said, "But we can never depend on Coyote, he doesn't know what he's doing he's liable to do anything and lose out anyway." There were two little fellows who hadn't sang yet, Bat and Chickadee, so they called on them. They called [2] on Chickadee but his song wasn't good enough. Then they called on Bat. "Oh I can't sing any song," said Bat. But they kept after him. So he started out with his song. When he had finished, all the people hollered, "That's the song we want!" "Sing it again."

So they all jumped up and war danced to Bat's song. "Now we'll have to fix a road to get up into heaven," they said. Of course they all had bows and arrows. "We'll have to try to make a road of arrows to climb up on." They tried and tried and tried to make a road. The big animals used all their arrows but they couldn't reach the sky, so they came to Bat and Chickadee again.

The big animals laughed when Chickadee stepped up with his bow and arrow. He took aim and shot carefully. All the people watched. His arrow reached the sky and stuck there. He shot another arrow, it stuck in the first arrow and stayed there. He shot a third arrow and it stayed in the second arrow. He kept on shooting. When he emptied his two bags of arrows, the long chain reached almost to the ground. He used other people's arrows to finish the road.

Then they climbed up to heaven to steal fire and bring it down to earth. Grizzly Bear was the last one to start up the arrow road. "I must take a bag of food with me," he said. "There may not be any food up there." So Grizzly Bear started up with a bag of food, but he was so heavy that he broke the ladder and fell flat on the ground. Grizzly Bear had to stay at home. [3]

When all the other people got up in the sky, Eagle was boss. He was the one who first had the idea of getting the fire and bringing it down here. Like all bosses, he stayed behind and he sent his people out to look around. It was night when the people got up there. "Who's going to see about the fire?," asked Eagle. Then he sent people out in pairs. Dog and Frog were partners. They were too lazy to look, they lay around, and lay around, and lay around, and, of course, didn't find anything. Then they went back. "We didn't see anything." Eagle got disgusted, "We've got to do better then that, I'll go myself. Beaver you come with me." "Alright!"

Beaver traveled on water and Eagle flew overhead. He got on a big tree close to the Sky People's houses. Beaver swam down the river to a fish trap, he went into the trap and played dead. Early the next morning a man went down to see what was in his trap. "Oh, there's a fine Beaver dead here." So he took it up to the Chief's house. "See the Beaver," he said. "Doesn't it have nice soft fur?" "I'm going to skin him right away." Eagle was up in a cottonwood tree looking down. He moved and some men saw him. "Oh, what a pretty bird, we've got to get that bird, we must kill it so that we can have its feathers for a headdress." The men went to the lodge to get their bows and arrows.

The man with Beaver took him into the chief's house. That's the house the fire was in. Soon they had him almost skinned. Beaver was afraid they were going to take his hide entirely off. If they took it off he wouldn't be able to put it back on again.

Outside the house Eagle was scared that the men were going to [4] hit him. Their arrows were coming closer. Just as Beaver's skin was almost all off except around his jaws, the men outside called out, "Come on and shoot, see who can hit him. Eagle's going to fly off soon." The men skinning Beaver heard them and ran out with their knives in hands. Beaver jumped up, rolled over and into his skin and put it all back on. It was just as good as ever. He took the fire, stuck it under his fingernails and rushed to the river. Everybody was looking at Eagle way up there in the air. No one saw Beaver until he was almost in the water.

Eagle watched his partner come out of the house. He kept dodging the arrows until Beaver got into the river. Then he flew away. "Oh, we missed Eagle," the Sky people hollered.

The man who had been skinning Beaver ran back into the house. Beaver was gone, the fire was gone also. "Oh, we've lost our fire," he hollered. "Our fire is gone."

Eagle and Beaver rushed back to their people, they were gathered near the top of the arrow road. We have the fire," said Eagle. "Let us get down before the Sky People get here." "The ladder is broken," the people told him. Grizzly Bear and his bag of food were too heavy for it." "The birds can fly down and the little animals can ride down on the big bird's backs, the rest of you get down the best you can," said Eagle, who was the boss.

So the little animals rode down on the big bird's backs. Coyote made his powers and turned himself into a pine needle and floated down. But soon the pine needle was going very fast, too fast to suit Coyote. So Coyote called on his powers again and changed himself [5] into a leaf, then he floated down slowly. He made a nice landing. But Sucker did not, he jumped from the last arrow where Grizzly Bear had broken them. Sucker landed on a rock face first, flattened his mouth, and shattered all his bones. Suckers have a flat mouth to this day and so have to suck their food. They are still very boney.

When all the people had reached the earth, they had a big gathering at the place where they had war danced to Bat's song. "Who has the fire," they asked. All looked at Eagle. "I don't have the fire," said Eagle. "We don't have the fire, sang Magpie and Crow. "We don't have the fire," sang Chickadee and Bat.

They all sang with their hands spread out open. Then Beaver stepped out in front. He spread his hand out, wide open and began this song.

> "I am holding what we went for
> I am holding what we went after."

But no one could see anything in his hands. His daughter went up to him and looked at his fingers. His oldest daughter looked at his first finger but there was no fire there. Beaver kept on singing,

> "I am holding what we went after
> I am holding what we went after."

His second daughter looked at his second finger but there was no fire there. His oldest daughter looked at his third finger and found some fire hidden in his double fingernails. His second daughter looked at his fourth finger and found some fire hidden in his double fingernails.

Beaver then stored the fire in the wood of many trees. What Beaver brought down from the sky is still with us. Fire is in every tree. Whenever we want fire, we can get it from wood.

Grizzly Lady[16]

Living in the Methow was a heavy-set lady about 55 years old with two equally heavy-set daughters. All were single. The mother may have been widowed, and the girls were fairly good looking. All were scouting around for son-in-laws. Meeting a young man, the mother said, "We need somebody to marry my youngest daughter so we can have support and food." In those days, young men carried bows and arrows, some the sharp arrow points of professional hunters, always prepared to hunt. Every offer was accepted, but to bad consequences. A young hunter would go home to the lodge, and share the bed of the youngest that night.

While he slept, the mother switched his stone arrowpoints for ones made from pitch, looking identical because of how she painted them. Made from pitch, they are harmless. That was her plan for his destruction.

Early the next morning, the oldest daughter went to a nearby hillside to dig up white roots. Once outside, the oldest girl became a grizzly bear, ready to kill. The mother then shouted to wake up her son-in-law, "There's a big grizzly bear out there, on the side of the hill. Please kill it as we need fur blankets and meat." Jumping up, with his bow and arrows at the ready, he leaves as his mother-in-law warns him to carefully approach the grizzly from the lower down hill side, and never to go above it. [2]

The hunter sneaks up under the grizzly within shooting distance, takes aim, and shoots an arrow, only to see it hit the bear and shatter, the point fell to pieces. Defenseless, the grizzly killed him quickly, tossing his body under a wind-fall log. These women plotted to destroy all of the young men because they were mean tempered, allowing each a one night stand with the youngest girl to further weaken a hunter.

Coyote knew what was going on, as always. He decided to visit his son living in the south, telling him, "I want you to go up there, accept their proposal, and kill the eldest girl." Being sensible, of course, the boy didn't want to do this. Coyote talked long and hard to change the mind of Muskrat, a man with an exceptional combination of youth, power, and intelligence. He was devoted to Sweathouse teachings, so, out of duty, agreed to come up to the Twisp River, where favored white roots grow. He wandered near their home until the lady saw him and proposed marriage with her youngest. Muskrat accepted, knowing, on his father's advice, to have extra strong stone arrowpoints ready to replace those substituted by the woman.

Like others, he went to bed with the youngest girl, who discovered she really did love him. [3] Also, the daughters were getting fed up with their mothers tricks, arguing "We have got to quit this," but their mother was ruthless. Late at night, the mother exchanged harmless pitch points for stone ones. At first light, early in the morning, she shouted for him to kill the grizzly. He arose, already knowing her plan. Taking his bow and arrow, he heard the old lady tell him to approach from the lower side. Once outside, however, he replaced his stone points, and took to the higher ground. The mother got more and more worried it was taking so long.

Muskrat came down on the grizzly from above, got within shooting distance, and made a kissing sound with his lips to get the bear's attention. When Grizzly looked up and saw her threatened position, she said in her human voice, "You're really not going to kill me are you?

---

[16] Relying on TBC. Specifically set in the Methow, its audience visualized its landscape as these episodes unfolded. As always, native stories illustrate what not to do by offending modesty, as well illustrated by public indiscretions of Coyote herein and elsewhere.

Your own sister-in-law." At the same moment, he released the stone arrow, killing her instantly. As she was falling over, he sprinted for the river (the source of his power), running for all he was worth, tossing his bow and arrows away. Divining into the swift current, swimming under water, he quickly and safely escaped.

But the Twisp river there flows crooked so mother Grizzly could take a short cut, [4] watching the mud flows to trace his trail underwater. Muskrat always kept ahead. Grizzly got very tired and ready to give up, but Coyote laughed aloud from his hiding place on top of a hill, shouting, "*Wah wah, wah, wah*. Now your daughter is dead, you killed far too many." Really angered, the mother got a second wind and chased Coyote, who came to the edge of a deep canyon and could not go on. As usual, he called out his sisters, and, after some disagreements, they told him to use part of his male member to become a log over the canyon. He did so, they reentered his gut, and he crossed to safety. When Grizzly approached the canyon, she saw the log was still there and started to walk over. Near the end, as she jumped off, the log jerked up and caught her right between her legs. It felt very good, so, thrilled, she tried it again, this time really rocking and straddling the log. She repeated this experience three more times until Coyote realized she wasn't behind him. Doubling back, he laughed loudly at her doings.

Getting her even madder, Coyote was in serious trouble so he again called on his sisters, who told him to build a bear trap. When he balked, the sisters built the trap for him, using grease for bait. The tracking Grizzly mother edged carefully into the trap to take a bite of the grease, and the trap crashed down on her front end and left her rear end sticking straight up in the air. Coyote was nearby, ready for the kill. His sisters were telling him to "Hurry up" because they were losing strength trying to hold down half of her. Responding, Coyote took a stick, rubbed it, and called out *wii-yxk-sas*, probing her rear end. His sisters kept shouting more frantically "Hurry and kill her." [5] Sure enough, they weakened and bear escaped. Grizzly rushed at Coyote, who instantly pulled back his foreskin ("skinned himself"), causing a fog. Darkness made it impossible to see even the fingers of a hand. Coyote sprinted miles away, but she kept charging. He made fog several times, but his power weakened, making only twilight.

As Grizzly closed in on Coyote, a badger hole appeared and he jumped inside the small hole. Grizzly was much too big to enter. Determined, she sat there all day and many days after. After ten days of starvation, he called upon his sisters, who told him to act like a leader, a chief haranguing his people, with the sisters pretended to be a crowd, responding "ii" and sounding like a whole town of dogs and people. Coyote spoke of a river and a boat to take them away to *taq^{w}iyma'*, where there was lots of food. He sounded real authentic, like a radio blasting.

Grizzly was on her guard and heard it all, thinking Coyote was with lot of people and lots of food. Just to be sure, she waited through another night. By then he was skin and bones, but, at dawn, he announced, "We're moving to *taq^{w}iyma*, we're going to *taq^{w}iyma* across the river." The first boat filled and there was the sound of them sailing away, but it really was just Coyote rolling around. Finally, only whining dogs were left behind. Grizzly was convinced, but to be absolutely sure, she stayed for a day or two longer, without hearing any other sounds.

Finally, late in the afternoon she left. Coyote could barely make it out of the hole, weak and staggering, but his special power had saved him, even though the only food then available to him were grasshoppers. And so …

"Rain for tomorrow, before it clears up so the sun shines."

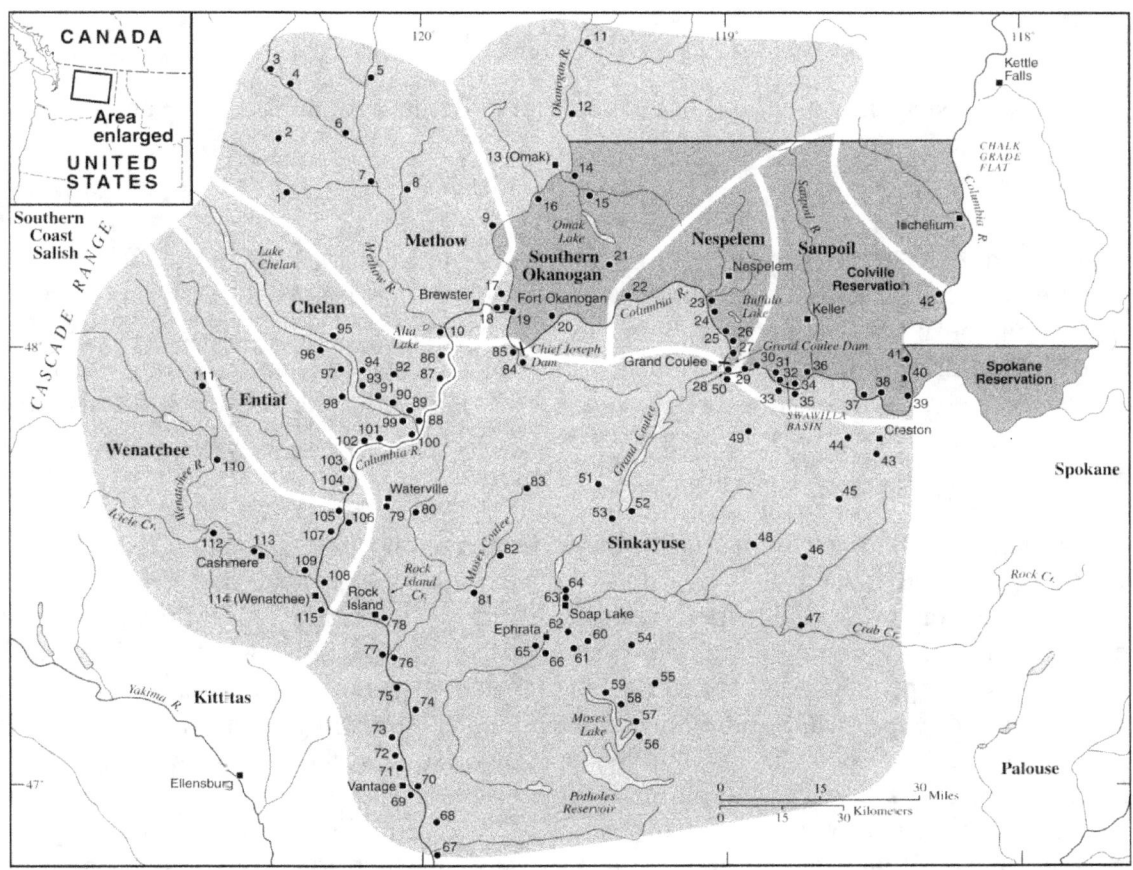

Methow Winter Villages among Middle Columbia Interior Salish

1 ntqʷləks ??

2 k̓aʔsáłqn 'twin peaks'

3 nkʷaʔłtank 'water on cliff'

4 ntə́tə́qʷús 'brush next to bank'

5 cwax 'creek'

6 stix̱ʷyyáp ??

7 txʷə́c̓p Twisp

8 łc̓əpc̓əpús ??

9 sləxíʔst(m) 'bluff with holes'

10 nxə́n̓cin 'bluff at the river mouth'

ROUTINES

Seasons, tasks, and community needs provided Methow rhythms of time and place.

Daily Round

The summer day often began before sunrise in the Methow household. With the aid of dry pine needles or sagebrush bark an old woman, always the first to arise, brought to life the fires which had been banked the night before with hardwood and knots. This accomplished she wakened the children, prodding them on the soles of the feet with the fire tongs if they were slow. Immediately upon leaving their beds the boys and girls ran to their respective bathing places on the river. They plunged into the water two or three times, the bolder ones diving, then hurried back to dry themselves around the fires. While they stood there they were tutored by the old woman in the knowledge and ideals of their people. Men were allowed to rise at their leisure but the old woman called and chided the younger women if they were not soon out of their beds. Babies were permitted to sleep as long as they would.

The younger women, departed immediately to pick berries or discharge other duties while the morning was yet cool. The children soon left to play in the sands of the river bank. The old women swept the floors, rolled up the unoccupied bedding and kept the fires burning. When the men arose they went to their sweat lodges or to the fishing platforms to spear salmon. Old men bathed and returned to sit around the house. As soon as the babies awakened they were bathed in baskets of warm water and placed in their cradles.

About ten o'clock those who had been away returned. The women turned to preparing the morning meal. Water was brought from the river in which to cook the salmon. The fish were cut up and put in the cooking basket with hot rocks with which the water was boiled. After the water had been kept boiling for about twenty minutes the food was ready. The salmon were removed from the basket with a sharp stick to be placed on the eating mat which had been unrolled on the floor. Fresh berries were served in a basket. If camas had been cooked with the salmon the cooking basket itself was placed on the mat along with a large horn spoon. The men and children were called and all seated themselves around the mat. The men sat with their legs beneath them, or outstretched; women sat on one foot or folded their legs together under them. Children ate with their elders only it no strangers were present. Invalids were fed later.

After the meal was finished the mat was laid out in the sun and the baskets were washed and hung on pegs in the lodge. Men devoted the remainder of the morning to dressing. Women did not take as long; when they were through they combed their husbands' hair. The early afternoon was given over to social activities, particularly gambling and visiting.

The evening meal was served at dusk. It differed little from the morning meal. Afterwards the children gathered around the reclining old people and begged for stories. The young men went out to smoke and discuss affairs of the day with their comrades. The young women attended to small duties about the [30] house. Bedtime came soon for the children; they were not allowed to remain up after dark. The men retired soon after dark and after them the women; this order was observed because the women would have been ashamed to be seen in bed by men who were still up.

The daily routine during the winter was much less diversified except for the ceremonial season when life was fullest. The time of arising, as in the summer, was before dawn, but the actual hour was later. Children bathed in the icy waters of the river; adults washed, in baskets of cool water or went to the sweat lodges. The morning meal was dispensed with during the winter. One meal a day was sufficient during this time of inactivity and shortage of food.

Morning tasks included cleaning away freshly fallen snow outside the house and along paths to water and fuel, using a paddle-like shovel of wood and brooms of sagebrush.

Men departed early in the morning if a hunting expedition had been planned. Otherwise they spent the day mainly indoors, smoking and chatting. Children played outside in the snow. Women attended to the household tasks and made baskets.

The daily meal was served late in the afternoon (some families preferred to have it in the morning). Dried foods were boiled. Often salmon alone constituted the meal.

Smoking and story telling occupied the evening. All went to bed soon after dark.

Yearly Cycle

Life began anew for the Methow with the coming of each spring. Selective "indigenous incendiarism" (Ross 2011: 267) burned lowlands after birds had nested in spring and uplands in the fall. After extreme inactivity of the winter months the first signs of spring were occasion for rejoicing. Moreover, fresh food would soon again be available to replace the winter diet of dried products broken only by an occasional meal of venison. The underground houses were deserted at the first opportunity. Temporary camps were established nearby for the sake of a change in surroundings and fresher air. This transfer of residence was usually made during the month called "time that the buttercups bloom," which corresponds roughly to March. The new quarters were occupied for two or three weeks during which time the men gathered shell fish and hunted fowl and rabbits. At the same time the women were digging the few early edible roots which had appeared on the warm sandy hillsides near the river, and were gathering prickly pears, which were eagerly eaten after the spines had been burned off and they had been roasted. At this time those who had spent the winter away from home returned to their own villages.

During the early part of the following month, "time that the leaves come out," there was a general removal from the Columbia to the root digging grounds on the plains south of the river. Before leaving, the winter mat houses were dismantled and all goods which were not to be transported were cached in trees or on elevated racks and platforms. Village groups did not move in a body across the river but bands formed of four or five families each and journeyed to their favorite spots. Each band before leaving notified the chief of its intended destination. The largest group usually went with the chief.

The root digging activities opened with the celebration of the first roots ceremony at which the first products of the ground were ceremonially eaten. For the women the ensuing period was one of industrious labor. A whole year's supply of roots had to be gathered and dried. It was necessary to move camp often in order to be near fresh fields. This was a considerable task in itself even though the mats for the conical shelters were fairly light and the hut designed to be erected quickly. The men did not assist in this work. Indeed, the man's life at this time was as leisurely as his wife's was arduous. He occasionally hunted rabbits and antelope but spent much of the time lolling about camp gossiping or gambling with other men. His time of intense activity, the summer fishing season, was yet to come.

The old and ill and crippled remained during this time at the winter camps on the river along with a few able bodied persons to care for them. The extensive travelling during root digging made it impractical to take the incapacitated along. When the travellers returned home with their products they were shared with those who had had to remain. [28]

The summer fishing season began about the first of May, when sturgeon and small fish were available. Trout and salmon appeared soon afterwards. Most of the members of each winter village built summer mat shelters at the fishing grounds nearest that village but some preferred to go elsewhere. The largest traps were located at the mouth of the Methow river, the mouth of the Spokane River and at Kettle Falls. These places always drew persons from far and near. Like the root digging, the salmon season was initiated with a ceremony, the first salmon rite. This observance was the most elaborate ceremony outside of the winter season. During a five day period of feasting and celebration the salmon was handled and eaten in a rigidly prescribed fashion. Social as well as economic life was intense from the opening rite to the end of the season at the end of August. Each day was punctuated with the distributions of the salmon at which time everyone gathered together. Visitors were constantly coming and going and gambling was rampant. The greatest amount of travel occurred toward the end of the season when the fish became scarce. There was always the hope that some distant site might prove more productive. The women were far from idle while the men were fishing and gambling. Their tasks were cooking and drying salmon, and gathering berries during any spare time.

About the first of September the dried salmon were temporarily stored on the flat tops of the summer shelters and a general disbanding of the group took place. Some went into the mountains to gather the fall roots and to hunt. Others went directly to the fall fishing grounds where they speared the silver and dog salmons from canoes or caught them with seines. The shelter used at this time was the same type as that in the spring, a conical mat hut. A closed structure was necessary for the fall salmon had to be dried indoors by the heat of the campfire. The heat from the sun was no longer great enough.

Winter villages were reoccupied about the middle of October. All dried foods were placed in their permanent storage places, the underground houses were cleaned and repaired, the long winter mat houses were rebuilt and general preparations were made for a winter of seclusion. Most of the work at this time fell to the lot of the men. The winter houses were made exclusively by the men except for the mats which were woven by the women. Men cut or gathered the supply of wood but women carried it in, as well as rye grass to cover the floors.

Mats of cattail tules, used for all purposes, were made in lengths up to twenty feet. Prepared cattails were laid side by side and sewed together with hemp cord, using a needle of hardwood. The latter was elliptical in section, slightly curved, and from six to twelve inches long. Five or six tules were pierced at a time and the thread drawn through. Seams were separated by intervals of about six inches. The edges of the mat were often twined with willow cord for added strength. Mats used for the final stage of salmon drying after the fish had been removed from the racks were made of slender young branches of willow twined with hemp.

The three midwinter months were descriptively named: "time that it snows"; "time that it gets cold"; and "time that it is white." It was necessary to spend most of the time indoors because of the severity of the weather. Women made baskets and mats, fashioned and mended clothing and prepared the meals. Men went on occasional hunting trips but were left with much unoccupied time which they spent playing games, telling stories or sleeping. There was one welcome break in the monotony of the season. The great ceremonial period of the year came at midwinter. Dances were held in continuous succession for as long as two months. Families travelled from one dance to another for the duration of that period. Guardian spirit, songs [29] were sung and shamanistic performances executed. Emotion was built up and released. At the end of the series of dances all were more content to await the coming of spring.

Salmon[17]

"It is dinner time, fresh Salmon from our very own personal fishtrap. Time to enjoy our own special delicious food," said the youngest of the five sisters who lived together near the mouth of the Columbia River.[18]

"Good idea," agreed the others. "You go down and bring up a Salmon while we get the rest of the food assembled for our meal." And the youngest sister did so.

When she returned with the clubbed salmon, the other sisters had put out cooked roots, fresh vegetables, and berries for the meal. The salmon was boiled and all ate from the same kettle. Afterwards, all of the bones were gathered up and placed back into the fishtrap set in the river. As soon as the bones hit the bottom, they turned back into a salmon. If any bones were lost, the salmon was crippled until the bones were found and added to the water.

These sisters were shore birds and they enjoyed the only access to salmon in the world at that time. During the day, they scattered out along the plains and dug roots, picked greens, or gathered fruits. In the fall, they harvested many kinds of berries.

They lived well and were content. If strangers came by they were made to feel unwelcome. The sisters did not want to share the secret of the salmon. Yet word had leaked out that these women had something special. Eventually Coyote heard about it.

Coyote was greedy, selfish, and powerful. At the beginning of the world, he was the first creature to think for himself and so was given particular powers by the Creator. Unlike other beings, whose center was their heart, Coyote's power was in his intestines. When he needed help, he called to his "little sisters" who came out and spoke to him.

"Come out, come out, my little sisters," Coyote said as he squatted down. Reluctantly, the sisters came out.

"What do you want, Coyote," they responded. "You always ask for our help and when we give it, you always say that you knew it all along and that we were no help to you. But we know that we do help you, regardless of what you say."

"Quiet, little ones," ordered Coyote. "If you will not be silent, I will call the rain to wash you away. Be careful and pay attention. I need to ask you something."

"We will listen," they gurgled.

"I hear that there are some lovely women down the big river and that they have a special food, a very tasty food. They will not allow anyone to visit them. They will not share. They are bad women and no one has been able to get the better of them. What should I do to trick them out of that special food?"

The sisters stood for a moment and then said, "Coyote, you will have to change yourself. Anyone who knows of or about you will know your ways and send you packing. You will not have a chance. You must look innocent and harmless. You must become a baby. Those women would probably fuss over a baby. That will be how you will trick them."

---

[17] This epic is still told among the people of the Colville and Yakama Reservations. Though it has mostly appeared in academic reports, other aspects of Colville literature appear in Mourning Dove (1990), a local native author whose pen name derives from the mourning widow of Salmon, as his body returns to the sea.

[18] Set at the mouth of the Columbia River, the lifeline, along with the Fraser, of the Plateau, Coyote's trek upriver provides a systematic conceptual map.

"No, sisters," shouted Coyote, "that will not work. I am too old to be a baby and I do not like messy diapers. I am strong and clean."

"You are mangy and hardly strong," replied the sisters. "Squat down so that we can get back inside. We've had enough. Either follow our advice or fail. Those are your only choices."

Coyote let the sisters return, and went on his way. After some time, he said aloud, "My sisters are no help. I will have to rely on my own cleverness. I will turn into a baby. That is something they did not think of. I will be bound in a cradleboard that will float down the river."

And saying so, he did so. He became a baby laced into a large wooden cradleboard and floated down the Columbia. After a time, he lodged against the fishtrap owned by the sisters. When the oldest went to get a salmon for their meal, she rushed back to their home, shouting, "Sisters, sisters, come quick. I have found a baby. A cute little baby. Abandoned and resting on the water against our trap. He will be ours."

"What is this about a baby. How do you know it is a boy, all I see is a soggy lump of wood and leather," said a middle sister.

"That is a mighty suspicious baby," questioned the youngest. "Look at his eyes, they are much too alert for any ordinary baby. It is some monster or someone else trying to trick us. Throw it back into the river and sink it."

"No. No, he is now mine," argued the oldest sister. "He has the cradleboard of a boy. That is how I know he is a boy. He is bright and intelligent to survive in the water for so long. That is why his eyes look as they do. Soon I will change him and make him dry, then we will know for sure. If you don't want him, I do. If you won't care for him, then I'll do it alone."

"No, sister," said the others, "that is not right. We are a family and will all be mothers."

"I will help too, but I remain suspicious," cautioned the youngest. "For now, though, we must be kind and keep the baby warm and dry."

They all helped to change and clean the baby, admiring his strong limbs and tiny body.

"Look, he has teeth," said the oldest. "He does not seem old enough to have teeth. He is truly advanced in growth and intelligence. Look how he watches us. Let us feed him bits of our food. Otherwise we will have to use salmon broth to feed him."

"Slowly, he eats our food," whispered a sister. "He will be easy to care for. He can eat solid food. He will be a very good boy."

Thus pleased with their new responsibility, the sisters retired for the night, leaving the baby in a warm, dry cradle. Coyote wished that the trick was over so that he could share beds with these sisters, but he knew that would defeat his plan and, for once, he restrained himself. Still, he thought, "That salmon stuff is very good. Roasted or broiled, it tastes wonderful. I can hardly wait to eat a whole fish by myself. These little morsels do me no good. I am a big man and I must eat in quantity to sustain myself. Tomorrow I will begin the work of freeing the salmon." With that he went to sleep.

In the morning, the sisters continued their discussions.

"I want to take the baby with me today," said the oldest.

"No, you can't do that, I want to take the baby with me," said another.

"Neither of you can because I will take the baby with me," responded a third.

The youngest took charge, saying "No. No one will take the baby with them as they wander over the plains. It will slow you down. We will get less food. We will leave the baby laced in his cradle and suspended from this tree. He will rock in the wind and be safe. He will be out of the way and we will all be able to get our work done."

After some reluctance, the other sisters agreed that this was a better plan. They would check on the baby at noon when they had lunch at home and if things looked dubious, someone would stay with the baby that afternoon. Then they left.

As Coyote rocked in the breeze, he debated whether he should nap while it was so quiet and comfortable or whether he should begin to free the salmon. He napped.

Noon came and the sisters found him sleeping peacefully. They liked their plan even better. During the afternoon, Coyote napped again.

For several days, that is all Coyote did; relax and enjoy attention by his five mothers.

Finally, he had had enough of morsels and was ready for a big meal of fish. For five days, he slipped out of his cradle and went behind the lodge to make antler picks. He made a single pick each day. For the next five days, he made stone bowls. Each day he took a boulder and carefully cracked off a flat side and hollowed it out.

During this time, the youngest sister changed the baby's diaper and said, "Sisters, come look. Do not these ripples over his body look suspiciously like muscles. How could a tiny baby develop muscles? All he does is rock, sleep, eat, and fill his diaper."

"It is because we are feeding him so well," replied the eldest. "We are putting meat on his bones. That is all."

"I do not think so, sister," said the youngest. "This boy bears watching. I still think his eyes are too clever by half and he is waiting to trick us."

Coyote tried to look innocent, but he knew that his moment had come. Tomorrow he must break through the weir and free the salmon. He would take them upriver and become a hero to the people. No longer would they despise him as a fool, a coward, and a trickster. He would earn his rightful place as a leader of men, and women too.

Next morning, as soon as the sisters left the lodge, Coyote released himself and gathered up his picks and bowls. He went down to the water and began to pick apart the trap. He worked in a hurry and made too much noise.

The youngest sister left that day reluctantly. Her suspicions were high. Her eye twitched and that was a bad sign. She did not go very far from home because of this and heard the sounds of the pick almost as soon as Coyote started.

"Quick, sisters. Come quick. Our fishtrap is being destroyed," she screamed again and again as she rushed to the river.

Coyote had already used up two of his picks. When he saw the sister coming and the others following close behind, he put the first stone bowl on his head.

The youngest sister swung her digging stick and pounded Coyote over the head, but the bowl broke the stick and the youngest retreated, screaming, "Hit him. Hit him hard, sisters. It is Coyote. He has been tricking us all along. I told you so. Kill him before he steals our salmon. It is all we have."

Each sister, in turn, rushed up to Coyote and slammed her digging stick down on to his head. Each blow broke a stone bowl he wore as a helmet. As the oldest sister struck, the last bowl broke, but so too did the trap.

Coyote dove into the water, calling back, "I will see all of you lovelies later when you have need of a man. For now, though, I will take these fine fish upriver and show them how they will fill the waterways with their nourishment. You should not have kept them to yourself. Now you will only have the memory of them unless you go through all the pain and labor of catching them in the future."

After swimming a ways upriver, Coyote went to the beach and laid in the sun, drying off. The salmon warmed in the shallow water. When he was dry, Coyote built a fire and said, "Come here some fine, young, firm salmon. I am ready to eat." Immediately a salmon jumped onto the sand and died. Coyote cooked and ate it, carefully returning the bones to the water where the salmon reappeared.

Coyote, of course, delighted in his new power over life and death. He continued upriver.

At the first village, he walked into the center shouting, "My people, I have a wonderful new food. It is a kind of fish called salmon. I will share it with you if you will share one of your maidens with me. I will marry her for the night and, in the morning, I will be on my way."

The adults met in council. A woman said, "This is Coyote. Remember who we are dealing with. He can not be trusted. How can we be sure that he will do as he says. I certainly do not want any of my daughters spending the night with that vagrant. He is vile and nasty on his best days."

"You are wise to be cautious, woman," responded an elder. "But if this salmon is truly as good as they say, we will be well served to play Coyote's game. I vote that we risk it. We must make sure to allow only a plain girl to share his bed." To this they all agreed.

Coyote had a wife in the village and, in the morning, he proclaimed, "Since you were not very generous with me, I will not be generous with you. Your fate is I leave smallish salmon in your river. You will have to catch many of them to make a meal or to store enough for winter."

Then Coyote continued upriver. At Chelan, he was refused entry to the village and proclaimed, "Hence forth, for your unkindness, you will have a waterfall between your lake and the river. You will only get salmon at the bottom of the falls. You will have no fish run of your own. That is your fate."

At each village and tributary of the Columbia, Coyote watched how people treated him and left them salmon or none accordingly.

At Kettle Falls, a huge gathering area, there were many people, much visiting, and abundant good times. Coyote married a beautiful, hard-working girl and he was delighted. In the morning, he said, "This is a wonderful place. I was very happy here so I will leave huge salmon at the falls. I bless the people who are here now and will be in the future." Then Coyote he went on with his adventures.

For many years, salmon remained in the places where Coyote put them. They never went everywhere the way salmon do now. This came about when Salmon contested with Wolves for the daughter of a Methow chief. Her name was Morning Dove. Salmon married her, but the Wolves enlisted the aid of Rattlesnake, who shot a magic arrow into Salmon's head, killing him. As Salmon drifted downriver in a canoe, his wife ran along the shore, sobbing and crying. Suddenly, she became a mourning dove.

Salmon went to the ocean and revived with the help of Mouse, who kept smearing grease over the bones. Since then, salmon have lived in the ocean, returning upriver to spawn and die. Every spring when the salmon runs begin, mourning doves greet them along the bands of the many rivers, welcoming them home.

Salmon & Mourning Dove

An elderly chief lived in a village along the Columbia River somewhere between Vantage and the mouth of the Methow River. In his possession were a set of mountain sheep horns that he had tried to "break up into smaller pieces for use as spear points. However, he had been unable to do this for several seasons. He decided to hold a contest to find someone able to break up the bone. He sent a runner to announce this up and down the Columbia. In return for his strength and skill, the winner would receive the beautiful daughter of the chief for his wife. People gathered from far and near, attempting to win the chief's daughter by finishing the required task. The first big strong men failed at the task. They were Grizzly Bear, Cougar, and Wolverine. After them came other young and strong men, but these too failed. Some tried several times to shatter the horns, but to no avail.

The traveler Coyote knew that his own strength was no match for that of all these big animal people, but he had his eyes fixed on the most beautiful daughter. Coyote gave it his best try, but he also failed.

Eventually, it became spring, about the month of May. The husky leader of the Salmon people sent a message by runner to the chief, saying he would arrive at the contest in two days or so. On that day, everyone gathered to witness the strength of Salmon. Runners were sent to other villages to tell people that Salmon had arrived. The chief's daughter could hardly wait to see the leader of the people who were coming from the ocean because she had heard a lot of good things about him. These ocean people came up the Columbia in their canoes, so people watched for them. In the village, all was ready. The chief had placed the horns in the middle of his big lodge, [2] where all the dryland people sat waiting for the red salmon.

The chief's daughter, a Mourning Dove, spent the day getting ready. She had two female slaves to look out for her. As she got ready, she would kid her slave by saying "This is the very last day that you will look after me because I am to be married to the most famous leader of the ocean people."

Finally, a lookout came running into the village, saying the canoes were in sight. Everyone in the lodge became even more anxious, knowing that the canoes were docking and they might witness a miracle.

Of all of them, the beautiful daughter was the most interested, keeping her eyes fixed on the door flap. The first person that she saw enter the lodge was a small man with a very light complexion, making him really handsome. Dove asked her slave if this man was called Salmon. She said, "No, that man is called White Fish." The second man to enter was tall, awkwardly built, and had a big nose. Dove learned from the slave that this was Squaw Fish. The third man was fairly good looking except for his big mouth and thick lips. He was called Sucker. The next man was very handsome with a light complexion and freckled face. Dove was sure that this was Salmon, but the slave said he was Steelhead. Beautiful Dove was disappointed that this was not the ocean leader, but forgot all this when the last man entered. He was the most handsome and perfectly built. He was Red Salmon.

He walked directly to the chief to receive instructions as to how the horns were to be exactly broken. Then he walked to the horns, turned them over in his hands just once, and blew into the open end so some of his spittle also entered into the horns. He gave the horn one strong twist with his bare hands, and it broke into suitable smaller pieces, each one inch wide. He laid all of these in the center of the lodge and stood up, telling the chief his job was done. [3]

Without further comment, he walked over to Mourning Dove, saying "we must go now." He and his beautiful new wife walked out from the lodge and started to cross the 200 yards or less that separated them from the canoes. Just then, the five warrior Wolf brothers attacked.

These brothers were disappointed at losing out for the beautiful lady Dove. The youngest brother was the smartest and in full control of the others. He arranged for the attack to be hand to hand, thinking that bow and arrows or other weapons might endanger Dove.

As the brothers moved towards him, Salmon pinned his wife under his left arm for safety and fought off the brothers with the right hand. Because Salmon was powerful and slippery, the brothers could not hold him long enough to kill him. Salmon moved slowly toward the canoes, where the other ocean people were getting in and pushing off, without lifting a finger to help their leader. Salmon got very close to his canoe and thought he was safe.

However, on the east side of the Columbia across from the chief's village there lived an old warrior. He was lying on his back, with his knees bent and his right leg over the left one. He was singing his very famous warrior song and felt very proud of himself. Eventually, his powerful senses and vision called his attention to the battle over Dove occurring on the other shore. "Oh yes, I see my grandsons are fighting one another over the chief's daughter," he said and he began to wonder which side he should help. He thought "One of my grandsons comes up in the spring and leaves in the fall, returning to the ocean until the following year, but the other five grandsons remain here year around because they are dryland people, therefore I will aid them." He got his famous bow and arrows, took out one of his fangs to put it an arrow, and shot it nearly a mile across the river. [4] His aim was true; the arrow struck Salmon behind the head.

Salmon knew he was hit, released his wife, and kicked the ground very hard with his powerful legs. He sailed high up into the air and landed in the Columbia, halfway between the shore and the middle of the river. His body floated down the river and into the Pacific Ocean, reviving when it got to the home of the Salmon. The next year in the spring, Salmon returned, fit and alive. He paddled his way up the Columbia from the Pacific. After many days, he came to a small lodge with smoke coming out through the smoke hole. He decided to stop and visit whoever lived there. He pulled up his canoe and walked the 100 yards to the house. As he approached, he overheard someone whistling a tune. He pushed aside the door flap and walked in, giving the kindest greeting he could think of. The small man inside stopped his work, looked up, but said nothing. He started to whistle again and became very busy. Salmon repeated his warm and cordial greetings, but the man ignored him, pretending he did not even exist. A third time, Salmon gave a greeting and said "My friend, my dear friend, what are you making?" Finally, the man answered "Just what do you suppose I am making? I am making a spear to catch Red Salmon." By then, Salmon was just about fed up with this strange little man, so he reached out, grabbed the man and flopped him on his stomach. Salmon took the spear and let the man have it right in his neck. The man quivered and died, Salmon carried the body down to the Columbia and threw it in where it became White Fish with a round mouth that makes it look like it is whistling. Salmon gave it this commandment; "When the human people arrive here in the future, they must use that same kind of spear as you were making to catch you."[19]

Salmon got back into his canoe and went further upstream. Several days later, he came to another small lodge with smoke coming out of it. He decided to visit there. As he walked slowing toward it, he heard someone singing a [5] warrior song. He stood beside the door flap and learned that the old man inside was really proud of himself, saying "Just one year ago I killed Red Salmon, the most famous leader of the ocean people." At that moment, Salmon walked in, but the old man pretended he did not see him after a quick glance told the old one it was Salmon. His song changed and he began to cry, singing "Just one year ago those mean people killed my beloved grandson Red Salmon." Salmon then replied, "Grandfather, there is no need to cry over me. I am very much alive and stopped in to visit you." The old man was very impressed by these kind words and the visit. It was early in the afternoon, so they sat together and told many stories until they finally got to the hand to hand battle with the five Wolves.

---

[19] This leister, intended for white fish, had inward barbs on a 6-8 foot pole of serviceberry.

Salmon said, "I need your help Grandfather to locate the home of the five brothers, and also to get even with them." The old man responded "I will gladly help you with information and advice for getting even. The five Wolves and your wife with her two elderly women slaves live in the high mountains. Leave your canoe near the base and you can climb up to their twin lodges by about midday. First you must talk alone with the elderly slaves to get them on your side. They will be convinced if you say you are only interested in your wife so you will leave the wealth and property for them. With their aid you will kill all five brothers, then leave with your wife. The slaves can have the deer hides, dried meat, fresh kill, and the two lodges. You must remember that the five are great hunters. They hunt every day, but each returns home separately. The oldest will arrive first, but instead of going straight to the home, he will go to the spring for water and to wash his hands. You must hide close to the spring to attack him easily. You will not have much trouble with the oldest or the next two, but the younger they are, the more smart, intelligent, quick, and accurate." [6]

The old man gave Salmon such information, advice, and encouragement until well past midnight. By then, the old man could hardly keep his eyes open. He told his Grandson to find a place in the lodge to sleep. Salmon said "I am just as happy simply to be with you Grandfather, to talk with you and to hear you talk." The old man was completely exhausted and did not respond. He fell over and slept soundly. Salmon made very sure he was asleep by pushing him around, but the old man continued to sleep.

Now Salmon planned to get even with his monstrous Grandfather. He had the necessary instructions, so he left the house. With his powerful vision, he could see in the dark and gathered much wood, rich in pitch. He piled this around the house, especially in the entrance so there could be no escape. When all was ready, he set it on fire. It flared and quickly engulfed the entire house. Salmon stood nearby and heard his Grandfather call "Grandson, we are on fire, please get out quickly to safety." But then it became quiet inside as the old one burned to death.

Salmon waited around until the ashes cooled off in the late afternoon. He picked out the remains of his Grandfather and with his powerful hands shrunk them until they were 2-3 feet long. Next he put the skull on a flat rock and used another one to flatten it. Then he tossed the remains among the rocks, where they came to life and crawled away in a crooked manner with a slight rattling. Salmon set this commandment: "From now on you will live in the rocks as a rattlesnake. In the future when the Humans arrive you will only bite them when they accidentally step on you while you are asleep. Otherwise, when you are awake, you must warn them with your rattles. Humans bitten by you need not die, except if they are very weak, young, or old. Some humans will secure power from you or by means of related powers will be able to cure your bites." [7]

Salmon returned, to his canoe and resumed his trip upstream. At the destination outlined "by the old man, he "beached- the canoe and climbed to the lodges. He met the slaves and got their help. Within 100 yards of the lodges was the spring and Salmon hid himself there – within jumping distance. His only weapon was a hatchet he carried on his body. Late in the afternoon, the eldest Wolf arrived, but when he got within 75 yards of the spring, he said out loud, "I smell a salmon." The two old women ran out of the house, scratching their bellies to indicate that there were no salmon around. They reminded Wolf, "Remember you have taken Salmon's wife so you are probably smelling her." Wolf decided that must be it, and went further to the spring. Before he dipped his hands to wash them, he jumped back once as a trick, just in case. Then he began to wash his hands. Salmon jumped once and cut off Wolf's head with the hatchet. He tossed the body under a big windfallen log some distance away and went back to await the others. The slaves had a harder time convincing the second and third brothers, but otherwise they were easily killed. The fourth brother was even harder to trick, but he too was killed. Finally, the youngest brother stopped 150 yards from the spring to say he smelled salmon. The youngest Wolf was extremely intelligent so he was not convinced and never got any closer than 20 feet from the spring. Salmon tried to jump him, but the distance was too great and Wolf too fast. Wolf ran away and Salmon followed him into the mountains but never caught up to him. Instead, Salmon gave Wolf this commandment: "From now on you will live in the high mountains. You are not to kill any humans when they arrive in the near future and they will hunt you only for your fur."

Salmon returned to the lodges, thanked the two slaves, telling them they would become lice but gave them no commandment. The youngest Wolf would never return so everything belonged to these women.

Salmon told Mourning Dove it was now time to go. She was the happiest person in the world then. They went back to where the canoe was tied. Salmon told her to sit in the front and to enjoy the ride and scenery along the river. It was then late fall, so he paddled into the middle of the river and said "I am going to rest." He laid down in the stern of the canoe and covered his face with a scarf. The canoe floated along on the swift currents of the river.

Dove was very happy; the most beautiful woman married to the most handsome man. She was content to just sit, watch, and think of her future life together with Salmon. This continued for many days. Sometimes, she would speak to Salmon, but he never answered so she let him sleep. Finally, they got near Celilo Falls.

Dove became very frightened as the canoe approached within 200 yards of the drop. She called to Salmon, shook his legs, but got no response. She lifted the scarf from his face and received the greatest disappointment of her entire life. Salmon had begun to rot. His face was eroded, all eaten by worms, with very little left of his head and neck. She cried and cried in utter despair. She thought only of herself, especially as the canoe got closer to the falls.

Suddenly Salmon called out. She turned and saw the same handsome man she had married. He walked to her, grabbed her by the arm, and said "You would have never drowned if you had kept quiet while going over the falls. Since you are scared to ride with me in the canoe, from now on you will follow me along the land. When I go south to the Pacific, you will follow along the shore. When I return the next year, you also will return. In the future, when the Humans arrive and hear you singing, they will know that Red Salmon is coming upstream." With this commandment, Salmon tossed his wife to shore just as the canoe went over the falls. She became Mourning Dove.

Returning Salmon Rite

Intimately connected [72] with the rite of the annual salmon return is usually a myth explaining the origin of the salmon, or the observances, or both. Excerpts from the Sanpoil myth may serve as charter for the ceremony as actually practiced.

On the Sanpoil River, a little way above the Columbia, an old man and an old woman lived.[20] The old woman was so stooped that she could almost walk around on her knees and elbows without bending over. The old man was crippled, too, but he could hobble around a little better than his wife. The old people had a grandchild that lived with them. She was a very good looking girl.

---

[20] Told by Bob Covington to Verne Ray (1932: 71-75).

One day Coyote came along and saw the old couple and the girl. He decided then and there that he wanted the girl for his wife, but he was afraid to ask the old people for her, for fear they would say no. It was early in the morning, so he decided to wait around until evening and then ask them. He sat around and lay around all day long. The old man and woman watched him. They saw that his hair was long and braided all the way down and that his forelocks were carefully combed back and that the few strands of hair in front of his ears were covered with beads. They noticed too that he was tall and strong. The old people talked about him to each other and decided that he must be a chief of some kind.

All day Coyote stayed there, silent until late afternoon when he spoke to the old man.

"Old man," he said, "what is that thing down in the stream a way?"

"Why, that's a fish trap," the old man answered.

"A fish trap? What is that? What do you do with it?" Coyote asked as if he didn't know.

"Oh, I catch a few bull-heads and sun-fish once in a while," the old man answered.

Coyote still pretended ignorance. "Is that what you eat, then? I don't know that I ever heard of them; are they big enough to eat?

"Oh, they're not much, but what else can we do? That's all we can get to eat," he said.

(Coyote then supplied the old people with grouse for dinner and real tobacco to smoke, very much to their amazement. He asked for their granddaughter and they agreed to her marriage.)

Coyote stayed with his wife that evening, making love to her. But late in the evening said to her, "I'm going out for a few minutes; when I come back we'll go to bed."

"All right," she answered, and Coyote went out.

He went down the stream to where the old man had his trap. In a little while he made it over in the form of a weir-trap, piling up rows of rocks to guide the fish into it. When he had finished he called out, "Salmon, I want two of you to be in this trap in the morning, one and one female." Then he went back.

The next morning Coyote asked the old man what time he went down to the trap.

"I usually go down about the middle of the morning; sometimes I find one or two little fish then," he answered.

A little later, just after sun-up, Coyote told the old man that he thought that he should go down and look at the trap to see if any fish were in it.

"There won't be any this early," the old man answered.

"Well, I think that you had better go and see, anyway; I heard something during the night and I think it was some fish in the trap," Coyote said.

So the old man went down to the trap. It was a little way off shore, but from the bank he could see something big moving around in the trap. He took off his moccasins and waded in. Sure enough, there were two big salmon in the trap. When the old man saw them he became so excited that he hardly knew what to do. He floundered out of the water and stumbled up the trail towards where he had left Coyote. He hobbled along, his body all bent over, and stumbled from one side of the path to the other in his excitement. [73]

When he reached Coyote he cried, "Say, there are two great big fish in the trap − bigger than I have ever seen."

"What?" exclaimed Coyote, "You must have stuff in your eyes; you must be dreaming."

"No," the old man insisted, "my eyes are clear." He rubbed them and said. "You had better come down and see."

Coyote went down with him. When they reached the trap Coyote looked in and said,

43

"Sure enough, you are right. These are salmon, the chief of the fish. We'll take them out, but we won't take them to the house; we'll take them over to that flat place there and I'll show you what to do to them."

When they reached the open field he sent the old man up the hill to gather sunflower stems and leaves. "Those are the salmon plants," he said; "salmon must always be laid only on sunflower stems and leaves."

The old man brought back the sunflowers and spread them out on the ground; then they put the salmon down on them.

Then Coyote showed him how to prepare the fish. First he showed him how to put a stick in the mouth and then bend it back and break off the head. Next he showed him how to make long sharp poles to stick in the salmon for holding it over the fire and roasting.

Coyote said, "Now, remember this: for the first five days go down to the trap and take out the salmon, but when you are fixing one to cook, never use a knife to cut it in any way. Always cook the fish over the fire on sticks, the way I have showed you; never boil it. Then, after it is roasted, open it carefully and take out the backbone without breaking it. Also save the back part of the head; never eat that, where rattlesnakes arrow struck. If you do not do these things as I have said, either a big storm will come up and it will rain until you are drowned, or you will be bitten by a rattlesnake; one of these things will be sure to happen to you. After you have taken the backbone and the back of the head, wrap them up carefully in cattail tules and put them somewhere in a tree or some place where they can't be bothered.

"If you do as I say you will always have salmon in your trap. I'm telling you these things because I am going to die some time and I want you to know what to do. After this, men will always place traps up and down the river to catch salmon; the man who has the first trap in the river will be chief and you should always do anything that he tells you to do.

"After the first week you can boil your salmon or cook it any way you wish, but always take care of the bones; never leave them where they can be stepped on or stepped over, especially by women."

For the next few days each time the old man went down to the trap in the morning he found twice as many salmon as on the day before. Coyote showed him how to dry them and prepare them for use in the winter. Before long a large scaffold was filled with drying salmon.

The people round about saw the fish and noticed how well the old man and woman were doing. They went home and told the other people about the big red fish and the tall young stranger who was staying with the old people. Soon a large bunch of them went to see for themselves. The old man and woman invited them in and gave them a feast. Then they told them how they got the fish."

The actual observation of the ceremony diverged very little from the program set down by Coyote in the myth. The Salmon Chief superintended all of the preparations for the rite as well as the performance itself. The building of the fish trap was not properly a part of the ceremony, but necessarily immediately preceded it in time.[21]

------

[21] Rituals marked each stage of weir building, from tree cutting to setting deflector walls.

Exceptional Woman

Power was often brought into play at the fisheries (Spier 1938: 160). Michel's father told the people during a winter dance that he intended to go salmon fishing near Malott. When the season came they all helped him to make the weir. People came from Nespelem, Kartar, Sanpoil, and near Chelan. After they had caught a few salmon, dried them, and distributed them among the families, the salmon stopped running. Most of the fishermen then moved away, leaving only a few at the weir. Michel's grandmother, who had Salmon power, cleaned the weir and sat down near it. She sang no songs; she just "thought about her power" and went away. Very late that night the salmon began to run again and by the next morning they had filled the weir. The people took them out, but salmon came up abundantly for several days afterward.

Lucy Joe told the following anecdote which, she said, shows that the people long ago really did have power. Nmaskwist, her father's sister's son, once made a salmon weir at Malott. At first it was unproductive. Nmaskwist's grandmother, Sīkūntalūqs, said, "I'm going to the weir." She walked along the weir to the opposite bank of the river and lay down there. Soon after sunset she heard the kingfisher (ċris ~ *starēs) flying over the camp. She thought, "Now we're going to eat." She lay there and slept. The salmon came. By daybreak a great many had been caught in the weir, and she called to the people, "Your weir is going to overflow." Then the fishermen all ran down with their spears and other equipment, without stopping to put on their shoes, and took out two hundred salmon. When they had got these, the weir broke. Sīkūntalūqs took off her moccasins and went swimming just above it. The people said to her, "What's the matter with you? You shouldn't swim up there." But that was her power. She replied, "I was the one that made the salmon come. It's all right if I take a swim." When other camps heard that the fishing was so good there, they came from Nespelem, Similkameen, and other distant places. In the evening Sīkūntalūqs lay down again and "fixed the weir." In the morning a kingfisher was found dead on the bank, and the weir was full of salmon. The kingfisher must have been Sīkūntalūqs's guardian spirit. When she sang, she said, "I'm an Eagle and its little sister, the Kingfisher."

Though usually women should not come within half a mile of a salmon weir, those with salmon power, or who were attended by a man who had such power, could do so with impunity.

Berrying[22]

In general when women went together to gather plant foods, as they generally did, no one of them would, officially take the lead. One with more power might be more successful than her companions. Such power might be acquired by a child going near a dead horse. But there was no division of their gleanings to affect a balance. Each was entitled only to what she gathered. They went to much the came place year after year.

Service berries (siya? ~ *sī'a)[23] were picked in June, July and August. They grew best in

---

[22] Nancy Turner, Randy Bouchard, Dorothy Kennedy, *Ethnobotany of the Okanagan~Colville Indians* ... 1980 provides correct spellings and Latin bio-names, here after cited as TBK. Kurt Reidinger added updates, using images and descriptions @ WTU ~ Washington Territorial University, http://biology.burke.washington.edu/herbarium/imagecollection.php.

[23] siya¿ ~ Serviceberry ~ Saskatoon ~ *Amelanchier alnifolia Nutt* TBK: 120.

fertile soil along all the larger streams, and were seldom scarce. The women wore coiled cedar-root baskets (*stəxəRe'pa) tied to the front of the waist and used larger coiled baskets (*sənsaq'a'lkən) for packing them, equipped with a tump line. Occasionally a party would go away over night.

The drying took approximately a week, depending on the weather and the degree of ripeness of the berries. If there were large flat rocks nearby they were spread on these; otherwise on tule cattail mats or sacks laid on the ground or on racks ten feet long, four feet wide, and two or three feet high. They were taken in should it rain. They were never piled up; always one layer deep. They did not have to be turned over. When dry, they were put into hemp bags for winter storage, or into wooden or bark tubs if destined for summer consumption.

Today the fresh berries are boiled and eaten with sugar, though in the old days they were eaten raw or perhaps boiled for a half hour with bitter-root or salmon eggs. Dried berries were never cooked alone; usually they were mixed with bitter-root and boiled, often also with salmon, which was separated when served and placed on mats. A special delicacy was salmon eggs and dried berries, boiled or eaten cold, but never mashed. The dried berries were sweet and thus very desirable for mixing with the many bitter foods.

Red or orange foam berries ($sx̱^wsm + \mathit{lip} \sim$ *sxō'sem)[24] were gathered the last part of June and the first of July. They were dried two or three days on tule mats, then sacked and stored, but were sometimes used fresh. They were prepared by first being soaked in hot water half an hour, squeezed with the hands when soft, then stirred vigorously with the foam berry mop [paddle] for twenty minutes or so in a cedar root basket, until they foamed up like the whites of eggs. Dried service berries might be added for sweetening before soaking, the berries being very bitter. Grease will prevent the foaming. This dish is a delicacy, prepared in the evening when friends call, and eaten with horn spoons.

Thorn berries[25] were gathered during the last part of July and the beginning of August, being found along the river banks. Black thornberries (*cxwanī'q, swa'enī'k) were picked and dried like service berries. Salmon bones with some meat on them might be pounded in a basket mortar and mixed with these berries. Red thornberries (*x̱ax̱'x̱a'ī'ī) were mashed and formed into thin cakes to be dried in the sun for winter use. No thornberries were cooked.

Huckleberries (*stəka'lqx)[26] were gathered, all through August. Mary Carden's sites are Moses Mountain and the hills west of Twisp. They were gathered in coiled cedar-root baskets worn in front at the waist. Some were kept a week or so and eaten raw. They were not dried until Nez Perce Indians came on the reservation and taught how to dry them like service berries.

The berries of the red willow (*sti'q'tsu),[27] white in color, ripened in August. They were never dried or stored but always either boiled or pounded up and mixed with fresh cherries or service berries in order to sweeten them, for they were very sour. They were boiled only if eaten alone, since boiling the mixture would nullify the sweetening influences.

Oregon grape berries[28] were gathered in [26] mid-August into pine bark buckets or coiled

---

[24] foamberries ~ soapberries ~ *Shepherdia canadenisis (L) Nutt* TBK 99.

[25] thornberry ~ hawthorn ~ red = *xexa¢* ~ *Crataegus columbiana Howll* / black = *sxwa'nik* ~ *Crataegus douglasii Lindl* TBK 123 ~ *Crataegus columbiana* cf Turner & Kuhlmann 2014.

[26] huckleberry ~ mt bilberry ~*st'xałk'* ~ *Vaccinium membranaceum* Dougl ex Hook TBK 103.

[27] red willow ~ red osier dogwood ~ *stiktsx^w* ~ *Cornus stolonifera* Michx TBK 96.

[28] Oregon grape ~ barberry ~ *Berberis aquifolium* TBK: 85.

cedar-root baskets. After being squeezed in these containers, handfuls were spread on a rock to dry for several days, then stored in tule sacks for winter use. Never cooked, they were served raw or the dried lumps were moistened and softened within a mat.

Blueberries,[29] raspberries (*łała),[30] strawberries (*tq!emtqəm),[31] and thimble berries (*palpū'ləqxn)[32] grew in quantities insufficient to be profitably dried, hence were always eaten fresh. Elderberries[33] were boiled and eaten immediately. Bearberries (*skūlī's)[34] were used in soups; only eaten fresh.

Roots

Bitterroot (spīt!um)[35] was plentiful throughout the area, and gathered in quantity during May. It grew best in moist ground, not too sandy, usually among rocks. Four sites known to Mary Garden are (1) hills seven miles north of Pateros on the south side of the river; (2) all the way from Twisp to Winthrop on hills either side of Methow River; (3) all around Duley Lake, about twelve miles east of Monse; (4) on the east side of Columbia River in the hills east of Waterville.

The Kartaro people dug it at three places: (1) at the south end of Lake Omak; [2] meadows south of Kartaro Creek; (3) near the present post office of Kartaro. It was common in Northern Okanogan territory. A great many people would gather at those places, often more than the number at a winter village.

It was dug with the usual dogwood digging stick, just before it bloomed; one hand holding the top of the root while the other dug. The stalk would be twisted off, the bark skinned off, and the root put in a twined hemp basket (*stexōRī'pa) carried on the right side at the waist. They were packed in large tule baskets (*kwa'ī'īp').

These roots were washed and laid on mats or grass for two or three days to dry in the hot sun. They were never steamed, smoked, nor mashed. Then they were put away in tule sacks (Carden) or in pits lined with pine needles, and covered with more pine needles and rocks (Lucy Joe). Care was taken to pack them tightly enough to prevent air from circulating, since this would make them hard and dry as wood. At service berry time they were usually taken out and mixed with dried berries, about half and half, for if stored long alone they became very bitter. It took a person with good power to mix effectively. The mixture was then stored for winter use, usually in pits, packed tight to keep out the air. This was all women's work.

But some men had the power to mix. Some could also pick berries, set them out to dry and go hunting a few days, come back and find the berries dried just right,

Bitterroot was eaten fresh, after being boiled or baked a half hour in the earth oven. Nowadays it is steamed in small pots, resting on many little sticks which keep it out of the water. When dried it was usually boiled. In all cases it was cooked separately but mixed with other

---

[29] blueberries ~ Dwarf ~ sesapt ~ Vaccinium caespitosum Michx TBK: 102.

[30] raspberries ~ łagla˙ ~ Rubus idaeus L TBK: 131.

[31] strawberries ~ tq'imtq'm ~ Fragaria vesca / F virginiana TBK: 125.

[32] thimbleberries ~ palpelk'n~ Rubus parviflorus ~ TBK: 132.

[33] elderberries ~ ts'kʷikʷ ~ Sambucus cerulean Raf TBK: 94. now Sambucus nigra L

[34] bearberries ~ kinnikinnik ~ skʷlis TBK: 101. Arctostaphylos uva-ursi L Spreng

[35] bitterroot ~ sp'itl'm ~ Lewisia rediviva Push TBK: 114.

food when served, since it is very bitter, like ordinary pepper or mustard. It was never pounded, and never eaten dry, for it would swell up inside one and be very uncomfortable, forming gases. Bitterroot was never preferred for its taste, but it was considered "good for one, like pepper and mustard."

A small onion (*waīqwiu'p'ts*),[36] very sweet, was dug with *spitlum*, in the same places and at the same times. It was eaten raw but never preserved. Today it is steamed.

Camas[37] was gathered by very few families, since none grew nearby. Some was found on the upper Methow River and in Tumwater Basin [several miles due east of Okanogan town). The bulk was dug beyond the Columbia River in the hills north of Wenatchee, near Waterville, whence it was packed after being dried. Tule mats were taken for this trip, since in early May there was considerable rain and tipis were wanted each night. While the women dug; the men would hunt jack rabbits with bow and arrow, collect birds' eggs, and spend much time at their games. The northerly bands knew only dried camas, obtained through trade, like the southern bands, mentioning:

> *teaxūlō'sa*, white round camas at Watervllle;
> *ī't'xwa*, black round camas traded from Idaho, much sweeter;
> *ka'ūōs*, white camas with a long bulb.

Camas was dug with digging sticks before the faded flowers had dropped from the stalks. The stalks were twisted off and the skins rubbed off before the roots were place-in the basket at the waist. The best ones were dried on tule mats in the sun for two or three days, then stored. They could be eaten at any time without cooking, and would last for two or three years before spoiling. Roots of poorer quality were steamed for fifteen hours in a pit and dried in the sun. They were then very hard and slightly black in color. These were stored too but would not last as long and had to be boiled before being eaten, usually as a soup with dried deer meat or salmon, since it did not taste so good alone. While the former product could be eaten without preparation and is delicious in taste, much more of the latter was prepared because people preferred hot food in winter. Sometimes camas was steam-baked in alternate layers of black moss, all dried together and cooked by boiling with a piece of deer fat. Dried camas was also boiled with deer meat or dried salmon. When it was served, the meat was fished from the vessel to be eaten separately. Camas boiled with bitterroot was mashed before serving.

Each woman dried her own lot and carried it home, keeping it for her own family; or trading it as occasion arose. [27]

Wild onions[38] were dug along the rivers beginning in April, on the hills in May and in the mountains in June, before blooming. They were rolled on a mat to remove the dirt end eaten raw. Or they were steam-baked for half an hour, and before eating each person would remove the outer akin. For storage, the steamed onions would be pressed into little thin cakes and dried. These would be sprinkled and rolled on a mat until soft before being eaten. They were never boiled nor mixed with anything else.

A root (*stakcī'n*, literally "bitter" *taxt*)[39] grows in bunches like sweet potatoes or rose

---

[36] small onion ~ *saxk* ~ Douglas ~ *Allium cernuum* Roth TBK: 38.
[37] camas ~ *itx^wa'* ~ black ~ *Camassia quamash* Pursh Greene TBK: 41.
[38] onions ~ *xeliwa* ~ nodding ~ *Allium cernuum* Roth TBK: 38.
[39] root TBK: ?? Kurt Reidinger > Columbian Lily ~ *Lilium columbianum* Hort. ex Baker.

roots, each the size of a small fist. It was dug in early spring in rich damp ground. The plant is two and a half to three feet tall and looks like a lily, with thick leaves and a yellow flower three inches in diameter. The roots were not peeled but washed and steam-baked for five to six hours (overnight), then dried in the sun for three or four days, usually mashed and spread out in thin cakes. After steaming the roots are white and very good tasting, but as bitter as bitterroot. In winter it is boiled and put into meat soup, not to modify its bitterness, but to add to the good taste of the meats. It would be too hard and dry to eat alone. Today it is steamed in pots twenty-five minutes, held above the water by sticks.

"Yellow bells" (*səma'rata),[40] a green stalk eighteen inches high with a small yellow flower in springtime, but with no leaves at any season, was dug in small quantities in the mountains during the summer. It grew in dry areas in the Methow valley and around Lake Okanogan. The roots are rough and bumpy, white, and disc shaped, two inches in diameter, and one quarter inch thick. They were eaten raw or steamed in a pit seven feet in diameter for fifteen minutes and then dried on tule mats for two weeks. Trips to the Methow River were made for these if time permitted, for they had to be dried and ready for storage before being brought back. Several women would prepare their lots together. In the north the women did not go out of their way to get them and did not preserve them. When dug with a root called *cūī'x^w* {below}, they were eaten together; washed, but not peeled, and boiled.

Wild carrots (*sklō'kūm)[41] were dug with small digging sticks in early June, just before they bloomed, on gravelly hillsides. Carden's four sites were (1) from Twisp to Winthrop; (2) around Duley Lake; (3) Waterville area; (4) Bridgeport area, south of the Columbia River. They have a single or double stalked stem about one and a half feet high, and a root about three-eighths of an inch in diameter, roughly spherical. The stalks were broken off before placing the roots in the Indian hemp side basket. At camp they were washed and dried in the sun, usually on racks a yard high. There would be one vertical pole at each corner of the rack, supporting two short crosspieces on which lay three longitudinal poles ten feet long. Tule mats about three feet wide were laid on [27b] these. Sometimes the carrots were steam-baked instead for about an hour, then squeezed dry with the hands and spread out on mats of small tules in the hot sun for three days or so (Carden).

Carrots might be eaten raw and some were buried raw in damp ground for summer use. Fresh carrots were boiled or steamed for immediate use. Dried ones were boiled, often together with service berries, until thick. They were never cut open.

The root (*pcaī'k)[42] of a plant one and a half feet tall with thorns in the fall but only grass-like leaves in summer (roots like camas but smaller and sweeter) grows in damp areas, gullies, etc. It is knocked over with a stick and the roots dug.

A root (*cūī'x^w),[43] one inch long, smooth, growing only in rocky places, was dug only in the Methow valley, at the same time with *səma'rata,[44] and prepared in the same way.

---

[40] yellowbells ~ *g'a'temn'* ~ *Fritillaria pudica* (Pursch) Spreng TBK: 46.
[41] carrots ~ *stl'uk'em* ~ wild caraway ~ *Perideridia gairdneri* Mathia TBK: 71. Kurt Reidinger
    > Gairdner's yampah ~ *Perideridia gairdneri* (Hook. & Arn.) Mathias.
[42] root ~ TBK: ??
[43] root ~ TBK: ??
[44] ↑ yellowbell # 40

A root (*tcōkōlō'sa, white camas ?),[45] about as big as two fingers, was dug at Soap Lake during May. It was steamed, then peeled and dried.

Tiger lily bulbs (*stəxt'sīn)[46] were dug near Twisp in September, when the flowers had fallen. They were treated like onions and the inner inedible core discarded. While never eaten raw they were also steam-baked, or mixed with dry service berries and boiled. They were slightly bitter.

Wild "parsnips" (*mīcō'wī)[47] were dug in moist ground in the higher hills during late fall while the men were hunting. The roots are two inches long and look like carrots. As soon as dug, they were steam-baked nearby in pits eight to ten feet in diameter. Fires were made inside these pits, stones heated in the fire and when the flames had died, covered with weeds and grass to a depth of eight inches, especially the large leaves of water lilies. Then the roots were laid in, followed by another six or eight inches of leaves and grass, with two feet of dirt on top. Water is poured on the hot rocks down the holes left by four sticks, which are now pulled out, and the roots cooked for forty-eight hours. They are inspected by digging a small hole in the edge.

When done the root is jet black and has an unpleasant odor but a very sweet taste. It is stored for winter as such: if it should lose its moisture it would lose its sweetness. When eaten it should still be moist, but it is never dampened artificially: this would spoil it. It is wrapped in grass and tule mats for winter, stored in underground pits, and eaten cold and raw, dipped into soup, etc. It will keep one year.

When several women dug together they would make a common steaming pit, then divide up the product by arbitrary judgment. The same pits could be used year after year. [28]

A root (*tsīms'nelqx),[48] about twice the size of one's thumb, and growing in clusters, was dug near Oroville. They were dried two or three days on tule mats, or boiled and eaten fresh, but were then very bitter. They were not highly prized.

A root (*xənasta'tkwa)[49] could be found in certain springs in August. Mary Carden's sites were Elliot spring near Brewster Flat and Dan Canyon spring near the Columbia between Pateros and Brewster. These long white roots were eaten raw and even preserved a few days by keeping them wet in a tule sack. They could, of course, not be dried for storage.

Other Plant Foods

The cambium layer of large pine trees (*tsīxwī)[50] was gathered in early spring (Johnnie stated in June only). If a tree is found to contain much sweet sap, its bark is scored all the way around with a knife as high as one can reach and again at the base, a vertical score made and the sections of bark pried and cut from the tree with special wooden knives four feet long called *n'tsīxwī^tn. Incidentally this kills the tree. The pieces are laid on the ground and scraped with

---

[45] root ~ TBK: ??

[46] tiger lily ~ stextsin ~ Lilium columbianum Hanson TBK: 46. Kurt Reidinger > Lilium columbianum Hort. ex Baker.

[47] parsnips ~ alapiapes ~ Cymopteris terebinthinus Hook TBK: 60. Kurt Reidinger > Cymopterus terebinthinus (Hook.) T & G.

[48] root ~ TBK: ??

[49] root ~ northern bugleweed ~ xinxen ~ Lycopus uniflorus Michx TBK: 109 < Coeur d'Alene.

[50] pine cambium ~ ts'ix^wi' ~ Pinus contorta Douglas TBK: 28.

knives of deer rib a foot long (called *nəkakamū'n), the soft cambium and sap being collected on dry grass (a long pine grass called *qūaqūaqūnī'lp). The matter is carried to camp wrapped in soft pliable bark with grass to lend it flavor and moisture. It must be eaten the same day for it soon loses its moisture and sweetness, but even then it is stringy and tough.

Sunflower seeds (*mī'ktū ~ smuk^{w}a'xn)[51] were collected as soon as the flowers had fallen off and the seeds were hard and dry, mostly in June and July. These plants grew so abundantly and widely that trips were never made to get then. (The sunflower plant was called c'mū'qūak'n.)[52] The women used a beater (*klepta'n) made by bending a flexible stick back on itself and covering the space with a piece of old buckskin. They walked about with a birch bark basket tied to the waist, bending the tops of the flowers over the basket and beating them gently to knock off the dried seeds. The baskets are rather cone-shaped, with large mouths. The seeds rarely have to be dried further, but if necessary they can be dried on woven hemp mats for two or three days, or browned by pouring them on a flat buffalo skin on which a hot rock has been placed, and pulling up the edges of the skin to toast them on it. They are winnowed by being poured from one basket into another in the wind. They had to be kept in air-tight containers, such as the wooden tubs, else they would dry out too much. The seeds would last for six years.

They are prepared by being pounded to powder in a basket mortar or buckskin bag and perhaps mixed with deer grease or pounded dry service berries. The food was eaten raw, not even moistened, and was regarded as a delicacy, served in horn spoons between meals. Today it is sugared, but used very seldom.

Choke cherries (*tlōxtla'x^w)[53] were gathered in mid-August, along the rivers. They might be treated like service berries, dried for a day on tule mats, etc. Alternatively they might be pounded to pulp with a pestle in a buckskin bag, seeds and all, then dried in the sun spread out in thin cakes on tule mats or a wooden rack. When dry they were often pounded up with salmon heads, tails, or eggs, or else soaked in water several hours. They were not cooked.

Black moss (*skwalī'p)[54] was gathered in the fall after harvesting other vegetable foods, though it does not vary from month to month, can be collected at any time of year, grows on smaller branches of pine, fir, and tamarack trees, and is collected from the last two, since it has an unpleasant, pitchy flavor if taken from pines unless the branches are dead.

Young boys climb high into the trees to get it, several clusters to the handful. While it may be eaten raw, it is then bitter and becomes green in the saliva, with a consistency like fresh soft dough. The large supply is steamed in pits three feet deep and ten or twelve feet in diameter. Hot rocks are covered with green leaves, then grass; then the moss is put in and over it is placed more grass, leaves, and a foot of earth. Four poles are left against opposite sides of the pit resting on the bottom, which are now pulled out to leave holes down which water is poured to the rocks. The moss is steamed from twelve to twenty-four hours, after which it has the consistency of stringy fresh dough. It is spread thin and pressed down until one inch thick, cut into pieces one-half inch square and then allowed to dry.

When hard, the shrunk and very black pieces are stored in sacks for winter use, lasting

---

[51]   balsamroot, locally called sunflower, source for "Methow" as a name   TBK: 80.   Kurt Reidinger > *Balsamorhiza sagittata* (Pursh) Nutt.

[52]   sunflower whole plant ~ smuk^{w}a'xn ~ "lump on the foot"   TBK: 80.

[53]   chokecherries ~ łex̱^{w}łax̱^{w} ~ *prunus virginiana* L   TBK: 127.

[54]   black moss ~ sqel'ip ~ lichen ~ *Bryoria fremontii* Tuck   TBK: 10.

three years if well preserved.[55] Boiled in soup and sugared, it is delicious.

Pine nuts (*sq!aū'q!u)[56] were gathered in September at the head of the Twisp River. Girls of sixteen could climb the trees and throw down branches. The cones were carried to camp in sacks. A hole in the ground would be dug, three feet deep, hot rocks put in the bottom, and on this was laid two inches of green grass and two inches of green tale. The cones were poured in next, covered with eight inches of dry pine needles and one foot of dirt. They are dry-baked over night and dug out in the morning, with care lest dirt get on the cones, laid on tule mats, and rolled under pressure of an open palm to free the [29] nut meats, which are pulled out, left in the sun for the rest of the day, and then stored for winter in tule sacks.

Some people ate pine nutlets as they were gathered from the fallen cones. They were not pounded or stored, but used as a tidbit while they lasted.

Two kinds of mushrooms were used, kła panter and pi'tlxk'n.[57] The former was boiled, the latter eaten raw. Neither was dried or preserved.

Prickly pear fruits (*siwi'ïna, Opuntia?)[58] were eaten, the spines being burned off.

Starvation Foods

When all the stored foods ran low in winter, or when they had neglected gathering because of preoccupation with the Dream dance, the people used other sources, according to their proximity. Mussels (sk^{w}k^{w}ɾina? ~ *skokōī'na)[59] are of first importance. Large beds of these were found in the Okanogan River every three or four miles, of which the two best known are just below the mouth of Omak Creek and a mile above Oroville. The mussel is three to four inches long, dark blue in color like the salt water varieties and similar in shape, but with thinner shells. Starving people would camp by these beds and gather them with a forked stick through holes in the ice if wading was impossible. They were easily opened and were boiled. Some few people liked them so much that they gathered and baked them in times of plenty, though never in hot weather. Shell heaps have been reported all along the Okanogan River.

Trout were speared through holes in the ice, with the small single-pointed spear with two prongs (called *wī'tck). If a bad winter was feared, the location of shoals of trout would be ascertained before the ice came.

Winter hunting was resorted to by men with good power, sometimes after a woman or even a child had dreamed that game was near. The hunter took no dog, and planned to follow the first deer tracks he found to the bitter end. It might take several days to overtake one. If successful he must divide his quarry equally, keeping only the heads for himself.

Less valued famine foods were black moss (see #54), eaten raw if the people were too

---

[55] Described for Okanagon by Wilkes party in 1841 (Wilkes, *Narrative* IV: 434) L Spier #16.

[56] pine nuts ~ *t'est'esiłp* ~ Engelmann ~ *Picea engelmannii* Parry TBK: 28. Kurt Reidinger > White Spruce ~ *Picea glauca* (Moench) Voss is rare locally, lodgepole pine ~ *Pinus contorta* Douglas ex Loud / Ponderosa pine ~ *Pinus ponderosa* P & C Lawson (Spier 1938: 29-30) are more likely sources since heat opens their cones..

[57] mushrooms ~ *łagpnta'* ~ *p'etl'qin'* cottonwood ~ *Polyporus sulphureus* Bull TBK: 16.

[58] prickly pear ~ *sx^{w}iyina* ~ *Opuntia fragilis* (Nutt) Haw TBK: 92.

[59] MidColmbia mussel shells are about six inches long, and middens near old villages show frequent use. See *Freshwater Mussels of the Pacific Northwest* Portland: Xerces Society.

weak to boil it; the stalks of cactus plants with the spines burned off, from which a soup was made; and sunflower root shoots, eaten raw and on the spot. If there were not too much snow the first buds of *cwa'ya (see #43) might be used. This was like the carrot plant but with a longer stem. The early disc-shaped bud was eaten, but apparently was far from nourishing. It grew near rivers. Even coyote, skunk, and the like have been eaten in time of starvation.

There has been no dying of starvation since the coming of the whites, but it seems to have been frequent before that.

How one's power would save him from starvation was related by Suszen:

The power of any animal might help a man. If his power was the salmon, he would wish for salmon to eat; then anything he ate would seem like good salmon. A man who had beaver power would think of this. It would tell him to eat little twigs or pieces of bark just as a beaver does. The man would dream this. Those things he ate then tasted like berries and meat. He could not give this food to anyone else, not even to his family, for it would be just wood to them. But they were content to see him eat it.

First Foods Ceremonies [32]

First food ~ fruit ceremonies were held after the first big gathering of camas, service berries, and bitterroot. The ceremony was called *cqəpōmnsinm. Most of the band would gather at the chief's house, where he would stand up and speak; perhaps other older men, would too; and then the people would eat the newly harvested food. The chief might have asked a few able women to cook some of his supply, or food which had been taken by common work. This was then eaten at noon, the men being served first as usual. In later days they prayed (*skūm) before the speech making. There was a special prayer for camas, said by about eight or ten women who were the first to go out digging, but usually only one ceremony was held for first roots, berries, and small game collectively. The night following there would be much sexual intercourse between husbands and their wives, but unmarried girls were supposedly closely guarded. At Kartaro more people gathered for this ceremony than the number which usually composed a winter village.

The ceremony symbolizes the first time that the Indians learned to eat these foods (said Suszen). Probably the prayer is a recent feature, introduced by chief Sūīpəqēn after a dream. His prayer was, "We are not the ones who made the berries and bitterroot grow. There must be another person in another world who makes the berries and bitter-root grow. And then after we get it, we eat it. You are not like birds, to just go over there and eat all you want. After somebody talks to you, then you can eat." This chief may also have introduced the idea of an "Other Person," the creator, in this rite.

In the northern part of the area, said David, there were no first fruits ceremonies other than those over salmon. This may be doubted because he also denied their existence elsewhere. Michel and Johnnie stated that the rite was practiced by both Sinkaietk and Northern Okanagon, but not by Colville.

Fall

Fall was a busy time, stocking larders for Winter. Men hunted, women gathered berries, both fished, and whole families engaged in slicing, drying, and smoking to preserve foods. In a real sense, they harvested what nature provided, without planting, though they did enhance conditions by burning, replacing rhizomes, and spreading nutrients.

Hunting

When choke cherry leaves were yellow and wilted, it was time for a fall hunt by teams of friends and families. Choke cherries had been gathered from bushes in gullies and small ravines, dried, and stored in hemp sacks. After natives adopted plow farming and livestock, the oats, wheat, and grain harvest was finished, and stacks of bunchgrass and sheaves were stood to dry. Horse packsaddle were loaded, and camping gear was packed. Pack saddles were made out of heavy, dried, forked thorn branches, whittled down with a sharp knife to fit horse haunches, nailed them together, covered with stretched wet rawhide, and sewn up with buckskin thongs, making holes with a bone awl. The girth was twisted from horse hair, first in small strands, then woven together in a wide strip to fit the large iron rings used as a cinch. Padded cruppers fit snugly under the horses tail, to keep the load from slipping off on a steep trail. Gear included empty flat parfleches {rawhide envelopes}, extra ropes, and buckskin thongs. Pet dogs, some specialized hunters, joined the caravan.

Climbing trails into the mountains, families went to favorite camps at small clearings on bench land, where drying scaffolds allowed meat to be smoked and dried over slow fires. In camps of mixed tribal members, each observed its own hunting taboos and practices, though this sometimes led to offense.

All hunters were celibate during this time. Couples slept apart. A man's bedding was considered sacred so children were forbidden to play on or around it. The main entrance was too busy with constant traffic, so a fresh kill had to be brought in through the lifted rear of the tent and placed on a bed of boughs; never near the doorway where women walked. In this way women contributed to the continued hunting success of men. Only after the game had been welcomed and cut up on a layer of fresh fir boughs could the meat then be taken out the front door to be dried and processed (cf Hill-Tout 1907: 167).

Colville hunters always string up deer heads on high limbs, with the nose pointing up so it could not smell the camp. They were never cooked or eaten until that hunt was over. Only men, and maybe a very old woman, could do this with deer heads and kidneys. Only older adults, never children, could eat bone marrow to prevent youngsters from getting weak legs and lungs. Only old people, often with few teeth, could eat unborn fawns, relishing their tenderness.

In her autobiography, Mourning Dove tells a story of one of her family's hunting camps where her mother favored an older Spokan couple. The old woman breached taboos by skinning a deer head inside the tipi beside the fireplace. Especially offensive was her gouging out the eyes and throwing them out the door, where the dogs eagerly gobbled them up. This was very disrespectful, and the mother, as housekeeper, carefully cleaned up the spot where the eyes fell while offering profuse prayers in apology. Among the sources of this friction were very different faiths between the couples, with Catholic Jesuits among Colvilles and Protestant ministers

(Walkers, Eells) among Spokans at Walker's Prairie.[60]

Another Spokan violation in that camp involved a pregnant bride. Hunters were especially wary of having a husband with a young pregnant wife join their group because they believed that everything she touched transmitted bad luck, the forces of life opposing those of death. Moreover, this couple shared the same bed and threw deer bones out the doorway for the dogs. Soon unsuccessful hunters blamed this couple for their bad luck, but always in private.

These camps moved multiple times every fall as the constant hunting scared the game further away. Once people had pack horses, trails were straightened out and widened through dense areas to keep from banging loads against trees, rocks, and high stumps, bending gear and metal cooking utensils all out of shape. By evening colorful parfleches were blackened from burnt trees. In some areas, families shifted from smaller deer trails to those of elk, which better accommodate horse size.

As hunters filled all of their packs, they moved to a usual winter home, sheltered from snow and cold. By February, stored food was mostly consumed, and parfleches flattened out. Family food was rationed, and meals served only when it became absolutely necessary. Mothers spared themselves in favor of the youngest and oldest. Men hunted on snowshoes in good weather, to add some protein. Kills continued to be brought through the back of the home. Regardless of the time of day, an impromptu meal was served of this fresh meat. The next day, the remaining meat was divided equally with everyone else at the winter village. All bones were picked clean. Yet rules of hospitality prevailed and guests were fed the best food available, as children were sent out of doors to save whining or embarrassment.

Horses also enabled long bison hunting trips into Montana, under the leadership of the Split Sun ~ Moses family and its confederacy. Other tribes also joined them as they moved east, returning home when they had enough dried buffalo. Some of this hunting skill may have been learned locally, since Okanogan (Spier 1938: 25) believe that buffalo once lived in the vicinity of Moses Lake. Ross Cox, the early fur trader, reported, "The Indians allege that the buffaloes were formerly numerous about the plains [of the Palouse in Big Bend and Spokane counties] and assert that remains of these animals are still found. There is also a painting of a bison on the wall of a cave in lower Moses Coulee.

---

[60] The families of Rev Elkanah Walker and Rev Cushing Eells led a Protestant mission among the Spokans at Tshimakain, also called Walker's Prairie, 1838-49, until abandoned in the aftermath of the massacre of Rev Marcus and Narcissa Whitman and 8 others at the Waiilatpu mission (Walla Walla) on 29 November 1847. See Drury (1940, 1976).

Winter Revivals

Any success relied on power from a spirit, who came closer to its human partner every winter and their bond was publicly expressed as individuals gathered to sing the songs given to them at their vision quest encounter. While this happened when a person was young, the song was not "brought out" in public until he or she were old, respected, and indeed successful, proving the power of a spirit. The final gatherings of the late winter became a known as a Chinook Dance to call the warm winds up the Columbia River.

A special sacred pole was set up in the middle of a large home.[61] Once the home filled, an old man or woman went up to grasp and shake it, singing while everyone also sang and drummed along. A man might go up, sing softly, and pause to pray, before repeating his song at full volume, symbolizing the whole tribe following a wise chief, shaman, or task leader for the benefit of all.

Some elders had several songs. Thus, a visionary might sing for an hour before abruptly changing songs, slowly getting up while shaking the pole, and engaging in a few quick steps around the middle area. This was a sign that others could get up and dance in the same way, moving in place before resuming their seats. Attendees came forward and gradually closed in around the singer, first dancing slowly with his voice easily heard, then growing more intense as they absorbed spirit and song within their bodies, moving faster until they joined in the joy of dancing, imitating various animals: open fingers over the head, swinging from side to side, for alertness of deer or elk; divided forefingers for running hooves of antelope.

Men largely imitated animals important to successful hunters. Women often represented powers important for their own tasks as berry pickers, basket makers, or baby doctors. Some appealed for health, gambling luck, a life-long love, and so forth. After about an hour, the leader in charge called a halt. All went back to their seats, awaiting the next singer. If there were many shamans, dancing continued all night long. On occasion, permission was given for intermissions when visiting, talking, and smoking were allowed, especially at midnight. Anyone who left without permission was vulnerable to attack by the spirits attracted to such gatherings and ready to kill, harm, or punish; or to gain companions in their loneliness.

During long nights, young men wearing animal masks, often of actual treated heads, entertained the congregation with antics that helped to keep everyone awake and alert. They served to propitiate actual animal species, as their elders were invoking spirit ones.

After two or three nights, shamans were ready to initiate a budding medicine man or woman. After a childhood when a person's supernatural power rested, it came back to adults, appearing as a dream or vision to remind them of the initial contract, saying "Sing my song and the world will shine for you."

Though a person might be reluctant to take on the obvious responsibility, ashamed to sing in public, or too poor to give gifts at the initiation, they knew they would die if they did not

---

[61] This sacred pole put up for each Winter Dance has ramifications throughout Interior Salish religion and culture, relating to the tree or pole set up by the Creator at the beginning of the world to serve as its main *axis mundi*. It is also represented by the posts or poles marking graves and sacred places. Prophet Cults from the 1800s include flag poles with ritual banners. In Salish, Sunday is called Flag Day because of this overlap in sacred associations. Ray (1939: 120, 126, 129) also refers to crucial center posts.

comply. Personal indications were being generally moody, deep in thought, lacking ambition to work, or do anything else. Soon, they fell seriously ill, lingering on the brink of a long, slow death until a shaman recognized the spirit power and declared the need for a public initiation during a Winter Dance in the month of January. Such a native doctor could only delay death until the initiation by continuing to try to identify the necessary song. If this warning was ignored, suffering increased, peaking during the winter until either death or a fatal accident. When such lives were in danger, a clear warning came from their spirit guide. If they were alone, the spirit might actually appear to them, strengthening personal fortitude.

Most rarely sang until their hair tinged grey with age. If too anxious to sing, a more powerful older shaman was likely to get angry at such crass showing off, punishing them by taking away their power to sicken or kill them outright, which is called "biting off their head".[62]

In preparation, a novice collected robes, clothing, and ponies for a year before their Give-Away (*Snee-wh-am, "Drop In") at the Winter Dance,[63] when these special gifts were called En-we-mun. The dates of these dances were set by the leading shamans of the tribe at a joint meeting. Usually, each area continued according to the relative sequence and date used for past decades.

At an initiation, the leading shaman sang first in low tones to a silent audience. As his voice grew louder, he walked to the medicine pole holding a strip of fur or other token representing the power of the initiate. He attached it and continued to sing until his strong, confident song vibrated throughout the people. Next, he motioned the initiate forward to the pole, where he or she usually forgets the song in all the excitement until this lead shaman started it off so the initiate could take it up and transcend their surroundings as they became caught up in it, becoming ever stronger as everyone else joins in.

This was an especially dangerous time. Thereafter, a novice was guarded and coached by a stronger shaman during the entire winter season, taught mastery and ownership over their power during the nights of dancing while seated beside experienced shamans to aid them when they worked on patients. The song was perfected, along with careful instruction in the rules of this Medicine Dance. Surviving the next full year proved that one was a full-fledged shaman.

---

[62] Powers should never be made explicit in public because encouraged fatal attacks of sorcery. Only the most powerful of shamans presume to hint more than vaguely about the nature of his or her partner(s). The clearer impression that people had about it (them), the more likely it could be lured away, leaving the person defenseless. Instead, visionaries took the expedient of only evoking or simulating some tiny aspect of a power in the most obscure way. Every power conveyed a token to the person, but usually this token was not as direct an emblem as it might appear at first. Certain animals were considered "friends" of others, so the token might be that of a friend of the partner, rather than a bit of itself. The evocation {snču¿čuwis©tm} and emblem-token {siya°t} remain vital to traditional religion.

[63] The Give-Away has long been a vital feature of Interior Salish culture and society. Its value rests on the general view that sharing is the most important of all the expressions characteristic of humanity. There is a rich and complex vocabulary for sharing in the Colville languages, specifying whether it was done in the contexts of Winter Dances, marriages, funerals, and other seasonal or life events. A unique feature of the Plateau Give-Away was that the audience came forward to choose their own gift, rather than receiving one from the host, as at Northwest Coast potlatches.

The last two nights became a general curing of those afflicted. Grabbing the pole and singing, a senior shaman asked those in need of his services to come forward into the middle of the lodge. For each, with his quivering fingertips, he placed his hands into a basin of water and touched the patient at the tip of the head, moving the hands slowly down the sides of the body, tracing the outline of the seated patient, to brush off any lingering illness. Such treatment covered the whole body. If he missed anything, he dipped his hands in the water again, sang in a low tone, and repeated the brushing off cure. When successful, the patient suddenly jumped up.

Four to six chosen men came to the shaman's aid, holding down his feet as he fought for control over the illness, held in his doubled up fists braced in front of his body. If the sickness came from a very powerful shaman, a curer's feet actually rose off the ground. These men held him until he could plunge his hands into the water basin, dissolving the disease object. Sometimes it looked like a worm covered with blood or a bloody feather, shot into the body to make the person sick or die. If the cause was too powerful, more shamans came to help. Sick people were always at liberty to try another curer if they were not fully cured or felt dissatisfied.

After midnight recess on the last night, host shamans chose members of the audience to distribute the presents assembled by shamans and patients, making sure everyone received a gift, according to their standing in the community. A popular man or woman received large and expensive gifts, such as robes, blankets, silk handkerchiefs, clothing, bridles, saddles, ponies, and trade goods.

In 1932, a woman at Monse, became suddenly ill and sent for a white doctor. He told her she had appendicitis and needed an operation at once to avoid a fatal rupture. Instead, she sent for a shaman with Bluejay power. He cured her, but it took six young men to hold him during the treatment.

Indiens had a staunch belief that God made the world according to a divine plan that gave power from the Animal World to native ancestors and their kin. Shamans understand this power better than anyone else, able to cause good things like nice weather and cures. But some shamans were bad, using it to kill so as to take on other's powers.[64]

The very best power came when all were gathered together for a feast of First Foods during the summer or, most especially, for a Winter Dance when many powers were strongest. Since everyone there was aware and watching, only good could come out of these gatherings.

In their most elaborated form, Revivals included a special rite blending strong faith, Houdini-like feats, and predictions for the future, some with warnings.

---

[64] Thefts or duels between shamans were conducted on planes other than that of ordinary reality. All that some people ever know is that a person died, not how or why. For example, shaman X decided to kill Shaman S by plucking a dead eagle at a Winter Dance and passing out the feathers among the audience. Since S had Eagle Power and died shortly after, X is considered to have been the cause of his death among those in the know. Later X himself died in a contest with a shaman from the coast because he thought he was fighting a battle with Spider power, instead of actual Octopus power; and this misjudgment killed him. Some shamans died defending their families from hostile shamans. Every family kindred supposedly included at least one shaman among its members because most relatives could be trusted, but not other people.

Seancing

A hallmark of the Plateau, shared with shamans of the Plains, Great Lakes, and Siberia, was the Seancing ~ "Behind the Blanket" rite, when a tightly bound shaman went into trance, receive many spirit visitors, and emerged untied. Held midwinter, the rite was initially condemned by Jesuits, who later accepted it.[65]

Formal invitations were given to community members by designated messengers. Families camped beside the long, three-fire, mat lodge set up for the ceremony, often after the area was cleared of deep snow. The lodge looked like a long slanting hay stack, covered by canvas, tule cattail mats, and fir boughs; and tightly seating a hundred people.

Men entered first and sat along one side, then women came in to fill the other side. At the rear sat leaders and shamans, sometimes smoking their pipes decorated with fur and feathers to indicate their special spiritual powers. In the very center stood a sacred pole tied to the top of the lodge by buckskin thongs and covered with strips of fur, feathers, copper bells, beads, hooves, and claws representing various spirit powers of each shaman who was going to participate in the dancing. The pole was about eight feet long, had red face paint on places where the bark was peeled off, and could only be touched by shamans going to sing and dance their spirit powers.

A shaman always wanted a large crowd attending any dance he sponsored, because this showed his power and popularity among the people. Only in this time and place could doctors safely acknowledge their powers in public, and novices be initiated within a safe haven. Otherwise, stronger shamans preyed on the powers of a lesser one, killing him or her. Those sick and afflicted came for cures, usually choosing one shaman to start off, then asking others to help if the case proved difficult. If the patient were poor, a gift was promised for later delivery or relatives came to the rescue with payments or gifts to "gladden the heart" of the curer to assure a quick and safe recovery.

When the lodge was filled, a host came forward and sat down by the doorway to guard it until midnight. No one could leave during the singing and dancing was in progress. If someone really had to leave, only the head shaman could give permission to the guard, causing public attention and some embarrassment.

The leading shaman then walked to the center, grasped the pole, moving it back and forth to rattle animal hooves and tiny bells tarnished with age, while deep silence filled the room, except for the crackling fire. All were still, alert and waiting until, suddenly, his song broke forth, first in grunts and undertones as he gasped for air and his voice became stronger to carry the tune at full volume. One song followed another, the start of each signaled by pole shaking.

---

[65] This rite is the most sensitive chapter in Mourning Dove's novel. This ceremony, usually called Conjuring Rite, is still closely guarded among the Lower Kootenay (McLeod 1971, Schaeffer 1971). Only they and the Colvile proper practiced it on the Plateau (Ray 1941). Earlier, Ray (1939: 116-119) described the Kootenay rite, compared it with the Ojibwa Shaking Tent (*Djisakid*), and noted that the Colvile included it within their Winter Dance, while the Kootenay held it separately. Along with tribes in the Great Lakes, such as the Ojibwa, and Plains, such as Lakota *Yuwipi* (Hallowell 1942, Primitive Man 1944, Densmore 1932, Powers 1984), its distribution is Circumpolar, common among native peoples of the northern hemisphere.

Men and women joined in and sang louder and louder until the lodge sides shook too. For some songs, the crowd stood and danced toward the center, faster and faster. Their motions and sounds imitated animals; hands in front of his head, palms out like deer antlers, arms flapping like eagle wings, wiggling like a swimming salmon. Dancing continued until the leader abruptly stopped and slid his hand from the top of the pole, just beneath the furs and feathers. He bowed to the pole and motioned to the ground, following his hand down the pole before he sat down. All the other dancers seated themselves under the lodge eaves, awaiting another shaman to shake the pole and sing his song.

One seancing ended ten nights of revival. During the day, people slept, families visited, and others gambled. The tenth night climaxed after the room filled and a guard settled at the door. A double grey blanket hung along the rear, with doctors sitting on either side. The shaman to be bound sat down in front of this curtain, head bowed, and sang his song alone. In silence, he spoke of his spirit power, summoning it into the lodge to "come in person".

Starting a new song, beginning as grunts, two men came forward, each using strong buckskin thongs to tie him up while still singing. His thumbs were tied tightly together behind his back, then his toes together, before doubling him up bent backwards to tie his thumbs and toes together. These men lifted him up and threw him roughly behind the curtain. Moments later, they lifted the blanket to reveal him sitting there, singing and holding all of the loose thongs in his hands. They did this several times, always with different men acting as assistants, to prove it was no trick.

All the hosting shamans took turns exhibiting their skill and untying themselves. Finally, when one of the leaders announced that his spirit helpers had arrived, he was bound up while singing and left behind the curtain. Animal spirits began arriving, heard but not seen by their calls. The lead shaman then imitated it and named which other shaman it belonged to. Many animals came and told their stories through the tied-up shaman. At last, the chief spirit arrived, shaking the back end of the lodge and promising to cure all for free.

Assistants then removed the curtain, with the shaman still tied up behind it, bundled in a dead faint. Using smudging herbs, the lead shaman slowly revived and joined the singing as he was untied, and led over to grasp the medicine pole, ending the dance for that year.

The assistants gifted the crowd with blankets, robes, silk handkerchiefs, clothing, and cloth, provided by the spirits of the shamans. Often, at dawn, dogs chased a deer into the camp to be killed and served as a breakfast feast celebrating the cosmic success of the dance.

1954 Riverside

The Okanogan Indians inhabit the Okanagan Valley in the Plateau region of British Columbia and EasternWashington. The Winter Dance described by Lerman was held near the small town of Riverside, WA along the upper Columbia in February 1954.[66]

The Winter Dance is one of the few surviving practices of Okanagan aboriginal culture. As recently as forty years ago the dance was performed in its traditional manner. In the past the performers wore costumes, ate Indian foods, and sang and danced in an elaborate manner. At

Norman Lerman

---

[66] His research was funded by Agnes Healy Anderson (1860 - 1940), who also bequested Seattle and Christian Science non-profits, and built Anderson Hall for UW School of Forestry.

the dance which I wish to describe daily work-clothes were worn, European foods were eaten, and only the older people performed or had any true interest in the ceremony. Thus the dance is now only a residue of the Okanogans' most highly developed artistic and religions spectacle.

The dance is held each year during the months of February and March. Each dance session occupies two to five nights of the week, usually on the week-end. The dance begins around 7 o'clock in the evening but does not get into full swing until after 10 o'clock. The end of the night's dancing is at dawn, about 7 o'clock. On all nights except the last one the dance follows the regular pattern. On the last night, just before dawn, has gambling and gift giving.

The dance is held in the largest room, usually the living-room, of a male or female shaman's house. In the centre of the room is a bare pole affixed to the ceiling and floor. This pole acts as the centre point for all activity during the dance. Only a shaman may touch this pole, and consequently only shamans can lead the singing and dancing.

Before performing, a shaman will begin humming a song softly while he sits or stands in some part of the room. As he sings louder he approaches the pole. He may walk around the pole singing to it or hold out his arms to the pole as he sings. When he grasps the pole in both hands he has become one with his guardian spirit. As long as he is holding the pole, his words are not his own but those of his guardian spirit. Guardian spirits speak unintelligibly and in a low voice, and, therefore, the guardian spirit's words must be transmitted to the audience by another person. For this purpose an interpreter {repeater} stands by the shaman and repeats the guardian spirit's speech in a loud voice. The interpreter may be anyone in the audience and is sometimes another shaman. This pipeline from the guardian spirit via the shaman and the interpreter continues for as long as the guardian spirit has something to say to the audience. As a rule the guardian spirit makes prognostications of the future, gives free advice, and makes comments on present events.

When the guardian spirit has had its say, the shaman began to dance while still grasping the pole. This is a sign for the assembled people to begin dancing. The shaman is at the pole, the interpreter near by, and the people shuffle, hop, or stomp around these two and the pole. After three or four minutes the shaman moves his hand down the pole and says, "Hoooo," which is a signal for the dancing to cease. After another exchange between guardian spirit, shaman, and interpreter dancing resumes. The performance continues until the shaman becomes exhausted. Everyone may then take a short rest, but at the height of the evening's excitement, when one shaman leaves the pole, another may jump out from the dancers and immediately continue. This pattern for the dancing and singing held true for all performers. However, each one had his or her own variations. For instance, the hostess shaman had a small stick with ribbons and small bells attached with she shook during the dancing. She was the only one to utilize any musical instrument aside from the human voice.

A number of special events occurred at the dance. One shaman attempted to cure a girl with a sore foot. This was done by having the girl and some of her relatives march solemnly around the pole during a guardian spirit-shaman-interpreter exchange. This same shaman was also responsible for one of the most important incidents of the night. [35]

While at the pole he begun to sing one of his dead grandfather's songs. The power of the song was so great that he lost consciousness. When this happened, everyone stood around in shocked silence, not knowing what to do. Finally, the shaman's hands were placed in cold water, and he revived to continue where he had left off. Everyone thought the occurrence highly irregular, but nevertheless awesome.

At 1AM a shaman went to the pole and began to chant; everyone sat down, and food was served. The lunch consisted of bologna sandwiches, water, candy, nuts, and halved oranges.

When everyone was served, the shaman and the servers of the food sat with the food in a circle around the pole and ate. When everyone was finished eating, the shaman resumed his chanting and the door was opened. The opening of the door let in fresh air and signified a short break.

During the evening various shamans distributed small strips of cloth. For each strip of cloth the shaman put up a dollar, or he may have had a blanket stand for all his strips. About 4 am all those with the same coloured strips began gambling for the shaman's prize. The gambling was on a blanket with a card game called "*waluks*." When one person got all the strips, he had won the shaman's prize. The shaman collected the strips and saved them to augment his power.

When the gambling was completed, the shamans took turns at the pole to sing and give away gifts. During the evening a few shamans gave away small things, like silk handkerchiefs, but the gift-giving did not begin in earnest until just before dawn. The presents were given to specific individuals or piled on the shaman and people came up and took them. The things given away were yardage, blankets, cigarettes, money, silk scarves and handkerchiefs, jackets, hats, and anything else the shaman had with or on him. The last gift-giver was the shaman who was host. This shaman usually is more lavish in his presents. The last things given away by the host shaman were the blankets covering the windows. When these blankets were ripped off, the light streamed in and the dance was officially ended.

University of Washington, Seattle, Wash. [36]

Dominant Cultural Pair

Twin hallmarks of Methows – pacifism & gender equality – vitally affected the life of every member, coloring a whole outlook upon the world and determining the attitudes taken toward it. Conservatism and radicalism, faith and skepticism are defined in terms of these concepts throughout the Plateau (Ray 1932: 25-27).

Pacifism was carried to such a degree that heinous offenses by raiding parties were left unrevenged. After one such raid the offenders were pursued for a short distance but the chief soon dissuaded the injured ones from attempting retaliation. "Our children are dead and our property is destroyed. We are sad. But can we bring our children to life or restore our property by killing other people? It is better not to fight. It can do no good." The Methow returned home. Such action was not unusual. The most eloquent speeches of Methow chiefs were delivered in the interest of maintaining peaceful relations with all peoples. These efforts were successful. Theory was put into practice. No warfare, either offensive or defensive, could be recalled by the father of any living man. Nor was the principle of pacifism applied only to foreign relations. On the contrary, this ideal was even more important in fashioning daily lives. From earliest infancy the child was drilled in the tenets of peaceful existence with his fellows. The pugnacious man was a public enemy with whom respectable people associated as little as possible. Clearly principal duties of the chief – counselling his people, arbitrating petty differences, and presenting a good example by his own conduct – saw that the peaceful life of the community was not disturbed.

The success of the principle was especially evident within the household. Groups of ten or twenty persons lived together over periods of many years without a single serious altercation. A safety valve was provided by a person's privilege to leave at any time to find a home elsewhere. One could not remain and demand his "rights" when he developed a grievance. As a result family trouble was unheard of.

Insignificant matters and major problems alike were decided with reference to what action would make for the greatest harmony. Even in the mythology this basic attitude was reflected. For example, the man who decided not to take revenge upon his brother who had stolen his wife, was commended for his decision.

Methow insistence upon the gender equality was of an impressive order. Obvious class distinctions were unthinkable. Slavery was an unaccountable custom of foreigners. When a new chief had to be selected any man was eligible. The selection was made by popular vote on the basis of moral character alone. He remained one of the people, as approachable as any other man in the group. His powers were preponderantly advisory rather than dictatorial. Every adult citizen belonged to the general assembly of his village. Nor did wealth carry with [26] it an advance in status. Indeed, wealth was rare. Only shamans could properly be counted rich men and whatever prestige they possessed was the result of their unusual supernatural powers, not their riches. The scarcity of wealth was again an outcome of the belief in the equality of humankind. Why should one man have more than another? Yet nature was bountiful — was not every man deserving of a living? The solution of these questions was a modified, communistic organization. The huge catches of salmon made each summer at the great fish traps were always divided equally among all present, foreigners included. A man need have taken no part in the fishing activities to be entitled to a share in the daily distributions. Likewise the meat obtained on a hunting expedition was divided evenly among all those who had taken part, regardless of what members actually killed the game. Allowance was made, however, for individual initiative. Salmon taken with a spear was the property of an individual spearman (every man was given his turn on the fishing platform). And game taken by the individual hunter was his personal property (except that the first deer killed by a boy had to be divided among the townspeople to the exclusion of himself). Women always retained the products of their individual labors at berry picking or root gathering. Yet it was never necessary for a person to go hungry if there was food in the village. A single meal or whole winter's lodging and meals were never denied.

Thus almost the whole economic life of the Methow was built around the principle that one person was equal to another. Other quite foreign aspects of life were affected as well. Social control was simplified. Stealing was practically unknown. Why should one steal? The usual executive, judicial, and police organization for dealing with criminals was minimized with the absence of one of the commonest of criminals: the thief. The deeply instilled dislike of conflict worked to reduce still more the number of torts committed.

In the quest of supernatural power we see equality again playing a part. Sponsorship was open equally to every man and every woman, not to only a privileged few as in other parts of North America. Very few Methows did not succeed in gaining at least one guardian spirit.

But all individuality was not levelled down by these dominating cultural tendencies nor by other cultural drives of consequence. Not all conformed alike to the ideals of peacefulness and equality. A range of individual variation was seen as in any comparable culture and greater than in many. There were nonconformists and skeptics, those who liked conflict, who deemed themselves superior to their fellows and who liked to accumulate private property. But these types were in the minority, as undesirable radicals who made social problems.

Of particular note, in the center of the Plateau, an area once considered a cultural mixture of Northwest coast and Plains traits, outstanding cultural trends directly contrast to the Coast with rigid [27] Coast system of classes and privileges, and to the Plains, where Methow ideals of pacifism are utterly foreign to the Plains boastful bravery in warfare.

Synergies

A specialized esoteric system of beliefs and practices, specified in the native languages, was provided by elders such as Jerome Miller to Dale Kinkade and myself. In keeping with the patterning by five throughout the Plateau, each person has five components: heart, breath, soul, spirit, and shadow. The Spier (1938: 168) fieldschool noted: The spiritual parts of the individual hardly lend themselves to rigid definition. Apparently there were five: the mind at the heart, the breath soul, the shadow soul, the immortal soul derived from Christianity, and the ghost. Related words refer to allied spirits and power.

Correctly transcribed,[67] these are

heart =	*spu'us*
breath =	*łx^{w}ncut*
soul =	*sn-piẃs ~ snka'ki'iẃs*
shadow =	*sqáqla'x^w*
ghost =	*k^{w}uska'm*
spirit =	*sumix*
ally =	*papaˤíwt* = ancestor's ghost
power =	*timx^w* (soul, spirit animal; cf timẃs navel, *tmn'* = corpse)
	txt'ncuttn (*xt'* = 'take care of')

Informing all of these beings, of course, is the creator God. Suszen stated that "before the whites came" God looked like the rainbow. He had a wife, son, and daughter (Spier 1938: 167). His continuing specific embodiment is the sweatlodge, as well as an abstract universal Mind, which resides in the inspiring heart, not the brain as thought by Europeans.

Indeed, many of these beliefs are mind-dependent, for good or ill. Some are specific to certain situations, such as grief or new starts. Each of these can be summarily characterized:

sumíx ~ sumáx = spirit power, usually obtained in mountains; after undergoing a sweathouse and fast, then going to mountains. Works for Indians, not Whites; works for horse, never cattle; no distinct types for killing, curing, only neutral put to various purposes.

na'acqamtn = questing places fixed from years back where trainees go and stay overnight to get power

sac'acxa'x^w = a person training for power

sk'^{w}əƛ́cím'x = new dancer; first time singing (in Chinook dance)

tər'tər'qmúl = dancer, person who dances a lot

---

[67] Mattina 1987: 65, 130, 186, 188, 201, 208, 237, 313, 338, 339. MD Kinkade, Columbian Notebook 3, Jerome Miller, September 24ff 1976.

ktər'qákst = person who dances in aid of an Indian doctor

kasktər'qákstəx^wkt = people dancing for an Indian doctor

nəwáy = when they give things away during a dance. Anyone may give things; if it seems insufficient, relatives chip in. Special pieces of rags or string given for gambling as tokens for actual things to be given later.

psiwst = self train to become a shaman.

ƛa'k^wilx = person with special powers, Indian doctor. Each visionary has a pipe, a wooden baton, and an emblem of its spirit power. The pipe has mystical abilities since its stem and bowl can be used as a place of refuge for ones own spirit when it is under attack, or, in contrast, used as a place to entrap the spirit of a rival shaman when he or she if offered a smoke. The baton is used during the medicine dance, when the emblem, often a bit of the animal embodying of a spirit species.

q'iwntm = power to kill. When a doctor was executed for loosing patients or stealing souls, he (never she) was clubbed, hanged, throat cut, or weighted with rocks to drown. Arrows and spears were useless (Spier 1938: 163).

sk'awáłca? = a spell

k'awən = bad wish, put a spell on someone, kill with a spell [Person able to do this has long hair; he rolls some in the palm of his hand, making an arrow of it, and shoots it into a person and kills him outright; can also kill a horse or dog. Doesn't work on Whites or cattle.

pá'a? = constraints on a person whose close relative has just died. When relative dies, one must sweathouse; boil fir-boughs or rose bush in big kettle and bathe with the water to be cleansed. Otherwise bad luck as deer or salmon will stay away, and you will lose at gambling.

stəx̲^wtluscút = giving things away after a funeral

smipnúm'təx^w = prophet

wi'wi'y'lxkn = name of the prophet who predicted that the present site of Wenatchee would become a city.

snk'^walmáya'tn = Indian legends, stories, the means of passing on history, memory, culture, often using negative examples, to entertain and train listeners.

In the Sanpoil language, the term for "ghost-spirit" (*pap'aiut*)[68] is the same as the word for "shoulder blade", as Ray (1933: 169, 174) wrote "A spirit-ghost was easily killed; an arrow shot at one never missed. At the spot where one had been killed here was always found a human scapula. Indeed, the native terms for ghost-spirit … meant scapula."

This is clearly a folk explanation, since the actual term for shoulder blade is *snn'ilkstn*. Based on previous insights, the terms for ghost-spirit and scapula are equated because, except for knee-caps, the shoulder blades are the bones, or at least the biggest bones to last longest, to occur on the edge of the body. They are also located upon the torso, the most vital part of the body since it is the locus of the heart, the abode of thought and emotion among the Salishans (Ray 1932: 169; Kinkade 1975). In short, as ghosts lurk at the edge between the living and the dead, belonging fully to neither domain, so too shoulder blades occur on the edge of the body between the skeleton and the skin, affixed fully to neither since they are separate when people find them with exposed skeletons.

---

[68] Corrected by Mattina, p64 # 67.

METHOW CULTURE

Methows, like other Interior Salishans and other Native Americans, were organized by language, drainage, and village – the most effective political unit. Each village had a leader, who was advised by an assembly of married adults, regardless of their origins or length of residence. Both seasonal and personal movement was common among these villages and affiliated camps, especially at berry, hunting, and fishing sites.

Leadership was hereditary among males, but the most likely candidate received approval from an assembly of all resident adults. Once selected, a chief held office until he died or left the village. Qualities sought were honesty, sound judgment, even temperament, and arbitration skills. Larger villages included subchiefs advising the chief in his roles of judge, arbitrator, and manager. A speaker and message runners also served the, community, repeating the words of the chief calling people to an assembly, or coordinating seasonal, movements.

As judge, the chief held open court, calling on witnesses, seeking evidence, and hearing the accused. Crimes included murder, stealing, perjury, assault, sexual indiscretions, abortion, sorcery, or sorcery retaliation. Under pressures from missionaries and federal agents, punishment often involved a three-foot lash braided of deer neck sinews (Ray 1932: 113). Murder was compensated for with goods, never executions. Other punishments might exclude someone from participating in a [16] ceremony, impose social ostracism for a set time, or demand specific acts such as providing food to the family of their victim.

In the Very Beginning

At end of age of the spirits, just prior to human arrival, the spirit leader who created the world gave names to all creatures at a dawn assembly. Coyote stayed up all night intending to be first in line to receive the name of Salmon, Bear, or Eagle. Instead, he fell asleep and was the last to appear. Yet because he thought for himself, the Creator put Coyote in charge of making the world ready for humans. The chief himself gave up his head and limbs so the ribcage become Sweatlodge, available to humans in need.

Boastful, foolish, wise, and devious, Coyote wandered the world putting it to rights. One of his greatest adventures was to steal Salmon from the trap of Bird Women at the mouth of the Columbia and bring them upriver. Every village at the mouth of a tributary stream was visited. Those who allowed him to marry pretty women received runs of large salmon, those who provided average women received average runs, and those who refused him found waterfalls blocking salmon migration into their streams.

Coyote also issued "commandments" about how the world was to be organized. He decreed the type and manner of salmon fishing in each stream, generally spears for clear water and nets for murky. Sometimes he left a spirit emblem or rock image at the [17] place to indicate these rules. Other times, he changed the landscape, as when he dropped all kinds of roots on top of Steamboat Rock.

While Coyote tried out for the part, a spirit council decided that the unnatural sons of Mole, Coyote's wife, would become Sun and Moon.

The world was populated with various dwarfs and monsters, including hairy, smelly, twenty-foot giants (Big Foot, sasquatch) who lived in the mountains (Ray 1932: 176). Various lakes and water obstructions had resident spirits, such as a nude woman with long flowing hair and exposed breasts or a hairy, longhorn being variously reported for Alta Lake, Omak Lake, and Annum (Buffalo) Lake near Nespelem.

Spirit powers *(sumix ~ shumix)* included all manner of entities, both animate and inanimate, such as driftwood and fish traps. Among the most powerful were and are Grizzly, Wolf, Badger, Skunk, Flying Squirrel, Pack Rat, Spider, Hawk, and Eagle. More dangerous powers were and are Grizzly, Bear, Wolf, Cougar, Badger, Summer Weasel, and Rattlesnake. Rabbit and Magpie were weak powers.

Life Cycle

First and subsequent pregnancy imposed strict taboos on the mother and father to assure the wellbeing of their baby. Often, the pregnant woman returned to the home of her mother until the birth. She undertook a regular regime, of walking, running, and [18] swimming, and eating sparingly.

When labor began the woman and an elder female retired to a birthing hut or a screened off section of the house. For delivery, the woman knelt against two stages and held on to the tops, or she braced against the forearms of the midwife, who knelt facing her.

The baby fell onto grass or a mat. The elder tied off the umbilical cord with deer sinew, bit through it, and buried the placenta. When the umbilical cord fell off, it was saved and tied to the babyboard. Later it was carefully buried by the father to insure good health for his child.

After birth, the baby was washed and massaged to shape features and limbs (Ray 1952: 125). For difficult deliveries, shamans were called to assist. If the fetus was born dead, it was buried immediately.

The mother was given an herbal tea to reduce bleeding. The father beat a dog or horse or ran a horse or himself into a lather so that the child would not cry a lot or convulse. At no other time was an animal injured out of fear of harming the child. A relative of the father usually made the cradleboard for a baby, but only after it was born healthy.

The mother rested for a week and relaxed for a month, drinking a fortifying herb tonic twice a day. After such confinement, she bathed and held a small feast for the baby, being forbidden to cook while she was loosing blood. Children [19] born out of wedlock were usually permanently adopted by relatives. Friendly families might betroth their infants to establish a permanent bond.

During naps for the first ten days, the baby was tightly swaddled in a hide. Afterward, at night, it was placed into a fawnskin bag and. during the day, bound onto a cradle board, nursing on demand. If the mother died, the baby was adopted by another nursing mother for about two years. Slight differences marked male or female cradleboards and bindings, in addition to the kinds of dangles hung from the protecting head loop. For a boy, the penis was exposed to extrude urine, while a girl had a buckskin fold between her legs (Ray 1932: 130) as a trough to allow urine to run off.[69] Baby bedding and diapers were made from birchbark or buckskin. During summer, children went unclothed until puberty. The contents of a baby's buckskin diapers were always emptied into the same hole to protect against its use in sorcery, and.

---

[69] Portman (1993: 20) misidentifies an obviously boy's cradle-board, giving too much emphasis to the beaded top, which is a decision made by the member(s) of the father's family who makes and decorates the baby holder for a newborn.

similarly, the umbilical stub was buried in the hills to keep the baby from harm.

Throughout infancy, the mother massaged the baby to make it grow tall and slim, with a fine nose and chin. Thick hair was especially prized, and made shiny with a sunflower root shampoo (Ray 1932: 54).

A healthy child from a prominent family was named soon after birth, but most babies were named later in their first year. Older children had their ears pierced. Baby teeth were given to [20] a dog with a prayer for new strong teeth (Miller 1990: 209, note 11). Parents threatened children, but whipping was only performed by an elderly man who came to a home by special request. In severe cases, he came disguised and the punishment was harsh.

Inside, children were to be quiet and unobtrusive, outside they could be boisterous and active, encouraged to swim and run.

Children helped adults wherever possible. Grandparents nurtured and protected their grandchildren, developing a close bond between them. During family meals, children were given meat or fish sections with the killing wound to make them strong (Ray 1932: 132),

A strong ethic, of sharing applied to all fish and meat (Ray 1932: 25), provided by men or women through a mutual division of labor (Ray 1932: 33).

When a boy killed his first small game or salmon, it was given away to an old man or served at a feast for old men to teach him the value of sharing. When he killed his first deer, it was cut up and pieces sent to every home in the community. When a girl gathered her first roots or berries, a feast was held for the old women (Ray 1932: 26, 133). A boy or girl never ate of their first efforts.

By puberty, all boys and some girls had acquired a guardian spirit by questing in the hills after dark. During a quest, piling rocks to keep busy, spirits appeared as humans to confer power before changing into their own species form as they departed. Good looks and a strong [21] body were particularly attractive to spirits (Ray 1952: 173), who left as one became old, weak, or sickly. When a human partner died, the spirit became a spirit-ghost in quest of another human, preferably from the same family unless it was lured away by a shaman. When a spirit-ghost was itself killed, a shoulder blade was found at the spot.

While a child received a spirit at eight to ten years of age, the encounter was forgotten until the spirit returned about fifteen or twenty years later, and the person sickened with feelings of loneliness and despondency. A shaman was called to fix the spirit in the patient, singing the song signaling their bond. In winter, the patient sang this song in public during a winter dance.

Some spirits conferred the ability to cure particular ailments, while shamans received power to heal persistent and supernatural illnesses (Ray 1932: 202), including animal attack wounds, fevers, mental upset, spirit return or loss, and magical poisoning by a jealous woman.

The shaman came to the patient and began by smoking a pipe to offer tobacco to the spirits, open communication, and consider the specifics of the case. Then he (sometimes she) selected a speaker and some helpers, one of whom brought a basket of water for washing hands. The basket was emptied and refilled between hand washings. The shaman sang, accompanied by the audience, while he inspected the patient. Once a diagnosis was made, the [22] shaman began other songs, sprinkled water, and used hand motions or sucking to cure the disorder. When a spirit or poison was extracted, the helpers forced the shaman to the basket and submerged his cupped hands to neutralize the intrusion (Ray 1932: 205). In return for the cure, the shaman received a generous payment agreed upon in advance.

At first menstruation, a girl was secluded for 10 days in a menstrual hut, wearing her oldest clothes and her braids in coils (Ray 1932: 134). She ran after dark because she was not to be seen. During the day, she pondered her future life. At the end, she was given new adult clothes and sent forth as a woman. Boys engaged in strenuous exercise during puberty but there was no special ritual observance. After a successful hunt or other good deed, he was pronounced a young man in public.

Women returned to the menstrual hut during each successive occurrence and were careful to avoid hunting and religious gear. If a weapon were contaminated, it was rubbed with coyote mint leaves to restore it (Ray 1932: 135). Girls from better families were watched and carefully chaperoned. The daughters of leaders wore long capes to hide their bodies, and might be secluded from public view until a marriage was arranged. Boys courted them with flutes and songs. For second marriages, love medicine was used to compel the spouse (Ray 1932: 136; Miller 1990: 79-90). Parents arranged marriages, and. as in-laws, exchanged gifts for the duration of a marriage. The couple lived with relatives of [23] the husband.

After courtship and betrothal, a time was set for the wedding. The bride-to-be moved to a mat shelter set up a distance from the village. Her family provided her with food and comforts, but she was to spend her time deciding on her future goals. She could not speak to anyone, nor they to her. After several days, or longer if she needed more time, two other lodges were build near her. One camp was that of the groom and family, and the other was that of the family of the bride because she remained in seclusion in her shelter until the actual wedding.

The groom's family carried a feast to the camp of the other family, and gave them gifts appropriate to women, such as baskets, woven bags filled with dried food, robes, blankets, and yardage. Prayers were said to bless the marriage, and to ask for long life and many healthy children. In private, the, bride was given a special feather to wear as a married woman.

The next day the bride's family carried a feast to the groom's camp and gave male related gifts, such as meat, tools, and weapons. Great care was taken to see that the exchange of gifts was even and that neither family outdid the other. For a life based on sharing together, both families had to start equal. The groom's hair at the side of his forehead was fashioned into a small braid to indicate that he was married. His wife assumed the responsibility of maintaining this braid during the marriage.

The marriage took place on the third day. Both families [24] prepared a lodge for the couple, supplying it with all necessities. The bride was dressed in fine garments and her feather. She was led out of seclusion to her horse, which was also elaborately decorated, and rode to the wedding lodge, where the groom waited. Standing together outside, leaders asked the Creator to bless the union and proclaimed them married. Sometimes, elite families used a wedding robe to wrap around the couple during the prayers.

After the couple was settled in their new lodge, the other-camps dispersed to give them privacy. At night, youngsters might come to serenade the couple or to engage in banter and joking, but this was all in fun. After a time, when the villagers moved to a new location, the couple rejoined the community and took an active role in its affairs.

To overcome parental objections, a couple might elope or allow themselves to be found in bed together one morning. Successful hunters, gamblers, shamans, and leaders had more than a single wife, sometimes in separate camps. Levirate (remarriage to a brother-in-law after death of husband) and sororate (remarriage to sister-in-law after death of wife) were practiced at the death of a spouse, although a sibling of the deceased could be refused after a proper mourning period was observed. Adultery and incest were offenses punishable by lashing, cutting off ears, or, in extreme cases, death. Jilted spouses might commit suicide. [25]

With children came family responsibilities and participation in the network of kinship obligations. Like other Plateau communities, these Salishans had a bilateral system pairing the duties of men and women on a mostly equal basis to form kindreds, requiring vast genealogical knowledge to keep track of relatives by descent or marriage throughout the Plateau and beyond.

Kinship terms stressed generation, gender, and collaterality (Elmendorf 1951). Parents and own children are distinguished from uncles, aunts, and niblings (nephews-nieces), yet all cousins are called siblings. When the death of a linking relative dies, special decedence terms are used for surviving collaterals to move their relationships closer together, much as the levirate and sororate reaffirmed family alliances by marrying a surviving sibling to widow or widower. In this case, terms meant "living uncle" and "living aunt" acting like parents.

Multiple wives, extensive mobility, and widely scattered resources contributed to the overall flexibility of this system so that kindreds were never localized and relationships were as broad as possible. Some evidence for cognatic corporate groups or totemic kindreds suggests more formality to prehistoric patterns.

Sorcery was dreaded, identifiable when a victim had a scared look in the eyes, was jumpy and twitched, and became delirious, often naming the shaman who caused that condition. Only a more powerful shaman could affect a cure. If the victim died, a family member might kill by magic or weapon the assumed malicious shaman, assured of acquittal by community consensus.

When near death, a person might call for an old man to act as confessor to keep his or her soul from wandering, tormented by past wrongs. At death, the body was wrapped in a rush mat or deerskin and placed in the branches of a tree. If a religious leader died inside a lodge, the mats were removed and the structure burned. As soon as possible in daylight, a grave was dug and the body carried there, followed by mourners. After the eulogy, a shaman swept out the grave with wild rose branches and the body was buried, flexed under wrappings of deerskins and mats. Important possessions, such as keepsakes and talismans, were added to the grave, but no clothes or food.

Afterward, at the home of the deceased, a feast was held and property distributed. Evergreen boughs and rosebushes were burned to fumigate the house and repel lingering spirits. Anyone who had touched the corpse underwent intensive sweating and bathing. The deceased's clothing, which was too personal, was buried separately. Mourners set up huts in the woods, sweating, bathing, fasting, and drinking a rosebush decoction morning and night for a year. An under bedding of fir boughs protected hunting luck while a man mourned his wife. A male mourner wore his hair loose, but a woman had hers cut off at shoulder length. Leather bands were worn around the wrists, providing a protective [27] circle, until they fell off.

At death, the soul, located near the heart, departed for the afterworld at the end of the Milky Way, or, if unabsolved, became an anguished ghost wandering the earth (Ray 1932: 171). The guardian spirit, as a spirit-ghost, hovered nearby waiting for another relative or a shaman to reestablish rapport with the living.

Ceremonies

The return salmon ceremony was the culmination of a ritual series for first roots, game, berries, and fish. For salmon, men gathered to thank forest trees then cut down and laid in a row to season, when another rite was held before they were carried to the river to build the weir.

While men assembled pieces for the trap, women gathered sunflower leaves to make a sunshade like a summer mat house without walls. The ground inside and outside of this shade was also covered with leaves. When all was ready, women, children, and young men withdrew for five days. Men wore no clothes during this time.[70] The "salmon *tyee*" spent five nights at the trap praying and singing to consecrate its use.

Every morning, men appointed by the tyee carried salmon from the trap and laid them on the leaves to be gutted. During days one through four. men feasted only on salmon flanks, which were boiled the first two days and roasted the last two, eating with a special triangular spoon made from a bent willow twig. [28]

Salmon heads, tails, fins, backbones, and roe were dried upon a woven willow platform until the fifth day, when they were mixed into a soup with service berries, bitterroot, camas, and water. This was the most holy meal of the rite since it included virtually all foods. Every man ate as much as possible. When not fishing or feasting, men gambled. After the fifth day, women rejoined the camp and fish processing began. Thereafter, women cooked all meals, and prepared all fish (Ray 1952: 71).

Harvesting each resource began with a public feast to thank and consume that new food.

The most elaborated of ceremonies was and is the winter dance, held in rotation among tribal communities during January and February. A large mat house was cleared, poles suspended along its sides to hold gifts, and a tree with only top branches, decorated with wrappings and dangles, was set up in the middle. Led off by the host, each visionary grasped the pole in turn and sang his or her song. Cooking and eating was forbidden during the ceremony and specially empowered men, called Bluejays and Owls, sat in the rafters watching for violations. They wore only breechclouts despite the bitter cold weather. After serving at dances throughout the season, they were ritually captured and restored to normal behavior.

Later in the season, dances were dedicated to bringing the Chinook or warm winds of spring. Within the house, men sat on the right and women on the left. The host was usually a powerful [29] shaman since displays of spirit powers often led to attempted thefts of the spirits by unscrupulous shamans, A speaker-announced for the host and others, calling out times for intermissions to drink water and smoke. In public, a novice proclaimed his renewed ties with his or her spirit by dancing, protected by a sponsoring shaman since he or she were particularly vulnerable while the power was new (Ray 1932: 192). After this initiation, the visionary would briefly describe the circumstance of the vision during a later intermission, or, alternatively, ask for guesses about what his song and motions had been evoking. On the last morning, gifts were distributed by the host to other performers, and to the audience as quantity allowed.

Foods

Every day, during summer, an elderly woman of the household arise to built up banked fires, then to wake the children, who ran to a stream to bathe, boys and girls going to separate locations (Ray 1932: 29). Children returned home to stand around the fire and hear a lecture by the matron on morality and leading a good life. Younger women of the house rose and began their cooking chores. Women rose and dressed first because it was immodest to be seen by males. Men got up last, going to bathe in the river or a sweatlodge. Babies were not deliberately awakened, being changed and washed when they awoke.

When warm, children went out to play at [30] playground on a sandbar or beach. The house was prepared for a day use after the women rolled up the bedding. Everyone returned for

---

[70] Naked evokes the primordial, with nothing between men and Creator, as they were born into this world, as does the simple bent willow stem spoon.

a late morning meal. Usually, salmon was stone-boiled in a basket and the pieces served on a sewn rush mat. Berries might be added to the broth. Sometimes, fish and camas bulbs were served in a cooking basket, eaten with the same spoon. While eating, men sat comfortably, while women folded their legs to the side and tucked in their heels. For an ordinary family meal, children ate with adults. At a feast, men ate first, before women and children.

After breakfast, women groomed the men, combing their hair. The afternoon was spent at routine tasks of provisioning, manufacturing, and repairing.

The evening meal was eaten before dusk, consisting of the same fare (Ray 1932: 106). For variety, food was stone-boiled, open fire roasted, pit roasted, steamed, smoked, or parched. Children usually heard stories during the early evening. Men gathered together in a home, often that of the leader, to smoke and council.

By dark, children were in bed because, night was a dangerous time, according to many stories and warnings about enemies and monsters they had heard. Men went to bed before women, who were the last to retire in modesty (Ray 1932: 30).

During winter, dawn bathing continued but only a single late afternoon meal was eaten because people were less active, with [31] some exceptions. After a snowfall, everyone worked hard to remove snow from the house roof and to make paths to the fuel, water, and canoe launches along the waterway. During early Spring, the pace quickened as people prepared equipment, tools, and materials for expeditions to fishing, harvesting, and gathering areas.

With spring (Ray 1932: 27) came the gathering of fresh shoots, such as balsam and prickly pear pods, which had to have their needles singed off. During the eighteenth century, people left their winter pithouses and dismantled mat lodges. The aged, handicapped, or ill remained at the winter site, using foods cached in trees or stored on scaffolds.

When various root crops were ready, families left together, telling the winter leader their intended destination. The largest number of people-went with the leader and his family. Along the river, men gathered shellfish and hunted rabbits and waterfowl. Special groups went to root grounds south of the Columbia River. Each camp sent women to dig roots, which were served at a feast, a first or return food rite giving thanks for the harvest and consecrating their efforts.

A return food rite was held whenever a fresh species of plant or animal became available (Ray 1932: 97). In each case, a leader designated a few women to gather the food, cook it, place it on mats. Everyone in camp sat around the food while an elder spoke about thanking food, carrying on tradition, and showing [32] respect. All food was then eaten. In some cases, special restrictions applied for the next few days. For instance, roots were steamed gently for two days after the rite to assure continued bounty.

During the next month, women dug roots every day with a digging stick (a dibble), collecting a supply for the coming year. A woman made her own dibble, measured from the ground to her bent elbow.

At the root grounds, every day, each woman dug roots from over half an acre. Related women were led by a senior matron, who planned and coordinated their movements to various areas. Once a spot was announced, women met there in the morning, after each finished her domestic chores. Attached to her belt, each woman had a small collecting bag. When it was full, she emptied it into a bag woven of sage bark or hemp. Roots were skinned, cleaned, and sorted every night. Those damaged were eaten or pulverized promptly, while others were placed on mats and turned frequently to dry in the sun. At the end of the harvest, bags of dried roots were taken to winter camps for permanent storage. Meanwhile, men visited, scouted, and hunted to supply the camps, anticipating fishing season.

To transport goods, in addition to packstraps (Ray 1932: 122), people relied on canoes, snowshoes, and improvised toboggans of deer and bear hides (Ray 1932: 118, 120, 122). [33]

Throughout the Plateau, staple roots were camas bulbs and bitter-roots (also called rock rose) (Ray 1932: 99). Several varieties of camas were and are recognized. The most distinctive were black camas, which was pit roasted and powdered for storage; and white camas, which was dried until cooked by steaming.

Other plant foods included various parts of the balsam sunflower harvested throughout the year. Also, there were prickly pear fruits, sunflower seeds, sweet coltsfoot petioles, pine nuts, hazel nuts, mints, and pine lichen (locally called moss), which was roasted in a pit with wild onions and camas (Ray 1932: 103). Today, they are slowly cooked in a stove oven.

May through August is the fishing season. While sturgeon and small fish were always available, the runs of anadromous salmon and trout provided the Plateau staple food (Ray 1932: 28). As an indication of their great importance, the return salmon rite lasted five days.

Five Columbia salmon species appeared in this region during May to November runs. These were chinook (king), averaging 32 pounds with a few of 100 pounds at Kettle Falls, during fish runs of May through July of silver (coho, white); pink (humpback); and chum (dog). Sockeye, which spawn in lakes, only ran in the Okanogan River on their way north. Steelhead trout, weighing 10 to 15 pounds, ran from March to July. The fall runs of both silver and chum, from September to November, provided a less productive last harvest. Both species weighed about 6 pounds, but pinks were sparse (Ray 1932: 57). [34] Water level was low then so silvers were speared or seined from canoes. Sometimes a shaded blind was built across a smaller stream to prevent moving shadows while spearing from the bank (Ray 1932: 60). Some night torch fishing was also done. These late runs of silver and chum salmon were smoke-dried in mat huts because the heat of the summer was gone.

Every fishery was utilized, with the largest camps and traps were at the mouth of Psk^{w}aws or Wenatchi River,[71] with others at the confluences of tribal namesake tributaries and the Columbia itself. The largest Salishan fishery was at Kettle Falls in Colvile territory, noted for large salmon taken during festive visiting, trading, and gambling. All Salishan tribes and their neighbors gathered there during the run.

Fishing technology utilized weirs and traps (funnel, basket, elevated, cf Ray 1932: 61).

A communal trap had weirs made of willow branches about 100 feet apart, held against the flow by intermittent cottonwood log tripods anchored by stones to a firm and smooth river bed (Ray 1952: 62). Construction was a highly skilled task, combining manual ability and supernatural sanction. Between the weirs, a woven fence led salmon to a basket trap near the shore of the upper weir, which included small gaps to allow some escapage. Such a trap was 3 feet wide by 6 feet long by 3 feet high. Every morning, confined salmon were driven into the small trap, clubbed, and thrown to the shore. The last few salmon were [35] speared out.

A funnel trap was privately owned and built on a small stream. A single weir – used for trout, whitefish, suckers – was emptied at mid-day and evening.

Open-twined willow basket traps were suspended at the base of waterfalls where leaping salmon fell into them, as at Kettle Falls. Access to the traps was by means of a willow-bark rope

---

[71] This sockeye fishery is contentious. Article X 1855 Yakama Treaty set aside six square miles at the Pisquouse ~ Wenatshapam forks until far off DC paid Yakamas for it, denying legal Colville Salish use until justice prevailed in recent court decisions (Bower, Hart 2000).

ladder. Those appointed to gather the fish would club them, string them on a rope passed through gills, signal to have them hauled up, and see that the catch was equally distributed among everyone in camp at that moment (Ray 1932: 653).

If the trap had few fish, the "salmon tyee," who was in charge of the fishing, wrapped himself in a robe and prayed at the trap all night. Everyone was ordered away from the waterway. During the fishing season, menstruating women stayed well away from the water and salmon because of a belief that menstruation odors repelled the fish. Regardless of the location, men caught and hauled all the fish, while women prepared each one for summer sun-drying. At the end of season, some people moved further upriver to harvest the last spawning fish.

Conservation was practiced at all fish weirs. Gates were left open at night to allow salmon free passage upstream to spawn and to be taken by other camps.

Salmon were prepared most carefully. The belly was cut and the guts removed before the body was placed on a drying rack for [36] an hour. Then the fish were taken down so the heads could be removed, split open, and hung up. The flanks were loosely separated from the backbone, slashed every half inch along the side to provide ventilation, and the layers were held apart by cedar splints. A peg was pushed through the tail and the fish was hung up to dry for about 2 weeks. Salmon heads and roe dried for a month (Ray 1952: 75). Drying racks were shaded with brush and leaves, and those holding chinook were particularly well covered since this fish spoiled easily.

Aside from traps, men used spears and nets, particularly at rapids along the Columbia River where fish had to move through a narrow passage. In some places, artificial channels were made as parallel trenches along the shore to allow for the rise and fall of water level. Children collected white rocks to line the trench bottoms .to aid visibility. In May, when the river was low, channels were dug to be 20 feet long, 3 feet deep, and six feet wide at top. Two other trenches were dug further up the bank. Salmon were taken with a spear from a triangular scaffold supported by pole tripods built at either end of the trench and braced against shore.

Along river banks, more elaborate fish platforms were built, owned jointly by the fishing camp, and occupied by only one man at a time. As each man speared a fish, another man took his place and did likewise. The eye strain of watching the water also kept allotted time brief. Spear size and shape matched [37] prevailing natural conditions, as dictated by Coyote's commandments. Thus, smaller fish were taken with a V pronged harpoon, but large salmon, such as chinook, required a 3 pronged leister. Harpoons were attached by a cord to fir shafts.

Nets were only used in murky or rough water, unless the nettle fibers could be dyed to match water conditions. Seines dragged for chum and silvers, while dip nets for salmon and suckers spread a mesh between handles. When this horizontal net was struck by a fish, the entire apparatus was pulled up. The mesh gauge varied according to the size of the intended fish. For eels and small fish, willow dip nets were two feet wide and one foot deep.

A seine, made of nettle fibers, measured 30 to 40 feet long and 6 feet high when suspended between twenty foot ropes on each side. A charred cedar block, called an "otter." floated at the end of one rope for visibility. The net was held vertically by sinkers made from flat stones tied within a willow loop. Seines were only used at night where a stream bed was smooth. Two men dropped the net from a canoe, letting it fill out, then hauled it in from land. If a seine was loaned to another, part of the catch was given as a gift when the net was returned. While Ray (1932: 69) suggested that seining technology was borrowed from the Pacific coast, Salishans believe that it was given to humans by supernatural Spider people who lived near modern Vantage.

In the fall, after the sun was less intense, salmon was [38] dried and inadvertently smoked inside houses. During this time, pine was not used for fires because the smoke was too sooty. Salmon heads and flanks, when dry, were stored in tule bags. If spoilage was a concern, then the bag was lined and food layers separated with dragon sagewort. All bags were sewn shut and taken to winter village locations for storage. Roe was sewn into salmon skins and hung up or stored on platforms at the winter camp. Prickly pear pods were tied around the four support posts of a platform to deter mice and other creatures from climbing up. For greater safety, some storage houses were built on islands.

Other significant water resources were sturgeon, sucker, eel, trout, and roe or eggs.

Late in Summer, some people moved from the fisheries into the mountains for fall hunting, berrying, and the digging of late roots. Fall foods included serviceberries. huckleberries, blackberries, elderberries, and chokecherries (Ray 1932: 101), which were used to make a pemmican mixed with salmon flour. Other pemmicans consisted of serviceberries, venison flour, and deer tallow; or salmon flour and berries; or sunflower seed flour, salmon flour, and berries (Ray 1932: 106).

While a few families stayed in the hills during the winter, often tending a trap line, most moved to winter sites near firewood, fresh water, and shelter from deep snow or brisk winds.

Hunting was the major occupation of fall and winter. Deer [39] were taken from November to March, along with some elk. Communal hunts were the most productive and required the most preparation. Prior to leaving, hunters entered the sweatlodge morning and evening for ten days to remove body odors offensive to deer, singing and praying for success. They also practiced sexual continence, which was especially important for the hunt leader.

During the day, weapons and gear were made or repaired. Each hunter took along clothes, snowshoes, and packs with mats for a hut, robes for bedding, and a only little food because hunters expected to eat fresh game. For longer hunts, women went along to keep camp, sleeping separately from men in the same huts. The leader coordinated all activities and assigned all tasks, designating runners to serve as drivers to chase game to the hunters waiting at the end of a canyon or draw. During hardship, a guardian spirit might appear to a hunter in a dream to offer advice and luck.

Deer were also driven into the Columbia with dogs and killed in the water. A hunter skilled in the use of dogs could command them by gesture and sound. Deer were also taken at a watering spot or a saltlick, using a blind, or by waiting near a game trail (Ray 1932: 82).

Each deer was carried into the house through the back and placed on a fresh bed of fir boughs. It was ritually butchered, beginning with cuts down both forelimbs and removal of the fore hoofs. Then the body was slit down the neck and along the [40] underside, down the hind legs, and the back hoofs were cut off. A final cut was made around the neck and the entire skin was removed in one piece (Ray 1932: 91). A special prayer was said as each cut was made.

The meat was divided equally to everyone in camp, but the hides belonged to the hunter who made the kill. Deer meat for winter use was dried on four foot high willow scaffolds, or, for less meat, upon a willow dome. Dry meat was stored in tule bags, or, later in time, leather parfleches. Bear meat was so fatty it was stored on elevated platforms with fir boughs between layers. Fat and tallow was tamped into paunches, boiled, and allowed to harden for storage.

When everyone returned to the winter village, a special feast was held for the elderly of stewed hoofs, lower leg muscles, head, and lungs (Ray 1932: 92). Young people were not invited because eating this food was taboo to them, under threat of becoming crippled.

Women worked hard dressing the hides of deer, elk, antelope, and buffalo. A hide was left in water until the hair loosened, propped up wet, dehaired with a rib scraper, and dried before it was left in watery deer brains, twisted to remove excess liquid, stretched on a pole frame, and, finally, rubbed smooth while warmed by nearby fires (Ray 1932: 94).

Black and grizzly bears might be killed, but the meat had a [41] strong taste and was only eaten as a matter of personal preference. Rather, bear were prized for their hides. Bears were encountered in berry patches along Columbia, or smoked from dens using rotten pine wood. Special mourning songs were sung by a hunter when he killed a black bear. Grizzlies were much feared and hunted only by those with power from Grizzly, or allied spirits such as Mouse, Mountain Squirrel, and Gopher. Woodchucks were shot with a sharpened arrow shaft with attached wooden flange to secure the arrow through the body and keep the animal from fitting through the opening of its den. Women sometimes poured water into burrows to drive out animals to be clubbed. Eagles, used for feathers and meat, were grabbed at their nests after a hunter had climbed down on a three-strand willow rope.

Along with Spokan, Flathead, and others, Columbians went to hunt bison on the northern Plains. Their leader, Split-Sun, emerged from such expeditions as the nominal leader of an intertribal Salishan confederacy.

In addition to spears or bows and arrows, hunters also used traps, deadfalls, and snares set over game trails (Ray 1932: 85) for mink, fisher, martin, badger, and otter. The deadfall consisted of angled cedar planks, weighted with rocks on top, and held up by a light pole with bait attached. Stakes driven into the ground on either side kept an animal from escaping the blow when the pole dislodged and the rocks came crashing down. For the larger fox, lynx, wildcat, cougar, coyote, and wolf; a log [42] deadfall was used to crush the animal's back. A deadfall over a pit was set for the biggest animals, including the occasional bear. Bait included salmon gills or rotten meat with a strong enticing odor. Shellfish was used as bait for otters, beavers, and muskrats.

Snares were set for grouse, coyote, lynx, wildcat, and some deer (Ray 1932: 86). A noose of willow bark rope was suspended from & flexible pole over a game trail, and partially enclosed by a half circle of brush opening to the snare. A coyote snare was counterbalanced by a stone weight.

People did not eat snakes, gophers, mice, wood rats, frogs, dogs, insects, hearts of fool hens, or deer eyes. Women were specifically forbidden to eat deer kidneys and deer blood (Ray 1932: 90), presumably to avoid excessively bloody menstruation.

Famine foods included rose hips, hides, and tree-cached bones of fish and game previously left as offerings (Ray 1932: 107). In desperation, deer might be driven over crusted snow firm enough to support a man but not deer, but this was considered disrespectful of the game. Similarly, at such times a rolled leaf was used to make a fawn-like bleat to attract deer. Famine was rare, usually precipitated by religious fervor following a natural catastrophe keeping people from gathering winter stores. The worst famines occurred after Mount St Helens ashfalls in the early and middle 1800s and the 1873 earthquake. [43]

Housing

In recent centuries, mat houses were used both winter and summer, replacing ancient semi-subterranean pithouses. In addition, menstrual lodges, sweatlodges, and camping huts of mats or skins were built (Ray 1932: 31).

The most ancient dwelling was a pithouse, with a circular pit about ten to sixteen feet wide and four to six feet deep, having either a flat roof or a conical one with a center post and pole stringers set two feet apart along the edge. The roof was covered, in turn, with planks of driftwood, if available, or with willow mats, a six-inch layer of grass or brush, and an outer covering of dirt taken from the pit excavation, sometimes plastered with clay as waterproofing. Entry was by a hatchway, which also served as a smokehole. A log ladder rested near the central fire. During storms, the roof hole was covered with a mat.

The flat roof, less common because of poor drainage, was made of parallel poles, laid across a deeper hole, covered over by layers of planks, brush, and dirt. The door was on the side. as was the ladder and fire. The floor was covered with rye grass.

The best known winter house was mat-covered and gabled. The frame was an inverted V with rounded ends. about sixteen feet wide by twenty to sixty feet long, capable of holding two to eight families. The framework consisted of upright crossed [44] poles, tied at the top, with parallel side poles tied three-feet apart along the sides. The ends were made by leaning poles against the frame, like a half tipi held in place by horizontally tied willow poles (Ray 1932: 32). The lower walls were covered with grass and dirt; the upper walls with tule mats tied to the uprights. A foot-wide gap along the roof ridge vented smoke and light. At the ends were double doors, an outer one between the curved poles and an inner door between end mats hung over the square end of the main frame.

Inside the house, the round ends served as storage compartments for families living nearby on the same side. A bare central aisle ran along the inside, dotted by a row of fireplaces, each one serving two families living on either side. Mats covered the floors of the living compartments, and beds consisted of slough grass mats, robes, and blankets. During the day, bedding was rolled up toward the wall. Every spring, these mat houses were dismantled and the mats claimed by their owners for use as camping tent covers. Each single family hut was built on a three pole foundation and covered by two rows of mats. In good weather or emergencies, a mat windbreak with willow uprights could be quickly put up.

Summer mat houses, built at fisheries, were rectangular, with a flat roof, and nine feet wide because there was only a single row of beds and a passageway. Side poles were forked to hold roof cross beams. The upriver half of the house was used [45] for drying fish because prevailing winds blew odors away. Fires were maintained outside. Mats hung along the back, sides, and roof, while the open front faced the river (Ray 1932: 34).

A sweatlodge consisted of a six to eight feet dome made of bent willow saplings covered by dry grass and six inches of dirt (Ray 1932: 55). Rocks were heated in an outside fire and carried to an inside basin where water was sprinkled on them to create steam. Menstrual huts were like mat huts.

In special cases, at vision questing sites on mountain peaks, cliffs, or shores, stone walls built of talus basalt rocks marked sacred precincts.

Clothing

Aboriginal clothing, often minimal, was made of animal skins for winter use or of woven plant fibers for the summer. Most recently, after horses, Salishans used tailored deerskin styles adapted from Plains tribes (Ray 1932: 45). Except for emergency repairs, sewing was done by women, who lavished much care and attention on their sewing kits.

In the past, in summer, men often went nude among themselves, otherwise they wore a sagebark sheath or pubic cover. Women wore a belted poncho and aprons woven with a bark and deerhair warp and a hemp weft. The poncho had a diamond-shaped opening for the head.

Sandals, worn by men and women, were woven from sagebark or fresh rose branches and left to dry. Men wore sandals when visiting other towns, travelling barefoot across [46] country and putting on footgear, to be dignified, just before walking into the community.

Women wore wrap-around skirts and hemp leggings, while men wore leggings formed of the entire inside-out hide of a badger, beaver, coyote, or small bear.

The loose skin poncho was worn by both men and women. In winter, men also wore an overrobe of bear or deer hide. Double coyote skins sewn at their shoulders provided a winter wrap. Woven willow or sage bark or a trimmed hide served for breech clouts for men and women. Leggings were used in winter or for hunting in scrub thickets. Men wore their leggings above the knee, tied and wrapped at the top and bottom, while women wore theirs below the knee and wrapped at the top.

Leather moccasins were simply made of a folded rectangular skin, sewn up the heel and along a pointed toe to an instep insert, which flared the shape to fit a foot. Narrow ankle flaps were added. An outer tab, made by shaping the heel, was decorated with a cutout pattern. Winter moccasins were more roomy so grass or fur insulation could be padded around the foot. Ceremonial moccasins had simple geometric designs done in feather or porcupine quills arranged over the front.

Fur caps were worn in winter. Male caps had front and back visors, but women's caps had no visors. Caps were made by stretching and shaping the green skin, which was gently pounded over a round rock. The skin was flexed to keep it soft, except [47] at the ends, which stiffened to be trimmed into visors.

Mittens were made of coyote and other skins, except rabbit, which was too thin. For safety, in the cold, mittens were tied to a cord around the neck on long trips. Robes and blankets used deer, bear, coyote, and rabbit hides. Some woven rabbit fur robes were also made, and rabbit skins were preferred for babies.

Beaded yokes were worn by women over their dresses during ceremonies, tied at the waist in several places to a long, sleeveless, buckskin dress. The yoke was made for a 'girl and pieces were added to the bottom and sides as she grew older. Feathers, quills, beads, rocks, and shells provided other decorations.

Ornamentation depended on the instructions from a guardian spirit. Caps were made from the species skin of the spirit, if possible. Scallops or fringes appeared on the clothes of curers. but not all shamans. For example, a woman able to ease menstrual pain wore a wide red band around the hem of her dress (Ray 1932: 49). Shamans had red bands around the arms or chest, and red feather bursts over the shoulder blades on robes. Powerful shamans wore feathers and porcupine quill decorations because only they dared to call attention to themselves. Random perforations in a shirt touted immunity from weapon wounds, as among the Nez-Perce.

During ceremonies, wearing a string or thong about the forehead announced an intention to become shaman. A string [48] holding up a forelock or dangling from a penis indicated fishing ability. Eagle, hawk, and owl feathers were worn for head decoration, along with feather and shell wristlets and otter skin belts (Ray 1932: 50).

Men and women wore headbands. Some women donned basketry hats, like Sahaptians. Necklaces strung shells, claws, and rocks, with shell earrings preferred (Ray 1932: 51).

Face painting was used for protection from sun and wind. At public gatherings, it evoked guardian spirits (Ray 1932: 51). Eyebrows were plucked and painted (Ray 1932: 52). Paints consisted of red ochre mixed with coyote or otter fat, dry yew wood and fish oil, black charcoal, blue and white clay, and green and yellow minerals from Mt Tolman in the Sanpoil. Shamans painted their face and neck all red or split red and yellow. A white forehead indicated ability to withstand cold. Hides and sticks were also marked with paint as calendars and to record significant events.

Girls learned to dress their own hair, while mothers, then wives, did this for men. Women wore bangs, sometimes with three braids (at the sides and back). Men plucked their own facial hair with tweezers made of wood or small animal ribs (Ray 1932: 56). After marriage, a wife kept a small tight braid on her husband's forehead. Men's hair was worn in two braids, sometimes wrapped with fur (Ray 1932: 52). Women often painted or daubed their hair and treated it to indicate characteristics of age, [49] activity, and social position. Both men and women rubbed their hair with salmon oil or used a perfume made from deer marrow mixed with crushed hemlock needles. Men rubbed their hair and body with a leather pouch impregnated with beaver testes oil as a cologne. During mourning, hair was cropped short.

Games

Professional gamblers were admired. The most popular native pastime was and is the stick game (*slahal*), with bets matched by both sides before play (Ray 1932: 155). Equipment consisted of 20 counters, a single kickstick, and two pairs of deer tibia bones – one of each pair marked by a dark middle band – sized to hide inside a closed palm (Ray 1952: 155). Play involved facing teams beside long poles resting on the, ground, with fires in the middle during night games. Each leader took 10 counters and a pair of bones before each tried to guess the other to determine the starting team. A correct guess won a counter and both pairs of bones. Leaders sat in the middle of each row, selecting team mates to hold or guess the location of the unmarked bones. The team with the bones sang and beat time with sticks against long poles as the other team guessed.

The guesser on the, other team made expansive hand motions to reveal bones placements. In particular, he watched the eyes of the holders looking for cues. When a choice was made, the guesser made hand gestures, using thumb and forefinger, to indicate that bones were on the outside, the inside, to right, or [50] to left.

When the bones changed sides, the other team began to sing. A successful guesser or holder continued until defeated, and everyone on a team had a chance to hold or guess unless they declined. A team won by receiving all 20 counters and the kickstick, doubling their bets.

Women played dice games using four decorated beaver teeth or deer ribs that they made themselves. The bones were steamed, straightened, polished, decorated, and pointed at the ends (Ray 1932: 159). One side of each piece had four dotted circles, the other side had stripes, the four shaken in cupped hands and thrown onto a hide. Each woman threw until all pieces fell with the circles-side down. With about 50 counters, all had to be won before any woman could win. Scores tallied as all four circles-side up for two counters, three circle-sides up for one counter, one side up to lose a counter, and no circles up to lose two counters.

During winter, two teams of women stared at each other until one woman cracked a smile. Two women teams squatted on their heels and sang before hopping and clapping in place until only one remained upright won, after other players laughed and fell over (Ray 1932: 160). Other teams of women held their breath while touching every half inch along a yard wide spiral traced in the sand, until a winner touched more of the spiral over a longer time. [51]

Both men and women played ball and pin (Ray 1932: 151). The tule ball was held in the mouth to keep it moist, then dropped toward a thorn in the right hand. Every successful thrust was named for a month "to shorten the year." In summer, men played hoop and pole, using a pottery or wood disc and a bone-tipped hardwood staff decorated with bands of buckskin, along a runway dug six feet wide, sixteen feet long, and nine inches deep. The six inch hoop was wrapped in buckskin, with crossed inner thongs hung with colored shells. A heavier ring was made of clay[72] covered with buckskin, or of polished and pierced stone. Two players or teams took turns rolling or throwing the hoop underhand. Score was kept with stick counters, and computed by the contact of particular pole bands with ring shells.

Another game used a hoop twisted from a limb and a four-foot willow pole (Ray 1932: 164). Men stood and threw at the hoop target set about 30 feet away. Slings of buckskin and hemp cord or of shaved willow string were used for contests. A more quiet game was cat's cradle string figures.

In the spring, shinny was played by teams of ten to thirty boys or adults, using a buckskin ball stuffed with grass and sticks made from tree branches crooked at the end. The goals were robes set 200 feet apart on a level field.

Running was also a sport, sometimes with heavy betting. Marathons for small teams covered 15 miles (Ray 1932: 165). Men might race each other to a mountain top. Race courses were laid [52] out to a tree and back. In recent times, horse racetracks were used. Poker, monte, and other card games were modern introductions.

Men challenged each other at swimming, wrestling, jumping, weight lifting with stones, and tug of war, when two men sat with their soles touching, grasped the same stick, and pulled until one of them was lifted up. In winter, men tried to swim across the Columbia, accompanied by canoes for safety (Ray 1938: 166). Men and women had segregated swimming areas.

Children had playgrounds on sandbars or sandy beaches where they played house. Girls used stick dolls, with an added head and clothes. Boys had tops of wood, spun with a string, or a bark disc, twirled with the hand. Favorite diversions were stories, hide and seek, seesaw with crossed logs, willow whistles, snowball fights, and hide toboggans.

Recent History

The trade routes used for centuries between the coast and interior carried word of Spanish and Russian exploration during the 1600s, followed by the exchange of the first European goods. Wondrous news of the horse preceded its arrival by the 1740s, with a shift to settlements near good pastures and long-distance bison hunts on the northern Plains, particularly near Montana Blackfeet.

The greater mobility provided by the horse fostered the Salishan confederacy under the family of Split Sun (sə́qtałk̓ʷúsm also known as [53] Half Sun ~ Sooktolkowsum ~ implying 'eclipse') to coordinate bison hunts by Columbians, Pskʷaws, Entiats, Chelans, and others. With the murder of the father, the name passed to his sons in succession, the most famous being the man known as Moses.

Epidemics decimated whole regions, destroying communities during the 1770s, 1830s, and 1850s. In the next decade, the fur-trade encouraged men to spend more time hunting. Iroquois and other Northeastern natives, long immersed in the trade, came West in the 1790s. bringing word of the Catholic Mass and Euro-American avarice.

---

[72] Native pottery is discussed in the final Researches chapter.

During 1806, while Lewis and dark did not travel through Salishan territory, rumors of their presence reached upriver tribes. David Thompson of the Northwest Company came down the Columbia in 1811, the same year David Stuart built Fort Okanogan for the Astor company. Ross Cox served this fort in 1816 and left an interesting memoir. While in charge of the fort, Alexander Ross married Sally, an Okanogan woman, and their family rose to fame in the Red River settlement that became Winnipeg, while the local kin, eventually as CB Suszen Timentwa, assumed leadership.

The Northwest Company acquired the American Fur Company in 1812 and merged with the Hudson's Bay Company in 1821. After establishing Spokane House in 1810, the American Fur Company moved trading activities to Fort Colville in 1825, a better location near Kettle Falls, a major Columbia River fishery.

Intrigued by Flathead and Nez Perce treks to St Louis to plea for missions, Protestants, Congregationalists and later Methodists, arrived to [54] preach in the 1830s, soon followed by Jesuits north of the Columbia and other Catholic clergy on the south.

In 1841, members of the Wilkes Expedition, particularly Horatio Hale, sailing around the world under the American flag, visited Ft. Colville, where Fathers Francis Norbert Blanche! and Modeste Demers began a Catholic mission in 1838. Nearby, Father Anthony Ravalli established St Paul's mission in 1845, and Father Peter De Vos built the Catholic center of St Francis Regis in 1847. A mission near Cashmere served the Psk^{w}aws after 1872. In 1898 a Jesuit boarding school was built near Omak at St Mary's Mission, now owned by the Colvilles and named for DC lawyer Pascal Sherman, a Chelan.

After Washington Territory was founded in 1853, Isaac Stevens, simultaneously governor of Washington Territory, Indian commissioner, and head of the northern railroad survey, forced treaties in 1855. That of June 9 at Walla Walla ceded lands that included those of Salishan tribes along the Big Bend of the Columbia. Intermittently over following decades, in response to American oppression, warfare erupted, particularly the Treaty War of 1856-58.

For upper Columbia River Salishans, the Colville Reservation was set aside by executive orders in 1872, but within a month its boundaries were redrawn so the fertile Colville Valley and the Kettle Falls fishery were lost. In 1885, Chief Joseph and survivors of his Wallowa Nez Perce band who were under indictment [55] for murder in Idaho joined the Colville Reservation.

In 1879, the US army had a post at Lake Chelan before driving Chelans to the Colville Reservation and then relocating to Ft Spokane at that river mouth (Ruby and Brown 1965: 173). In 1886, Pateros was homesteaded among twenty native lodges and many Chinese dugouts, there to sluice for gold on China Bar from 1860-90. In 1875, Chinese miners at Chelan Falls were massacred by racist whites dressed as Indiens (Layman 2002: 84, 92).

The middle Columbia Salishans, led by Chief Moses, received, in 1879, a reservation west of the Colvilles, mostly on Methow lands, which was expanded in 1880, and relinquished in 1884 in favor of a move to the Colville Reservation. Many Entiats and Methows went, but Chelans, who were moved at gun point, later returned and took lake allotments at Wapato Point. Psk^{w}aws ~ Wenatchis also stayed in their homeland, suffering the bizarre US purchase from Yakamas of their treaty-protected fishery in 1894. Those homesteads and allotments not lost through taxes or outright fraud remain part of the reservation. Many Wenatchi did not live at Colville until 1904, but their chief, John Harmelt, never moved, dying in a burning cabin.

Prospecting for gold and occasional strikes disrupted the region during the 1850s and 1850s, especially when cattle herds were moved north from California to the Canadian Eraser and Caribou to sell to miners. The vegetation of the Okanogan Valley suffered from such overgrazing. During the 1890s, gold was found on the Colville Reservation, resulting in loss of the North Half in 1892 and allotment of the South Half after the 1905 McLaughlin Agreement.

Since the 1930s, reservations suffered consequences of [56] Columbia River dams, beginning in 1936 with that at Grand Coulee, whose back waters flooded the Sanpoil drainage.

In 1935, after defeated votes on an Indian Reorganization style constitution, the ancestral tribes on the Colville Reservation confederated and elected a business council to govern their affairs. Four voting districts (Inchelium, Keller, Nespelem, and Omak) were established to elect councilors, who serve two year terms. The first woman elected to the tribal council was Christine Quintasket, a novelist and folklorist writing as Mourning Dove. [57]

Colville Reservation

The Colville Confederated Tribes, mostly Interior Salishans, occupy a reservation, bounded on the west by the Okanogan River and on the east and south by the Columbia, now flooded behind Grand Coulee and Chief Joseph Dams. As a "legally-dedicated land base", within ancestral territories, the rootedness of Colville reservation encourages strong continuities in native traditions.

The northern boundary originally was the Canadian border until a twelve mile strip was claimed by Congress to affirm national borders and the North Half was taken away on 1 July 1892, except for allotted farms and for legally-won fishing and hunting rights. "The North Half, a land of high valleys, mountains and many lakes and streams, was prized by the Indians for its game and shelter. White miners found gold in the region and mines operate there to this day" (Yanan 1971: 17). Imposed by the government in the aftermath of the Dawes Severalty Act of 1887, a May 1891 agreement individually alloted the land. These allotments had not been approved in 1896, when the area was opened for settlement, and some people were forced off land where they had lived for countless generations because they did not then have clear title.[73]

Aboriginally, the Columbia River was the lifeline connecting many tribes, including those now known as Interior Salish. The lower Columbia was occupied by Chinookan communities, near its mouth, and Sahaptin ones upriver. The Chinook were devastated and dispersed by European diseases by 1830, and the Sahaptins, as a consequence of an 1855 treaty, were forced to relocate to the Yakama Reservation of Washington or to the Warm Springs and Umatilla Reservations of Oregon. The landmark dividing Sahaptins and Salishans was Vantage ~ Priest Rapids on the Columbia, although neighboring villages there intermingled languages, customs, and families.

Upriver from there, Salishans living along tributaries were the Snkyuse ~ (Moses) Columbians (whose main village was at Vantage), Pskʷaws (~ called Wenatchi by Sahaptins), Entiat, Chelan, Methow, Okanogan, Nespelem, Sanpoil, Colvile, and (Arrow) Lakes, who were mostly in modern Canada, which has tried to declare them extinct. Canadian neighbors were the Kootenay and the Fraser River Salishans. Salishan tribes to the west were the Spokan, Kalispel, Flathead, and Coeur d'Alene.

Two dialect chains (interlinked speech communities) make up Mid-Columbia Interior Salish, with the Methow as the buffer between them. The chains are distinguished by differences

---

[73] Comparable greed occurred during the opening of Oklahoma for homesteading, as described by Thomas Wildcat Alford, a Shawnee, in his book *Civilization*.

in vocabulary and inflection. In speech, a predominant vowel can be heard. Downriver, among Columbian, Psk^{w}aws, Entiat, and Chelan, it is "ay;" upriver, Okanogan, Nespelem, Sanpoil, Colvile (tribe at Kettle Falls), and Lakes use "ii," while the intermediate Methow have shifted from "ay" to "ii".

Kettle Falls has long had a strong if shifting Catholic presence. St Paul's church was an early mission station (later eclipsed by the second of the St Francis Regis missions), visited for brief services during the fishing season for salmon who need to be huge to swim that far upriver. Nearby was the soldier settlement, called Harney's Deport before 1860 and Pinkley City afterwards, in honor of Major Pinkley Lugenbeel, commander at Fort Colville. At least half of the soldiers there were born in Ireland and attended the local church. The major center for missionary activity, however, was St Francis, founded at a settlement of mixed blood Cree Metis now called Chewelah, Washington. Father De Smet visited there 4 August 1845 (Schoenberg 1962: 19, #126). The second mission of St Francis was built halfway between Pinkley City and St Paul's in 1869. St Paul's had been closed in 1858 as a full-time mission, but it was reopened in 1863 for occasional use.

In 1872, the Colville Reservation was both created and immediately shifted to the west side of the Columbia. (Ulysses S. Grant agreed to set the land aside in 1872, but, a month later, removed the eastern third of it by shifting the boundary west to the Columbia River to provide rich bottom land to pioneers.) This deprived these tribes of both prime farmland, coveting by white homesteaders, and the fishery at Kettle Falls, which was permanently lost when it was flooded behind Grand Coulee Dam in 1939. St Francis Mission was accordingly moved to the other side of the river in 1873, onto land given by Chief Kinkanawah on the stipulation that the church also include a school. This became the Goodwin Mission at Ward, Washington, administered by the Sisters of Providence (~ Charity). They ran a school for boys that closed 1 September 1908. Their best-known activities centered around the Goodwin Mission School for Indians and the Sacred Heart Academy for white girls, which closed 30 July 1921.

St Francis had many setbacks during its time, but it remained a regional hub. Grist and saw mills were added from 1875 to 1880. A larger church was built between 1877-81 and used until it burned on Christmas morning of 1888, the year Mourning Dove says she was born. Another building was started but not finished until 1911. It burned in June 1938. By then, St Mary's Mission near Omak, on the western side of the reservation, had long replaced St Francis Regis as the Catholic religious center.

According to Indian agent William Winans, when Chief Kinkanawah, Mourning Dove's great uncle, became too old in the estimation of the Jesuits, they advised the tribe to have him resign. He did so, and in his place the tribe elected Joseph Cotolegu, who "checked gambling, drinking, and other disorders and broke up illicit connections among the Indians". Two subchiefs, Chief Orphan [~ Aropaghan, also Arophan, Urpaghan] and Chief Bernard [the policeman] aspired for a time to leadership after Chief Kin-ka-nowha died. After Chief Orphan's death, Chief Bernard proved himself a fine Christian leader. Bernard was the nephew of Chief Kin-ka-nowha." Later in life, Bernard organized the Colville Indian Association to fight for natue legal rights (Raufer 1966: 224).

Along the western boundary, the Okanogan, without their consent or approval (as they say), are divided by an international border into American River Okanogan {middle O} and Canadian Lake Okanagan {all A-s}. The Canadian dialect is much more vibrant, than the US one which has few speakers, particularly encouraged by En'owkin native writing and research center at Penticton, jointly run by the six bands of the Okanagan Nation, in conjunction with

Okanagan College and the University of Victoria.

St Mary's Mission near Omak remains an important Colville center, where the school is now operated by the confederated tribes as the Pascal Sherman Indian School. Pascal Sherman, first named John Wapato, was a member of a prominent Entiat family at Lake Chelan, who became a lawyer for the Department of Labor in DC. His name was changed by a priest during Holy Week, when many Colvilles camped at the mission for church rites between Palm Sunday and Easter in spring weather.

Reconstructed aboriginal patterns provide a baseline for understanding Colville traditions. In ancient times, people lived in small communities or neighborhoods during good weather, then gathered in communal winter villages that were situated near firewood, fresh water, and sheltering terrain. In general plan, a village or encampment was arranged along a water course, with the large winter villages usually at the confluence of the Columbia and a major tributary. The chief, leader, or headman lived at the center in a bigger home, suitable for holding general council meetings of adult men and women. Every settlement had a speaker to broadcast news, and a series of scouts or lookouts watching the movements of game, people, and sky for expected and unusual occurrences. There were several types of housing, ranging from individual mat lodges to long multifamily dwellings with a fire trough down the middle. Locations within a lodge were generally assigned by age. Old people, usually a grandmother, slept nearest the door (other tribes say to be near "the way out"), older children further inside, and the married couple toward the back.

Dried or cooked food was always available for snacks, but usually a family took one or two daily meals together. During the day, women worked together gathering and processing food or craft materials, while men worked separately. Women cooked, wove, and sewed inside, but did their tanning outside and away from the camp because of the odors involved. Children had specially designated playgrounds, usually on a beach, sand bar, or cleared area along the river bank. Sweat lodges and menstrual or birthing huts were set away from the camp for seclusion and privacy. Graves were placed in the nearest talus slopes, marking the continuity of living and dead with the land.

A series of rituals was, and to some extent is, held through the summer to express thanksgiving for each of the native foods as they become available. These First Food Feasts continue as a special part of Colvilles' relations to the land. The rites are held in turn for first crops of roots, plants, berries, and fruits important in the aboriginal diet. Central to all of these was the First Salmon Rite, studied by Erna Gunther (1928), the revered founder of UW anthropology and long director of the campus museum.

For the Sanpoil First Salmon,[74] women prepared a ramada or shade, covering the ground below it with sunflower leaves. Then they camped away from the river for five days. During that time, the men went naked ("with nothing between themselves and the Creator") and feasted on fresh salmon. The first four days, they ate flank sections, boiled the first two days and roasted the next two. The fifth day they ate a special soup made from the dried odds and ends of all the previous salmon, mixed with roots and berries. It was particularly holy because it was so ecumenical, blending many foods and men. After this, women and children rejoined the fishing

---

[74] In the 1970s, since Grand Coulee Dam blocked salmon runs, Sanpoil First Salmon came by refrigerated truck from Quinault, where that chairman was married into Mourning Dove's Quintasket family and is buried at Piya mission.

camp and work began in earnest to dry salmon for the winter.

Different species were honored in different areas. According to notes left by Norman Lerman (File 2: 179), Riverside held the ceremony for suckers in April, Tonasket for rainbow trout in May, and Oroville for Sockeye in July. In an article in the *Nespelem Tribune* (Volume II (4): 1, 4) of 10 July 1935, Mourning Dove reported First Foods for bitterroot at Omak in April, for salmon at Keller in May, for serviceberry at Osooyos Lake in late June, for chinook salmon at Kettle Falls in July, and for dog salmon at Oroville when they arrived.

The plight of the Colville reservation during the 1960s attracted several scholars, who added to earlier research. All of these have noted that the dominant Plateau values were pacifism and gender equality. This context of equality allowed Mourning Dove and other Colville women to flourish, since changes brought on by the horse, fur traders, and missionaries intensified rather than diminished earlier female status. "Interestingly, those women who obtained a spirit helper found themselves in competitive positions with males and new doors opened to them."

Certain families were always known for their leadership abilities, both civil and religious. Their men and women acquired powers of varying strengths from sacred sites visited generation after generation. Men and women had different roles and careers in a statistical, but not an absolute, sense. Generally, men led in the public arena, and women in the domestic, but cross-over was likely. While men were often concerned with practical considerations, women tended to general welfare. For example, at marriage, a bride began keeping a calendrical ball of string to record details of family history. Like Mourning Dove, Plateau women were the recorders and conveyers of tradition.

Paralleling the Mediterranean notion that the honor of the family resides with its women, who must be modest and protected for the wellbeing of all, Billy Curlew, the late Columbian (Snkyuse) leader, always said, "My wife is my wealth," meaning that she had to be well dressed and have expensive horses so that she would properly reflect his (and her) status in the tribe. The marriage of widow and widowers to surviving siblings of the deceased spouse (sororate if sister, levirate if brother) was recognized in practice and in the kinship terminology. Such marriages perpetuate the alliance between the two families, and protect the children of the previous marriage from trauma. Families members safeguard each other, so a sibling is a proper replacement for a deceased spouse.

The use of the horse greatly increased mobility. The adoption of guns and the trappings of equestrianism gave some eastern Plateau tribes the look of Plains Indians, on horseback wearing the feather headdresses and beaded buckskins of popular media image. Some groups, like the Sanpoil and Nespelem, kept their Plateau orientation and acquired only a few horses; others, like the Columbians, used large horse herds to hunt bison in the Montana northern Plains and develop a growing confederacy to protect these interests. "While men were away, women, particularly senior ones, took on more responsibilities, and their social, domestic, and political importance grew as … males took long trips to the Plains to hunt bison" (Miller 1990: xxviii, noting Ray 1960). Young wives, of course, went along to dry meat and tan buffalo robes.

These Inter-Salishan bison hunts onto the Plains in Blackfoot territory took place after the horse reached the Plateau and enabled long distance overland travel. The original *sáq̓tałk̓ʷúsm* Split Sun (mistranslated as Half-Sun, the name actually refers to an "eclipse"), father of Chief Moses, organized such equestrian bison hunts and so formed the Columbian Confederacy among the Snkyuse, Psk^waws, and Chelan tribes, with some support among the Entiat, Methow, Okanogan, and tribes further east (Ray 1960, Ruby and Brown 1965).

While pacifism was an important value for Plateau tribes, they often had to defend themselves from Plains raiders. Once fur traders became established on the Plateau, they successfully discouraged warfare in the interest of having natives devote all their energies to pelts and trading. Some communities left traditional use areas and moved to newly established trading posts. After the traders came the missionaries, who worked to end overt hostilities, and, in doing so, inadvertently helped increase the covert use of sorcery.

Thus, aboriginal beliefs and institutions have been perpetuated, although now they are fit into an overall Catholic context. Guardian spirits, vision quests, shamanism, sorcery, and rituals reflecting a basic belief in power (*shumix*) remain entrenched. In the Plateau, as throughout Native America, rock art identifies locales of sacred significance. Often, they serve to verify the ancestral location of a mythological event or a communal ritual. Along with lightning-struck trees, these are loci of concentrated power. Even now, Colvilles are well aware of these sites as zones for power acquisition, although few use the decreasing number of locales still available. White settlement, massive construction such as Grand Coulee Dam, extensive flooding, and desecration have all taken their toll. On the other hand, Jesuit missionaries remain the tolerant towards beliefs not directly in conflict with Catholic doctrine. For example, Jesuits and elders cooperated in having a bulldozer operator for the Bureau of Indian Affairs fired after he covered a rock art panel with road construction debris.

While Mourning Dove believed in the superiority of Catholicism and many Plateau tribes were preconditioned towards it by converted Iroquois traders, Jesuits also had the advantage of being the only missionaries in the area between 1847-58, since all Protestant missionary families were removed from the war zone of the 1855 Treaty War by the US Army. As single males, Jesuits and a few Oblates stayed, either at their missions or in native camps, strengthening the impression that they were more dedicated and self-sacrificing. Because many of them were foreign born, in contrast to American Protestants, natives identified them with their own interests rather than those of the American enemy.

As George Gibbs long ago noted for the Plateau, "An additional source of coolness between them arises from a difference in religion − the Spokans being Protestants, or of the "American religion," and the Coeur d'Alenes Catholics" (Gibbs 1855: 414, 422). The distinction was already drawn among the Indians between the "American" and French religions, and, as in the case of the Coeur d'Alenes and Spokans, has already created ill feelings.

Colville remain predominantly Catholic and that was one of the appeals of their reservation for the Psk^waws since they had long their own Jesuit mission at Cashmere. While Rev James Wilbur was at Yakama reservation, however, Methodism was very predominant.

With the end of the treaty war, settlers moved into the region to stay. Although tensions were minimized by having natives concentrated at reservations, the Salishans continued to roam free because they lacked treaties. Chief Moses (*sə́q̓tatk̓^wúsm* ~ Split Sun) of the Columbians kept his people dispersed and concealed for their own safety. Also, natives lacked numerical strength to retaliate because they were still suffering from the depopulation caused by smallpox and other epidemics, such as those in 1832 and 1854-55. Alcohol also took its toll.

Eventually, these Interior Salish were assigned to two reservations by presidential executive order, in the Methow or Kettle Rivers. The Sanpoil, whose particularly conservative and inhospitable stance toward the government was encouraged by their prophet Kolaskin, became the nucleus for the final Colville reservation.

The vitality of traditional beliefs about mythic time and events is such that Colvilles still frequently remind each other that some day Coyote will return from the East and break up the 16 dams along the Columbia, restoring their ancient traditions, waterways, and foods. At present, the salmon can only reach upriver as far as Chief Joseph Dam, where natives are allowed a fishing station. Their belief rests on the epic of how Coyote initially broke up the first fish trap of seabirds impounding salmon near the mouth of the Columbia, releasing the primordial Salmon in the days when the world was young. The size and quantity of the salmon in each of the tributary rivers is said to be proportional with the beauty of the wife each village let him have. Those who refused him ended up with waterfalls entirely blocking any local salmon runs.

Chief Moses, on behalf of members of the Columbian confederacy, received a reservation in 1879 to the west of Colville, in the territory of the Methow, but he surrendered it for financial considerations in 1883 and moved with most of his followers to the Colville agency. Moses invited Chief Joseph and surviving Wallowa Nez Perce, returning from imprisonment in Oklahoma in 1885, to join him at Nespelem, since, if they returned to Idaho, they were subject to arrest warrants charging murder.

Invited by Chief Moses, descendants of those indicted Nez Perce loyal to Chief Joseph remain on the Colville Reservation near the grave of their beloved leader. Their saga is long and complicated. A disputed 1863 treaty deprived Old Joseph and his people of their Wallowa valley home in northeastern Oregon. Whites moved in and conditions deteriorated, aggravated by pressured from then senator and future US President James Garfield, until hostilities erupted on 14 May 1877. After a valiant defense, Young Joseph, the famous leader and son of Old Joseph, surrendered 5 October 1877 near the US border with an understood promise that they could return home. Instead, 431 survivors were shipped to Fort Lincoln, North Dakota, then to Fort Leavenworth, Kansas, and lastly to Oklahoma in 1879. Many died of the cold and then of the heat, desolation, and poor sanitation. After a national outcry, they were allowed to return to the Northwest, arriving at Spokane Falls (modern Spokane) 27 May 1885.

Colville elders say that Young Joseph and Chief Moses were briefly educated together by the Presbyterians at Lapwai, Idaho. They remained friends and Moses invited the Wallowas to come the Colville reservation to avoid murder indictments in Idaho, if they had gone to the Nez Perce reservation. By December of 1885, they had occupied prime land along the Nespelem River, where few members of that indigenous tribe survived.

The northern half of the Colville reservation was lost in 1892 and, by terms of the 1905 McLaughlin Agreement, the diminished southern half was allotted into 80 acre plots for each enrolled member. During the trauma of this allotment survey, Mourning Dove first menstruated. Incidentally, James McLaughlin, federal special agent for this strong arming, was a firm Catholic married to a Sioux woman who published a collection of Lakota tales. Famously, he instigated the murder of Sitting Bull by ordering his arrest in the last days of the Ghost Dance.

Mineral entry, allowing outsiders to make mining claims on the remaining Colville reservation, was legislated for 1896, and the unallotted land was opened for homesteading in 1900. All of these events are emotionally discussed in Mourning Dove's final chapters and my added footnotes.

Much of recent Colville history has been a fight for continued survival and economic stability. In one of her last letters, Mourning Dove wrote to McWhorter about her disappointment that the Colvilles did not approve their own constitution under the Indian Reorganization (Wheeler-Howard) Act and other reforms advocated by John Collier. A constitution was approved by Colvilles on 28 May 1937 and revised on 26 February 1938.

Mourning Dove was spared the bitter confrontations over the attempted 1950s termination of federal responsibility for her reservation a century after the Stevens treaties.

The Colvilles continued to achieve a measure of success by white standards until the Bureau of Indian Affairs tried to terminate their reservation under House Resolution 7190 of 1955. A 1960 Stanford report urged the liquidation of the Colville reservation and the dispersal of the assets among the members. Mercifully, this did not happen. Its consequences would have been catastrophic. Members of the reservation rallied and fought off the attack, halting disaster although bitterness is still directed at those enrolled Colvilles who advocated termination in self-interest. Many lived off reservation and had little or no ties with their homelands.

A renewed tribal council has implemented a deliberate strategy, building upon traditional values of flexibility and resourcefulness, to develop economic programs to encourage timber sales, mining, and industry.

Salishan customary specialties continue. As William Brunton observed, the Interior Salish have typically relied on encampment type gatherings, such as the July 4th PowWow, in preference to the feasts sponsored by the Sahaptins. The advantage of the Salish pattern is that it brings people together for longer periods with closer interaction, helping to make Salishans dominant in the modern politics of the Plateau.

Today, Colville is a reservation with an effective leadership and a complex diversity. Catholics remain in the majority, but shamans, Shakers, Peyotists, and Protestants are also in evidence. Far from disappearing, traditions recorded by Mourning Dove continue to thrive, both in her own family and in others, but they are mostly translated into English with a Catholic cast. Her Homeric efforts to transfer traditions from oral to written modes, with some editorial changes, were but a hint of the larger transformations all Colvilles have been undergoing since the World Change.

— Who Are The Colville Indians? —

This is Colville Indian Country . . .

We are the Confederated Tribes of the Colville Indian Reservation. We are the biggest and most advanced tribe in the Northwest. The Colville Tribe is comprised of eleven different bands of Indians. Ten bands are from Eastern Washington State and one band, the Nez Perce, is from Northeast Oregon. The eleven bands are: Wenatchee, Entiat, Chelan, Methow, Okanogan, Nespelem, San Poll, Lakes, Moses, Palouse, and Nez Perce. Many other different tribes came and visited, fished, and traded goods with each other in the area of Kettle Falls, Washington. In the early 1820's, the White people learned that our Indians were excellent trappers and stalker of game for the large fur trade era. For this purpose, a new fort was established at Kettle Falls by a man named Simpson. The new post was to be called Fort Colville, after the leading member of the committee of Directors of London, Andrew Wedderburn Colville, who advanced Simpson to his position of leadership. Andrew Colville was also in the rum and molasses business. The eleven neighboring bands were confederated as Colville Indians because of Fort Colville. None of the eleven bands are real Colville. We have no .such word in our language. It is as foreign to us just as the man Andrew Colville was; a man we never set eyes on.

Trading was developed at Fort Colville on a near daily basis. From 1826 to 1871, these furs from the following animals were traded, the fox, lynx, martin, mink, otter, raccoon, wolverine, badger, and wolf for guns, knives, food, cooking utensils, and other items of convenience. The weaver and otter were considered most important trades. The martin and bear fur became more popular when the beaver hat lost popularity to silk and pelts of other species in the 1840's. Many bearskins for hats worn by the British soldiers likely came from Fort Colville.

All of the eleven bands that would gather on the "now present" Colville Reservation were at least 40% dependent on the great salmon runs for their yearly supply of foods. The salmon could be eaten fresh or dried and stored for future used through the winter months. Salmon was our main diet for existence. Our main winter homes were built and set next to the main rivers. Drift wood was plentiful and sandy banks were used for digging pit houses into the earth. This style home was completed to get below the ground for warmth before the cold winter months arrived. We had the first "earth homes" in America. We built the first air conditioning, it was made out of the reed mat lodges. If it rained, the mats would swell up to keep the interior dry and when the sun dried the mats they opened to let air pass through. In the summer we traveled to hunt, fish, gather roots, berries, reeds for homes, and other supplies to build shelters or make clothing. Many of the elders stayed in our winter villages year round.

Grand Coulee Dam was constructed during the depression for Jobs, electricity, irrigation projects, and recreation. Then the Corps of Army Engineers and the public utility departments came and built more dams. The dams built blocked our natural salmon run, even though they supposedly planned fish enhancements. There can never be a way to replace our losses. No fish ladders could be put on Grand Coulee Dam, because the water behind it fluctuates as much as 100 feet a year. The fish eggs would be high and dry or freeze up. What happened was the destruction of our main salmon fisheries at Kettle Falls and on the San Poil Rivers. This loss of salmon fishing and the introduction of foreign foods affected our people's health for decades. It changed our diets ever since we lost some of the ability to hunt, fish, or dig roots in the usual places. Our personal systems were adapted to fish oils. Now most of us survivors have high cholesterol, high blood pressure, and onset diabetes because of the "new" foods introduced to us Indian people never had these health problems until about 20 years after the dam was in operation.

Our reservation was established by Executive Order in 1872, but it was not until the 1880's before seven of the bands joined the Nespelem, San Poil, part of the Okanogan and Lakes Bands on the reservations. The Lakes and the rest of the Okanogan, who were both allies slowly moved in, some of the bands moved to Canada. None of them signed the Yakama Treaty of 1855. In 1884, the Moses Bands began moving onto the Colville Reservation as directed by the United States Government. This was against the decision of the Okanogan, Lakes, Nespelem, and San Poil Bands. The supportive bands were the Moses Columbia, Wenatchee, Entiats, Chelan, and the Methow. Then Chief Moses later invited the Nez Perce to become a part of our Confederated Tribes. There was inconsistency, indecision, and friction among the eleven bands. They had encountered much difficulty understanding or getting along with each other. But, we still survive and have grown together to become one of the most successful reservations in America.

– TODAY –

• The Confederated Tribes of the Colville Reservation covers about 2,300 square miles, and is 1.3 million acres in size. It is bigger than the state of Rhode Island. Our main revenue is our Forestry Products. We have one of the most advanced sawmills in the world The Colville Indian Precision Pine Company which operates The Colville Tribal Resource Company, and Colville Tribal Logging Company. They produce about 80 million board feet of lumber a year. We have our own nursery to replant and grow new trees. There is close to $100 million in Tribal

Enterprises and the employment runs near 2,000 people. Three tribal owned grocery stores are situated in three of our four districts.

• We have a Tribal Credit Union with a loan program for our people.

• In addition to our Bingo Hall with slots in Okanogan; we feature two new Casinos, one in Chelan and one in Coulee Dam. The first casino is our largest and is located at Mill Bay in Chelan, Washington on Lake Chelan, which features a first class restaurant, The; Coyote Cafe. They have Blackjack, Slots, and other gambling devices. Then our newest addition is in Coulee Dam, Washington and has 200 Slots plus Keno. We also have a very successful construction company, the Colville Tribal Services Corporation. Our future is looking bright as we look forward to more jobs with more new enterprises being developed.

• The Tribal Fish Hatchery stocks all the lakes and streams in North Central Washington State. We market treated posts and poles all over the world. Our Convalescent Center is the cleanest and best in the state, and has won many awards. There is a long waiting list of Indians and on-Indians to become residents there. We have our own Child Welfare System and an Agency for the Aging and a Foster Grandparent program for involving our elders, too. There are four senior meal sites across the reservation.

• For recreation, we have some of the best fishing spots anywhere with over 18 well stocked lakes, and many creeks, and rivers. The Tribes own two large resorts off the reservation; one in Keller, Washington and one at Seven Bays, Washington, which operates a first class restaurant. We build houseboats, which we rent out along with fishing and ski boats and all the necessary supplies.

• The wildlife on the reservation includes elk, whitetail and mule deer, brown, black, and grizzly bears, moose, a few bighorn sheep, wolves, and coyotes, bald and golden eagles, and quails.

• The Indian culture and religions are very much alive and active. We have the Seven Drums, and the Indian Shaker religions as well as the Indian Winter Chinook Dances, the annual spring Thanksgiving Root Feasts, and the memorial giveaways in honor of our deceased.

• We honor over 800 Tribal Member Veteran's of every war, World I, II, Korean, Viet Nam, Falkland Islands, Persian Gulf, and Afghanistan.

The Confederated Tribes of the Colville Reservation is who we are, and we are proud to be Indian in America.

Colville Tribal Museum and Gift Shop

CB Suszen Timentwa
Lucy Jim
Sophia

Chillowhist Jim

Moses

MIDCOLUMBIA INTERIOR SALISH

The Middle Columbia River Salishans ('sālīshənz) lived traditionally along the middle Columbia River in northwestern Washington. Their population has been concentrated on the Colville Reservation since the nineteenth century. The component peoples of this regional grouping are the Snkyuse (sink^{y}ōōs), Psk^{w}aws ~ Wenatchee (wə'năchē), Entiat ('antē'ăt), Chelan (shə'lăn), Methow ('met'häw), Southern Okanogan (ōkə'nägən), Nespelem (nes'pēləm, nez'pēləm), and Sanpoil (sănpō'ĭl).

These groups were settled along the Columbia River and, except for the Snkyuse, also along its western or northern tributaries, which drain the eastern slopes of the Cascades and the area north of the Big Bend. The Snkyuse (or Columbias) were east and south of the Big Bend. Their main village was at the mouth of Rock Island Creek, and their resource domain was transected by Grand Coulee, Moses Coulee, Moses Lake, and the Potholes region. There were distinct subgroups at Creston in the northeast and at Quilomene Bar (locale of the defining Sunset Creek 45KT28 site) on the southwest, where a separate subdialect was spoken (the Quilomene band, *snq^{w}əlq^w'əlminəx^w*). The central location of their territory, with their winter villages set along its borders put them in contact with all the other Middle Columbia River Salishans.

The Southern Okanogan in the United States (or River Okanogan, spelt with a letter O in the middle) and the Northern Okanagan in Canada (the Lake Okanagan, spelt with letter A throughout) constitute a single people that was divided by the international boundary (Spier 1938).

The Snkyuse came to be known as the Moses-Columbias after their famous nineteenth-century chief. After settlement on the Colville Reservation the name Moses-Columbian or Moses came to be used for the Wenatchee and Entiat as well.

External Relations

Because the Snkyuse were located across the Columbia, they had access eastward and greater involvement with Flathead and Sahaptians. After acquiring horses, they led bison hunts onto the Plains which encouraged the development of a confederacy of Middle Columbia tribes under the leadership of the family of Spilt Sun (*səq́tałk̓^{w}úsm*, also known as Half Sun ~ Shooktalkoosum; Curtis 1911:67, Ray 1960, Ruby and Brown 1965). Salishans living along the rivers draining the western Cascades developed trade and marriage networks with Coast Salish, such as between the Skagit and the Chelan. Their hunting of mountain goats and other alpine mammals was important for the regional trade. The Psk^{w}aws traded through formal partners with Kittitas Sahaptians and the Coastal Snoqualmie. Raiding for horses and hostilities with Plains tribes like the Blackfeet, encouraged a warrior ethic among these tribes, although pacifism was a strong ethic among Plateau Salishans. Gender equality also remained important (Ray 1932: 25, 115).

Travel became more extensive with horses (Ray 1932: 117), adding features of equestrian Plains culture such as new leather clothing styles, pack and riding saddles, horsehair bridles, stirrups, the tipi, and travois. Skin bags replaced coiled baskets.

Trade centers for the region were located at Soap Lake, Waterville, the mouths of the Wenatchi River and Icicle Creek during the June salmon run, and the Dalles (Ray 1932: 116), along with Kettle Falls and modern Brewster (mouth of the Okanogan River). Shells from coast were traded through the Chelan, with the inland tribes trading tanned buckskins, dried roots, and, in particular, furs.

The Psk^{w}aws formal trading partnerships (*sċúq̓^{w}i?*) were passed on to family members in every generation. A man could only trade with his partner, and thus scheduled his visit during large gatherings when he could be sure the partner would be there (Spier 1938: 75). In October, Psk^{w}aws came to the mouth of the Okanogan to fish and trade with local friends.

Once the Psk^{w}aws had horses, the earlier trade in pipes, tobacco, hemp, dressed skins, and bows also included more bulky items such as ground root cakes, dried berries, and buffalo robes (Teit 1928: 121).

CULTURE

Subsistence

Access to the Cascade Mountains made mountain goat hunting an important specialty of the Psk^{w}aws, Entiat, and Chelan. The wool, along with dried goat meat, was traded as pelts or woven into blankets (Teit 1928: 113). Strips of white fur, intriguing and curious, were used to lure the goats close to the hunter. The slain goat was treated with great respect. The head was sprinkled with bird down and roasted (Ray 1942: 1236).

In summer, boys and girls awoke and ran to a stream to bathe separately (Ray 1932: 29), returning home to listen to an older woman lecture them on morality. At an ordinary family meal, children ate with adults, but, at a public feast, men ate first, before women and children.

During winter, dawn bathing continued but only a single late afternoon meal was eaten because people were less active, except when removing fresh snow. In early spring, the pace quickened as people began to prepare equipment, tools, and materials for summer fishing, harvesting, and gathering.

As the various root crops were ready, family groups left, giving the winter leader the location where they would set up camp. Throughout the Plateau, staple plant foods were camas bulbs and bitterroots (also called rock rose). A first food rite was held whenever a fresh species of plant or animal was ready to harvest (Ray 1932: 97, 99).

Throughout the year, other plant foods included parts of balsam, prickly pear fruits, sunflower seeds, sweet coltsfoot petioles, pine nuts, hazel nuts, mints, and pine lichen (locally called moss), which was roasted in a pit with wild onions and camas (Ray 1932: 103). Fall foods included serviceberries, huckleberries, blackberries, elderberries, and chokecherries (Ray 1932: 101), which were used to make a pemmican mixed with salmon flour.

At the root grounds, each woman daily dug up over half an acre for roots. A senior woman led each group, planning and coordinating their overall movements. At night, the roots were skinned, cleaned, and sorted. Meanwhile, men visited, scouted, and hunted to supply meat, while also preparing for the fishing season. At the end of the harvest, the bags of dried roots were taken to winter camps for storage before most people moved on to fishing camps.

May through August was and is the fishing season. While sturgeon and some small fish were always available, it was the runs of anadramous salmon and trout that provided the Plateau staple (Ray 1932: 28). Indicating its importance, the first salmon rite lasted five days.

Overall, five Columbia salmon species[75] appeared in this region during May to November runs. These were chinook (king), averaging 32 pounds with a few of 100 pounds, during a run of May through July; silver (coho ~ white); pink (humpback); and chum (dog). Sockeye, which spawn in lakes, only ran in the Okanogan River on their way north. Steelhead trout, weighing 10 to 15 pounds, ran from March to July. The fall runs of both silver and chum, from September to November, provided a less productive last harvest. Both species weighed about 6 pounds (Ray 1932: 57). Fall water levels were low so silvers were speared or seined from canoes. Lake Chelan had a small landlocked silver salmon. Pinks were obtained mostly in trade since this species was more common on the coast.

The largest fishing camps and weirs were at the mouths of the Wenatchee River and Icicle Creek, with others at the confluences of tribal namesake tributaries and the Columbia itself. The largest Salishan fishery was at Kettle Falls in Colvile territory, noted for large salmon taken during festive visiting, trading, and gambling. All Salishan tribes and their neighbors gathered there during the run.

Fishing technology utilized weirs, funnel traps, basket traps, and elevated traps (Ray 1932: 61). If the trap had few fish, the "salmon tyee" (Salmon priest) in charge of the fishing, wrapped himself in a robe and prayed at the trap all night. Men caught and hauled all the fish, while women prepared each one for sun drying. At the end of season, people visited upriver to collect the last spawning fish. Menstruating women stayed well away from the water and salmon because of a belief that menstruation odors repelled the fish.

Aside from traps, men used spears and nets, particularly at Columbia River rapids where fish had to move through a narrow passage. In some places, artificial channels were made, generally as three parallel trenches along the shore to allow for the rise and fall of water level. Children collected white rocks to line the trench bottoms to aid visibility. Salmon were taken with a spear from a triangular scaffold supported by pole tripods built at either end of the trench and braced against shore. Along some river banks, more elaborate fish platforms were built, owned by the whole fishing camp, but used by only one man at a time.

Nets were only used in murky or rough water, unless the nettle fibers could be dyed to match water conditions. Seines were used for chum and silvers, while dip nets, for salmon and

---

[75] These five salmon species have many localized common names; all within the genus called *Oncorhynchus* subdivided by these species:

O tshawytscha (chinook, king, spring, quinnat), up to 80 pounds, spawns in large streams or rivers, sometimes with spring and fall subspecies.

O kisutch (silver), usually 6-12 pounds, up to 30 pounds, runs in early fall but may not spawn until late fall, in smaller streams far from the sea.

O gorbuscha (pink), 3-10 pounds, spawns early fall, smaller streams near the sea.

O keta (chum, dog), 8-18 pounds, spawns late fall, smaller streams near the sea, lean and smokes well.

O nerka (sockeye), usually a few pounds, fattest species, spawns upriver in lakes; when landlocked, known as kokanee.

In addition, steelhead (*Salmo gairdneri*) is a sea-run rainbow trout, up to 36 pounds, that, like Atlantic salmon, spawns and returns to the sea. Pacific salmon spawn and die, nourishing local carnivores and generally poor soil (Suttles 1990: 24-25). Today volunteers leave previously frozen spawned out salmon carcasses in uplands to continue this soil enrichment.

suckers, had small mesh spread between handles. For eels and small fish, willow dip nets were made two feet wide and one foot deep. While Ray (1932: 69) suggested that seining technology was borrowed from the Pacific coast, Snkyuse believe that it was given to humans by supernatural Spider people who lived near modern Vantage, Washington. Indeed, the Snkyuse word $?áx^w in$ means = both web and seine.

Other significant water resources were sturgeons, suckers, eels, trouts, and roe or eggs. One technique for taking sturgeon involved killing a mountain goat on the cliffs above the Columbia River, letting it fall into the shallows, and spearing the fish that came to feed.

In late Summer, some people moved from the river fisheries into the mountains for fall hunting, berrying, and the digging of late roots. A few families might stay in the hills for the winter, tending a trap line, but most other families moved to winter locations near firewood, water, and shelter against deep snow or brisk winds.

Hunting occupied the Fall and Winter. Deer were taken from November to March, along with some elk. Communal hunts were the most productive. Prior to leaving, hunters entered the sweat lodge morning and evening for ten days to remove body odors offensive to deer, singing and praying for success while also practicing sexual continence ~ ritual chastity, particularly by the hunt leader.

During the day, weapons and gear were prepared or repaired. Each hunter carried clothes, snowshoes, and packs with mats for a hut, robes for bedding, and a snack because hunters expected to eat fresh game. For longer hunts, women went along to keep camp, sleeping apart from men in the same huts.

The leader coordinated all activities and assigned all tasks, appointing drivers to chase game toward the hunters waiting at the end of a canyon or draw. Like the Sanpoil, Snkyuse, who were closer to antelope herds, may have conducted communal hunts like the antelope drives of Great Basin shamans.

Deer were also driven into the Columbia by trained dogs and killed. Such dogs were guided by their owner using special gestures and calls. Individual deer were taken at a watering spot or a salt lick, using a blind, or along a game trail (Ray 1932: 82).

A slain deer was carried into the house through the back and placed on a special bed of fir boughs to be welcomed by family and friends (Miller 1990: 114-122). The animal was then ritually butchered in a precise way (Ray 1932: 91), as a special prayer of thanks was said as each cut was made. The meat was divided evenly among everyone in camp, but the hide belonged to the hunter who made the kill. Women, as always, dressed and tanned the hides of deer, elk, antelope, and buffalo.

Along with Spokan, Flathead, and others, Snkyuse went to hunt bison on the northern Plains under the leadership of Split Sun.

When the winter village was reoccupied, a special feast was held for the elderly, with the young excluded, consisting of stewed hoofs, lower leg muscles, head, and lungs (Ray 1932: 92).

Black and grizzly bears were hunted for their hides, but the meat had a strong taste and was only eaten as a matter of personal preference. Whether deliberately smoked from their dens using rotten pine wood or encountered in berry patches, special mourning songs were sung by a hunter. Bear and deer meat was sometimes baked in an earth oven. Psk^{w}aws used special poisoned arrows to hunt grizzlies.

In addition to spears or bows and arrows, hunters also used traps, deadfalls, and snares set over game trails (Ray 1932: 85) for mink, fisher, marten, badger, otter, fox, lynx, wildcat, cougar, coyote, and wolf. Shellfish was used as bait for otters, beavers, and muskrats. Snares were set for grouse, coyote, lynx, wildcat, and some deer (Ray 1932: 86).

People did not eat coyote, mink, wolf, land otter, buzzard, raven, crow, eagle, snakes, gopher, mouse, wood rat, frogs, dog, insects, the heart of a fool hen, or deer eyes (Ray 1942: 1350-1375). Women were specifically forbidden to eat deer kidneys and blood (Ray 1932: 90), presumably to avoid very bloody discharges during menstruation. Famine foods included rose hips, hides, and tree-cached bones of fish or game previously left as offerings (Ray 1932: 107).

A strong ethic of sharing applied to all fish and meat (Ray 1932: 26) produced by men and by women according to their mutual division of labor (Ray 1932: 33).

Technology

Native industries relied on different materials: fibers, stone, wood, skin, bone, and shell.

Fibers Considerable time was spent in the production of hemp cordage (Ray 1932: 44) which had a great variety of uses, including weaving into tumplines (Ray 1932: 120). Tule rushes (Ray 1932: 38) were sewn into mats for bedding, corpse shroud, housing, table runners, and berry drying. A willow shoot mat was made for drying salmon. Cedar roots, often traded from the Methow, were formed into coiled baskets, decorated in simple bands and triangles. Baskets served as containers for water, berries, and other foods, as cups, and as cooking vessels. Flat twined storage bags of bast, tule, or cattails were decorated by weaving in colored fibers dyed yellow from the inner bark of Oregon grape or blue from huckleberries, along with natural browns and blacks. Berry and root baskets were also made from the bark of birch, cottonwood, or pine (Ray 1932: 37). Tightly twisted sagebrush bark served as a slow match for transporting fire. Rushes and bark were used for torches during night fishing.

Stone Basalt or granite were pecked and ground into pestles and hammers; flint was chipped into knives, points, drills, gravers (Ray 1932: 35). Arrow points might be further baked, hung in a sweatlodge, or soaked in rose branch water to increase their efficacy. Pipes were made from polished soapstone (Ray 1932: 40). Dense rocks were used as sweatlodge stones, and flat lap stones provided a handy work surface (Ray 1932: 90). Granite schist, particularly from Kettle Falls, made excellent hide scrapers (Ray 1932: 95).

Wood Log mortars with a rawhide lining were used with hardwood or stone pestles to make flour of salmon, venison, and sunflowers. Carved sticks served as handles, and were bound together as fan-shaped combs (Ray 1932: 54). Dishes, spoons, forks, and firepokers were made from wood. Individual spoons were used at feasts, but, at home meals, a family shared a single one. Log mauls were cut with a handy branch to serve as the handle. A fire drill of pine was rotated over a base hearth of jack pine. Tinder was dried grass or antelope brush. Driftwood provided firewood, although a dense root was used to keep the banked fire going overnight. Long mat needles were carved from sticks, as were fire and cooking tongs (Ray 1932: 44). The largest wooden artifacts were canoes (Ray 1932: 122) or rafts. Snowshoes (Ray 1932: 120) were made by men from maple, and dibbles (digging sticks) by women, who pointed and smoothed a slightly curved hardwood stick and added a wood or horn handle. Three types of bows – sinew-backed, stave, and elk-rib – were used (Ray 1932: 87). Salmon skin or deer hoof glue was used to attach the deer leg sinews (Ray 1932: 88). Bowstrings were made of hemp or deer back sinews. Arrow shafts were straightened and smoothed before three feather vanes were added.

Wooden blocks served as net spacers or gauges (Ray 1942: 327).

Skin Pelts, hides, and skins served for bedding, clothing, and robes (Ray 1932: 35). An eight-foot packstrap or tumpline was made entirely of buckskin or had a bearskin center piece. Quivers were made of coyote or buck deer pelts (Ray 1932: 89). Parfleches, borrowed from the Plains, were made from buffalo or deer hides (Ray 1932: 44). Mountain goat wool was woven into blankets (Ray 1942: 3032).

Bone & Horn Pointed bones served as awls. Spoons were steamed and shaped from buffalo, mountain goat, and antelope horns. Elk horn and bone provided wedges and dibble handles. Smaller deer bones became needles and hooks, while deer ribs served as scrapers (Ray 1932: 95). Mountain sheep horn was steamed and molded into a bow.

Shell Fresh water clamshells served as spoons, and colored shells were used as counters in games. Abalone and other large shells were traded from the coast.

Buildings and Sacred Sites

Ancient semi-subterranean pithouses were replaced in historic times by mat houses, both winter and summer, because they were less work for the decimated survivors. Menstrual lodges, sweatlodges, and camping huts of mats or skin tipis were also built (Ray 1932: 31).

Distinctive of Psk^{w}aws towns was a special weaving house, built over a pit two feet deep and entered through a roof hatchway, where women spent the day together making coiled baskets and goat wool textiles (Spier 1938: 124), highly valued as trade items.

The pithouse, a circular pit about ten to sixteen feet wide and four to six feet deep, had either a flat roof or a conical one with a center post and pole stringers set two feet apart along the edge. The roof was covered, in turn, by layers of driftwood planks, if available, or by willow mats, a six-inch layer of grass or brush, and an outer covering of dirt removed from the pit excavation, sometimes plastered with clay as waterproofing. Entry was by a hatchway, which also served as smokehole. A log ladder rested near the central fire. During storms, the roof hole was covered with a mat.

Psk^{w}aws also built a pithouse over a square pit, a supplementary form shared with the Southern Okanogan and the Kittitas.

In recent centuries, the best known winter dwelling has been the mat-covered, gabled, communal longhouse. The frame was a peaked or inverted V with rounded ends, about sixteen feet wide by twenty to sixty feet long, capable of holding two to eight families. The framework consisted of crossed poles, tied together at the top, with parallel side poles tied three-feet apart along the sides. The ends were formed by leaning poles against the frame, like a half tipi held in place by horizontally tied willow poles (Ray 1932: 32). The lower walls were covered with grass and dirt; the upper walls with tule mats tied to the uprights. An open gap, a foot wide, along the roof ridge allowed for the passage of smoke and light. At the ends were double doors, an outer one between the curved poles and an inner door between end mats hung over the square end of the main frame.

Set up at the fisheries, summer mat houses were rectangular, with a flat roof, and nine feet wide because inside there was only a single row of beds and a passageway. Side poles were forked to hold roof cross beams. The upriver half of the house was used for drying fish because prevailing winds blew odors away. Small fires burned outside. Mats enclosed the back, sides, and roof, while the open front faced the river (Ray 1932: 34).

A sweatlodge consisted of a six to eight foot dome made of bent willow saplings covered by dry grass and six inches of dirt (Ray 1932: 55). Today, blankets and canvas provide the covering. Rocks were heated in an outside fire and carried to an inside basin where water was sprinkled to create steam. Menstrual huts were built like mat homes.

Only in special cases, at vision questing sites (see p69), would stone walls be built of talus basalt rocks to mark sacred precincts along the Columbia or atop mountain peaks. A few hollow boulders are regarded as Coyote's petrified sweat lodges of the Spirit Age. Shamans of great power painted pictographs on rock faces to memorialize their power and to provide a place where friends and kin could petition it for help (Spier 1938: 143-44; herein Ch 4).

Transport

In addition to packstraps (Ray 1932: 122), people relied on rafts, canoes, snowshoes, and improvised toboggans of deer and bear hides (Ray 1932: 118, 120, 122) before horses were introduced. Of note, people traveled barefoot in summer, putting on sandals or moccasins only as they approached a camp or village. In winter, padded and insulated footgear were worn, and travel often involved snowshoes.

Clothing

Aboriginally, clothing materials varied with the seasons. Animal skins were used in winter, woven plant fibers for summer. Most recently, with the addition of the horse, Salishans used tailored deerskin styles adapted from Plains tribes (Ray 1932: 45). In summer, men often went nude among themselves, otherwise they wore a sagebark pubic sheath or leather breechcloth. Women wore a belted poncho, with a diamond-shaped head space, and aprons woven with a bark and deerhair warp and a hemp weft.

Sandals, worn by men and women, were woven from sagebark or fresh rose branches left to dry. Leather moccasins were made of a rectangular skin, folded and sewn up the heel and along a pointed toe to an instep insert, which flared the shape to fit a foot. Narrow ankle flaps were added. A tab, made by shaping the heel, was decorated with a cutout pattern. Winter moccasins were more roomy so grass or fur insulation could be padded around the foot. Ceremonial moccasins bore simple geometric designs in feather or porcupine quills on the front.

In heavy brush or cold weather, women wore wrap-around skirts and hemp leggings, while men wore leggings of an entire inside-out hide of a badger, beaver, coyote, or small bear. Men wore their leggings above the knee, tied at the top and bottom, while women wore theirs below the knee and wrapped only at the top.

In winter, men also wore an overrobe of bear or deer hide or a tunic of double coyote skins sewn together at their shoulders. Woven willow or sage bark or a trimmed hide served for breech clouts for men and women.

Fur caps were worn in winter. Male caps, like the deer stalker style of Sherlock Holmes, had front and back visors, but women's caps had no visors. The cap was made from a green skin stretched and shaped by gently pounded it over a round rock, then flexed to keep it soft, except at the ends which stiffened to be trimmed into the visors.

The feathered headdress typical of the Plains was introduced as chiefly attire by Split Sun, a sign of his increased leadership during bison hunts and war expeditions into Montana.

Mittens were made of coyote and other skins, except rabbit, which was too thin. For safety, mittens were tied to a cord around the neck on long trips. Robes and blankets used deer, bear, coyote, and rabbit hides. Some woven rabbit fur robes were also made, and rabbit skins were preferred for baby clothes.

Particular ornamentation followed instructions from a guardian spirit. Caps were made from the pelt of the same species as a spirit ally. Powerful shamans wore feathers and porcupine quill decorations because only they dared to call attention to themselves. Random perforations in a shirt indicated immunity from weapon wounds, a warrior power like that of the Nez Perce.

Men and women wore headbands, and some women donned basketry hats, like neighboring Sahaptians. Eyebrows were plucked and painted (Ray 1932: 52). Face painting protected against sun and wind, invoking guardian spirits at public gatherings (Ray 1932: 51).

Girls dressed their own hair, while mothers, then wives, did this for men. Women wore bangs, sometimes with three braids (at the sides and back). Men plucked their own facial hair with tweezers made of wood or small animal ribs (Ray 1932: 56). Men's hair was worn in two braids, sometimes wrapped with fur (Ray 1932: 52). Women often painted, daubed, or treated their hair to indicate characteristics of age, activity, and status. Both men and women rubbed their hair with salmon oil or used a perfume made from deer marrow mixed with crushed hemlock needles. Men rubbed their hair and body with a leather pouch impregnated with beaver testes oil as a cologne. During mourning, hair was cut short.

Baby bedding and diapers were made from birchbark or buckskin. Children went unclothed in summer until puberty.

Wealth

Wealth items, never abundant, included clamshell beads, locally called wampum, and dentalia tusk shells (Ray 1932: 50) traded from the sea coast. Only shamans remained wealthy, retaining their "pay" for curings (Ray 1932: 26). Chiefs and other leaders were expected to be generous and so could not retain wealth while holding positions of responsibility.

Life Cycle

After conception, a woman was careful to lay on her side to prevent twins from forming. Eating eggs would result in a caul. If the fetus faced the mother's back, it would be left handed; if it faced her front, it would be right handed (Spier 1938: 121).

Thus, pregnancy imposed strict taboos on the mother and father concerned for the wellbeing of their baby. Often, the pregnant woman returned to the home of her mother until the birth. Her regular exercise regime featured walking, running, swimming, and eating sparingly.

When labor began, the woman and an elder female retired to a birthing hut or a screened off section of the house. For delivery, the woman knelt against two stakes and held on to the tops. The baby emerged onto a mat. The elder woman tied off the umbilical cord with deer sinew, bit through it, and buried the placenta. When the umbilical cord fell off, it was saved and tied to the babyboard, later buried by the father in secret to insure good health for his child.

The newborn was washed and massaged to shape features and limbs (Ray 1932: 125). In difficult deliveries, shamans were summoned to assist by using their spirit power to ease out the baby. If the fetus was born dead, it was buried immediately.

Herbal tea was drunk by the mother to reduce bleeding. The father beat a dog or horse or ran a horse or himself into a lather so that the child would not cry excessively or convulse. At no other time was an animal deliberately injured.

Close relatives of the father made the new cradleboard once a healthy baby was born. Often a man made the wooden frame and a woman made the leather sack attached to it. Slight differences marked male or female cradleboards and bindings, in addition to the kinds of dangles hung from the protecting head loop. For a boy, the penis was exposed, while a girl had a buckskin fold between her legs (Ray 1932: 130) to allow urine to run off. A baby's buckskin diapers were always emptied into the same hole as protection from sorcery, and, similarly, the umbilical stub was buried in the hills.

The mother rested for a week and relaxed for a month, drinking a fortifying herb tonic twice a day. At the end of confinement, she bathed and held a small feast for the baby, being forbidden to cook while she was losing blood. Children born out of wedlock were usually permanently adopted by relatives. Important families might betroth their infants to forge a permanent bond. If the mother died, the baby was adopted by another nursing mother for about two years, the two nursing babies becoming "milk kin" to each other.

Throughout infancy, the mother massaged the baby to make it grow tall and slim, with a fine nose and chin. Thick hair was especially prized, made shiny by using a sunflower root shampoo (Ray 1932: 54). Leading families named their babies soon after birth as a mark of status. Older children had their ears pierced. Baby teeth were given to a dog with a prayer for new strong teeth (Miller 1990: 209, note 11). Parents threatened children, but actual whipping done by an elderly man, sometimes disguised, in return for gifts from the parents.

Children were urged to help adults. Grandparents nurtured and protected their grandchildren, developing a close bond between them. During family meals, children ate pieces of meat or fish that included the killing wound to make them strong (Ray 1932: 132).

A boy or girl never ate their very first food efforts. When a boy killed his first game, depending on its size, he gave it away to an old man or served a feast for old men to teach himself the value of sharing. When a girl gathered her first roots or berries, a feast was held for the old women (Ray 1932: 26, 133). The Psk^{w}aws held a ceremony the first time that a child smoked a pipe (Spier 1938: 193).

By puberty, boys and some girls should have acquired a guardian spirit by questing in the hills after dark. At first menstruation, a girl was secluded for days in a menstrual hut, wearing her oldest clothes and her braids in coils (Ray 1932: 134). At the end, she was given new adult clothes and sent forth as a woman. Boys engaged in strenuous exercise during puberty but there was no special ritual observance. After a successful hunt or other good deed, he was pronounced a young man in public.

Women returned to the menstrual hut during each successive occurrence and were careful to avoid men's hunting and religious gear. If a weapon were contaminated, it was rubbed with coyote mint leaves to restore it (Ray 1932: 135). Girls from better families were chaperoned. Boys courted them with flutes and songs. For second marriages, love medicine was used to compel the spouse (Ray 1932: 136, Miller 1990: 79-90). Parents arranged marriages, and, as in-laws, exchanged gifts periodically for the duration of a marriage. The couple often lived with relatives of the husband.

To thwart parental objections, a couple might elope or allow themselves to be discovered in bed together. Successful hunters, gamblers, shamans, and leaders had more than a single wife, sometimes in separate camps. Levirate and sororate were practiced at the death of a spouse. Adultery and incest were offenses punishable by lashing, cutting off ears, or, in extreme cases, death. Jilted spouses might commit suicide, then as now.

Following courtship and betrothal, a time and place was set for the wedding. The bride-to-be moved to a mat house built away from her village, where her family provided her with food and comforts, as she spent her time quietly deciding on her future goals. After several days, two other lodges were built near her. One camp was for the groom and family, and the other was for her family. She kept inside her own shelter until the actual wedding.

The groom's family carried a feast to the other family, and gave them gifts appropriate to women, such as baskets, woven bags filled with dried food, robes, blankets, and yardage. Prayers were said to bless the marriage, and to ask for long life and many healthy children. In private, the bride was given a special eagle feather to wear as a married woman.

The next day the bride's family carried a feast to the groom's camp and gave male related gifts, such as meat, tools, and weapons. Great care was taken to see that the exchange of gifts was equal and that neither family outdid the other. For a life based on sharing together, both families had to start equivalent. The groom received his marriage braid.

On the third day, the couple married. Both families contributed to a new home, supplying it with all necessities. The bride was dressed in fine garments and her eagle feather. Standing together outside, leaders asked the Creator to bless the union and proclaimed them married. Some elite families wrapped a wedding robe around the couple during these prayers.

Once the couple was settled in their new lodge, the other camps dispersed to give them privacy. At night, youngsters might in fun come to serenade the couple and engage in banter and joking. After a time, when the villagers moved to a new location, the couple assumed a more active role in community affairs.

When near death, a person might call for one or more old men to act as confessor to keep his or her soul from wandering, tormented by past wrongs. At death, the extended body was wrapped in a rush mat or deerskin. If a shaman died inside a lodge, the mats were removed and the structure burned. As soon as possible after dawn, a grave was dug and the body carried there, followed by mourners. After the eulogy, a shaman swept out the grave with wild rose branches and the body was placed inside fully extended. Important possessions, such as keepsakes and talismans, were also placed in the grave, but no clothes or food, which were burned or buried separately.

Closely related mourners set up huts in the woods, sweating, bathing, fasting, and drinking a rosebush decoction morning and night for a year. Fir bough bedding protected hunting luck while a man mourned his wife. A male mourner wore his hair loose, but a woman had hers cut off at shoulder length. Leather bands, providing a protective circle, were worn around the wrists, until they fell off.

At death, the soul, located near the heart, departed for the afterworld at the end of the Milky Way, or, if unabsolved, became an anguished ghost wandering the earth (Ray 1932: 171). The guardian spirit, as an ancestral spirit-ghost, hovered nearby waiting for another relative or a shaman to reestablish rapport with the living (Ray 1939: 99).

Kinship

The birth of children brought increasing family responsibilities and participation in the network of kinship obligations. Like other Plateau communities, these Salishans had a bilateral system pairing the duties of men and women within kindreds, assuming extensive genealogical information to keep track of relatives by descent or marriage throughout the Plateau and beyond.

Interior Salish kinship terms stress generation, gender, and collaterality (Elmendorf 1961). Parents and own children are distinguished from uncles, aunts, and niblings (nephews, nieces), yet all cousins are called siblings. At the death of a linking relative, special "decedence terms" (Miller 1985) are introduced among surviving collaterals to move their relationships closer together, much as the levirate and sororate reaffirmed family alliances by marrying a surviving sibling to the widow or widower.

Polygyny, great mobility, and scattered resources contributed to the overall flexibility of this system so that kindreds were not localized and relationships remained as broad as possible. Faint memory of what seem to have been cognatic corporate groups or totemic kindreds suggests there was more formality to prehistoric patterns.

Social Organization

The rise of the confederacy under Split Sun *sóq̓taɫk̉ʷúsm* of the Snkyuse village at Vantage gave these tribes a greater political cohesion than their neighbors (Ray 1960). As his sons succeeded to the title and position, they arranged dynastic marriages with other leading families to extent their influence.

Throughout the Plateau, communities were organized on the basis of common language, drainage, and winter village – the most basic and effective political unit. Each village had a leader, who was advised by an assembly of married adults, regardless of their own origins or length of residence. People moved with the seasons or by personal choice among these villages and affiliated camps, especially to berry, hunting, and fishing sites.

Leadership was hereditary among males, with the most likely candidate receiving assembly approval. Once selected, a chief held office until he died or left the village. Qualities sought were honesty, sound judgment, even temperament, and arbitration skills. Larger villages included multiple chiefs and subchiefs, who advised the main chief in his roles of judge, arbitrator, and manager. A speaker, noted for his loud voice, repeated or reinforced the words of a leader. Message runners called people to an assembly or coordinated the seasonal movements of related groups.

As judge, the chief held open court, calling on witnesses, evaluating evidence, and hearing from the accused. Crimes included murder, stealing, perjury, assault, sexual indiscretions, abortion, sorcery, or revenge. Under pressures from missionaries and federal agents, punishment often involved a three-foot lash braided of deer neck sinews (Ray 1932: 113). Murder was compensated for with goods, never executions. Other punishments might exclude someone from participating in a ceremony, impose social ostracism for a set time, or demand specific acts such as providing food to the family of the victim.

The women of leading families also had high rank and, as the wives and daughters of chiefs, undertook leadership roles during female and domestic activities.

Games

In the spring, shinny was played by teams of ten to thirty boys, men, or women, using a wooden ball covered with buckskin and sticks made from tree branches crooked at the end. The goals were robes set 200 feet apart at the ends of a level field.

Men challenged each other to contests of swimming, wrestling, jumping, weight lifting with stones, and tug of war, when two men sat with their soles touching, grasped the same stick, and pulled until one of them was lifted up. In winter, men tried to swim across the Columbia, accompanied by canoes for safety (Ray 1932: 166). Men and women had different swimming areas and separate contests.

Women played dice games with four decorated beaver teeth or deer ribs that had been steamed, straightened, polished, decorated, and pointed at the ends (Ray 1932: 159, Ray 1942: 4034). One side of each piece had four dotted circles, the other side had stripes. These dice were shaken in cupped hands and thrown onto a skin. Each woman threw until all pieces fell with the circles-side down. About 50 counters were involved and all had to be won before a single player could win by getting them all. Score was made by getting all four circles-side up for two counters, three circle-sides up for one counter, one side up to lose a counter, and no circles up to lose two counters. Women made their own dice.

During winter, two teams of women stared at each other down until a woman smiled and her team lost. Sometimes, two women teams squatted on their heels and sang before hopping and clapping in place. The last one still upright won, as most players laughed and fell over (Ray 1932: 160). Other teams of women held their breath while touching along a spiral traced in the sand. The team won whose woman held her breath longest and touched more of the spiral.

Both men and women played ball and pin (Ray 1932: 161). The tule ball was held in the mouth to keep it moist, then dropped toward a thorn in the right hand. Every successful thrust was named for a month "to shorten the year." In summer, men played hoop and pole, using a pottery or wood disc and a bone-tipped hardwood staff decorated with bands of buckskin, along a runway dug six feet wide, sixteen feet long, and nine inches deep. The six inch hoop was wrapped in buckskin, with crossed inner thongs hung with colored shells. Two players or teams took turns rolling or throwing the hoop underhand. Score was kept with stick counters, and computed by the touching of particular pole bands and ring shells. A heavier ring was made of clay covered with buckskin, or of polished and pierced stone, as Herman Friedlander found at Omak Lake:

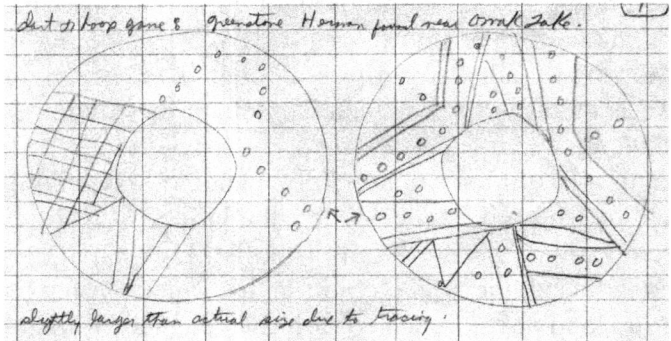

Another throwing game used a hoop twisted from a limb and a four-foot willow pole (Ray 1932: 164). Men stood and threw at the hoop target set about 30 feet away. Slings of buckskin and hemp cord or of shaved willow string were used in contests. A more quiet game was cat's cradle to create string figures.

Running was another sport, with marathons for small teams covering 15 miles (Ray 1932: 165). Men might race each other to a mountain top. Race courses were laid out to a tree and back, with heavy betting on the winner. In recent times, horse racetracks were used.

Children had playgrounds on sandbars or sandy beaches where they played house. Girls used stick dolls, with an added head and clothes. Boys had tops of wood, started with a string, or a bark disc, twirled with the hand. Favorite diversions were hide and seek, seesaw with crossed logs, willow whistles, snowball fights, and hide toboggans. Children played with shuttlecocks made from duck feathers, and used, at the request of elders, bullroarers made of wood or deer ribs to influence the weather (Ray 1942: 4064, 4094).

The most popular recent native pastime is the stick game (*slahal*), with bets matched by sides before play (Ray 1932: 155). Poker, monte, and other card games are more recent.

Traditional Literature

On Naming Day, at the end of Spirit Age, just prior to human arrival, the spirit leader, who created the world before becoming Sweatlodge, gave names to all creatures at a dawn assembly. Coyote stayed up all night intending to be first in line to receive the name of Salmon, Bear, or Eagle. Instead, he fell asleep and was the last to appear. Because he had thought for himself, however, the Creator put Coyote in charge of making the world ready for humans. The chief himself gave up his head and limbs, providing the sweat lodge for all humans in need.

One of Coyote's greatest adventures was to steal Salmon from the trap of Bird Women at the mouth of the Columbia and guide them upriver. Every village at the mouth of a stream or tributary was visited, and Coyote left salmon there according to the beauty of the woman he "married" during his stay (Boas 1917, Ray 1933, Spier 1938).

Coyote also issued "commandments" about how the world was to be organized. In some places, he left a spirit emblem or rock picture to indicate these resources and rules. At other times, he changed the landscape, petrifying monsters and scattering foods. A council of spirits decided that the unnatural sons of Mole, Coyote's wife, would become Sun and Moon.

The world was also populated with various dwarfs and monsters. Various lakes and water obstructions had resident spirits, such as a nude woman with long flowing hair and exposed breasts and hairy, long horned beings in Omak and Alta Lakes.

Cosmology

The earth was a sky dome over an earth disk, with the Columbia River through the middle and the Cascade Mountains and Plains along the edge surrounded by ocean.

Fundamental to everything, spirit powers (*sumax*) included both animates and inanimates, such as driftwood and fish traps. Among the most awesome are Grizzly, Wolf, Badger, Skunk, Flying Squirrel, Pack Rat, Spider, Hawk, and Eagle, with Rabbit and Magpie weaker powers. Dangerous powers are Grizzly, Bear, Wolf, Cougar, Badger, Summer Weasel, and Rattlesnake.

During successful questing, spirits appeared as humans to confer power before changing into their species form just as they departed. Good looks and a strong body were particularly attractive to spirits (Ray 1932: 173), who went away as one became old, feeble, or sickly. When a human partner died, the spirit became a spirit-ghost in quest of another human, preferably from the same family unless it was lured away by a powerful shaman. When a spirit-ghost was itself killed, a shoulder blade was found at the spot.

While a child received a spirit at eight to ten years of age, the encounter was forgotten until the spirit returned, some fifteen or twenty years later, and the person became sick with a feeling of loneliness and despondency. A shaman was called to treat the patient, fixing the spirit inside him or her by allowing the singing of the song signaling the bond. When winter came, the patient sang his or her song in public during a winter dance.

Though some spirits conferred the ability to cure particular ailments, only shamans received power to heal persistent and supernatural illnesses (Ray 1932: 202), including wounds from animal attack, fevers, mental upset, spirit loss, and magical poisoning by a jealous woman.

Ceremonies

The First Salmon Ceremony was conducted by two shamans when the first chinook (king) was caught at a communal weir. Prior rites of thanksgiving were held for the trees cut to make the weir, for the dried poles carried to the stream banks, and for the completed weir. The "salmon tyee" spent five nights at the trap praying and singing to consecrate its use.

As men built the trap, women put sunflower leaves on the roof of an open sided sunshade and over the ground inside and nearby. When the women finished, they took the children and withdrew from the river for five days. Men removed all their clothes and went naked during this time. All of the work, cooking, and feasting was then done only by men. The first four days, only salmon flanks were eaten, boiled the first two days and roasted the last two, with the men using a special triangular spoon made from a bent willow twig.

Salmon heads, tails, fins, backbones, and roe were dried upon a woven willow platform until the fifth day, when they were mixed into a soup with service berries, bitterroot, camas, and water. This was the most holy meal of the rite since it included virtually every food. A man was expected to eat as much as possible so these foods would be bountiful.

After the fifth day, women rejoined the camp and began the large scale processing of fish. Women resumed the cooking all meals, and prepared all fish (Ray 1932: 71).

The harvesting of any other resource was also begun with a public feast to honor that new food. After berry feasts, married couples increase fertility to bolster harvests (Spier 1938: 32).

The Winter Dance acted as a world renewal and all-purpose thanksgiving, hosted in rotation among tribal communities during January and February. Traditionally, a large mat house was cleared, poles suspended along its sides to hold gifts, and a tree with only top branches, decorated with wrappings and dangles, was set up in the middle. Led off by the host, each visionary grasped the pole in turn and sang his or her song provided by a encounter with a spirit. Participants and audience fasted during these recitations, but a feast ended the service. Later in the season, dances were dedicated to bringing the Chinook or warm winds of spring.

Today, the dance is held in a large public room specially built into the homes of hosting families. Within the house, men sit on the right and women on the left. The host was and is usually a powerful shaman since displays of spirit powers often led to attempted thefts of the spirits by unscrupulous shamans. A speaker announces for the host and others, stating intermissions and times to drink water and smoke.

In public, a novice proclaimed his renewed ties with his or her spirit by dancing, protected by a sponsoring shaman since he or she were particularly vulnerable while the power was new (Ray 1932: 192). After this initiation, the visionary would briefly describe the circumstance of the vision during a later intermission, or, alternatively, ask for guesses about what his song and motions had been evoking. On the last morning, gifts were distributed by the host to other performers, then to the audience as quantity allowed.

Witchcraft

Malevolent sorcery caused a victim to have a scared look in the eyes, be jumpy and twitchy, and became delirious, often identifying with and naming the shaman who caused the condition at the moment of death. Only a more powerful shaman could effect a cure. If the victim died, a family member might kill the malicious shaman by magic or with a physical weapon, assured of acquittal by the consensus of the community.

Population

Estimates by Anastasio (1975: 202) suggest 2500 in 1805, decreasing to 1300 by 1835, while (Curtis 1911: 68) reported 1000 in 1870. By 1835 only 350 Southern Okanogan are listed.

While only 139 Sinkuse {sic} "attached to the agency" are reported for 1888, Agent HJ Cole (ARCIA 1892: 487) noted 390 Moses-Columbia, including 139 males above 18 years, 150 females above 14 years, 9 children 6 to 16 years old, and 32 others. In 1889, Agent Anderson listed 311 members of the "Moses Band." In the 1990s membership in the Colville Confederated Tribes was about 8000, with about half living on the reservation, which included remaining allotments and homesteads on the excised North half, Moses Reservation,[76] Kettle River, Wenatchee fishery, and Palouse River.

After a bitter fight over 1950-60s termination, the Colville business council embarked on a policy of successful economic development. Today, Colvilles identify themselves as Catholics, Methodists, Pentecostals, Shakers, Seven Drums, Shamans, and Peyote (Native American Church). Recast traditions include pit oven recipes now done by slow cooking inside a stove, continued first foods rites, and tribal feasts, name givings, and funerals.

Synonymy

Snkyuse: Spelled Sinkiuse by Hodge (1910, 2: 576), who lists variants, the name is from Columbian *snq'aʔáẃs*; the Okanagan form is *snk'eʔíẃsx*. Another term for the Moses Band is *skwáxcnəx^w* = people of *skwáxcṅ*, a place-name meaning '(where people) live against the shore' used for Rock Island and the lower part of Moses Coulee. Another name for them was Isle de Pierre (Mooney 1896: 743).

Psk^waws ~ Wenatchee: Wenatchee is from the Sahaptin name for this group, which in the Yakima dialect is *winátšapam* "is flowing out" (Beavert and Hargus 2009: 285). The Columbian name is *snp'əsq^wáẃəx^w*, meaning = 'the people of the Wenatchee River' (np'sq^wáẃs "broad valley"). Hodge (1910, 2: 263, 932) lists synonyms in separate entries for Pisquows and Wenatchi, being uncertain of the synonymy of these terms.

Entiat: Entiat is the name of a settlement, *nt'iyátk^w* = 'grassy water'; the band was called *snt'iyátk^wəx^w* = 'people of Entiat village'. These are the Inti-etook of Alexander Ross (Hodge 1907, 1: 611) and the Entiatook of Mooney (1896: 734).

Chelan: Named for Lake Chelan, called *cəl'án* = an ancient Salish word for "lake"; the band is called *scəl'ámx* or *scəl'ámxəx^w* = 'people of Lake Chelan'. These are the Tsill-ane of Ross (Hodge 1910, 2: 826).

Methow: The name Methow is from the name of the Methow Valley, *mítxaw*; the Methow River may be called this or, explicitly, *nmitxawátk^w*. The Methow people are called *sp'aƛ̓múl'əx^wax^w* = 'people of Methow Valley', based on an alternative name *sp'aƛ̓múl'əx* = 'bitterroot country'. Mooney (1896: 734), who used the spelling Mitaui, included the Chelan and Entiat under this name. Ross spells their names Meat-who and Battle-le-mule-emauch (Hodge 1907, 1: 850). Ray includes them with Psk^waws.

---

76 Borg (2015) is a masterful review of Moses Allotments #20-28.

Southern Okanogan: In Okanagan the Okanagans are called *uknaqínx* = people of *uknaqín*, their traditional place of origin, said to be at or near Okanagan Falls (Teit 1930: 198; Anthony Mattina p.c. 1996; M Dale Kinkade pc 1997). Hodge (1910, 2: 114-115), who used the spelling Okinagan, gives spelling variants and synonyms. Mooney (1896: 734) used Okanagan. The Southern Okanogan have also been called Sinkaietk (Ray 1936: 122; Spier 1936: 10), a name based on that of the Okanogan River, *nqʕítkʷ* (Columbian *nqḥátkʷ*).

Nespelem: The name for the Nespelem in Okanagan is *nspílm* (Mattina 1987: 133). Hodge (1910, 2: 57), who used the spelling Nespelim, gives variants.

Sanpoil: The Okanagan name for the Sanpoil is *snpʕʷílxx* = people of *snpʕʷílx*, the name of the Sanpoil River and valley. Variant spellings N'pochele, N'pockle, and others are listed by Hodge (1910, 2: 451-452). Mooney (1896: 733) reported their Yakima name as Hai-ai'nima, which is the Hi-high-e-nim-mo of Lewis and Clark (Moulton 1983+, 6: 480, 488).

Curtis (1911: 66, 69) listed Sinkolkoluminuh (Quilomene), Stapisknuh, Skukulatkuh, Skoahchnuh (Rock Island), Skihlkintnuh, Skultaqchimh, Tsilan, Sintiatqkumhu (Entiat), Sinkumchimuh (mouth of the Wenatchee), and Sinpusqoisoh (Pskʷaws at Leavenworth).

Sources

Primary published sources on Middle Columbia Salishans are the classic works by Ray (1933, 1936a, 1939, 1942), with more limited work by Teit (1928). Ethnohistorical sources include Chalfant (1974), Ray (1936, 1960. 1974), Spier (1936), Ruby and Brown (1965, 1989), and Smith (1983). Voluminous government documents relating to the Colvilles are restricted in Gary Palmer (1991).

Meager museum collections can be found at the Thomas Burke Memorial Washington State Museum, Seattle; Colville tribal museum, Coulee Dam; and local historical societies in nearby counties and in Spokane.

Famous Colvilles include: Split Sun, confederacy chief Moses, heir Chief Joseph, patriot Kwolaskin (Squalaskin), prophet Mourning Dove ~ Christine Quintasket Pascal Sherman (Joe Wapato), DC lawyer Lucy Friedlander Covington Isabel Friedlander La Course Arcasa, elder Joseph Tonasket, leader Mel Tonasket, administrator Laurie Arnold, PhD.

PLATEAU TRIBES

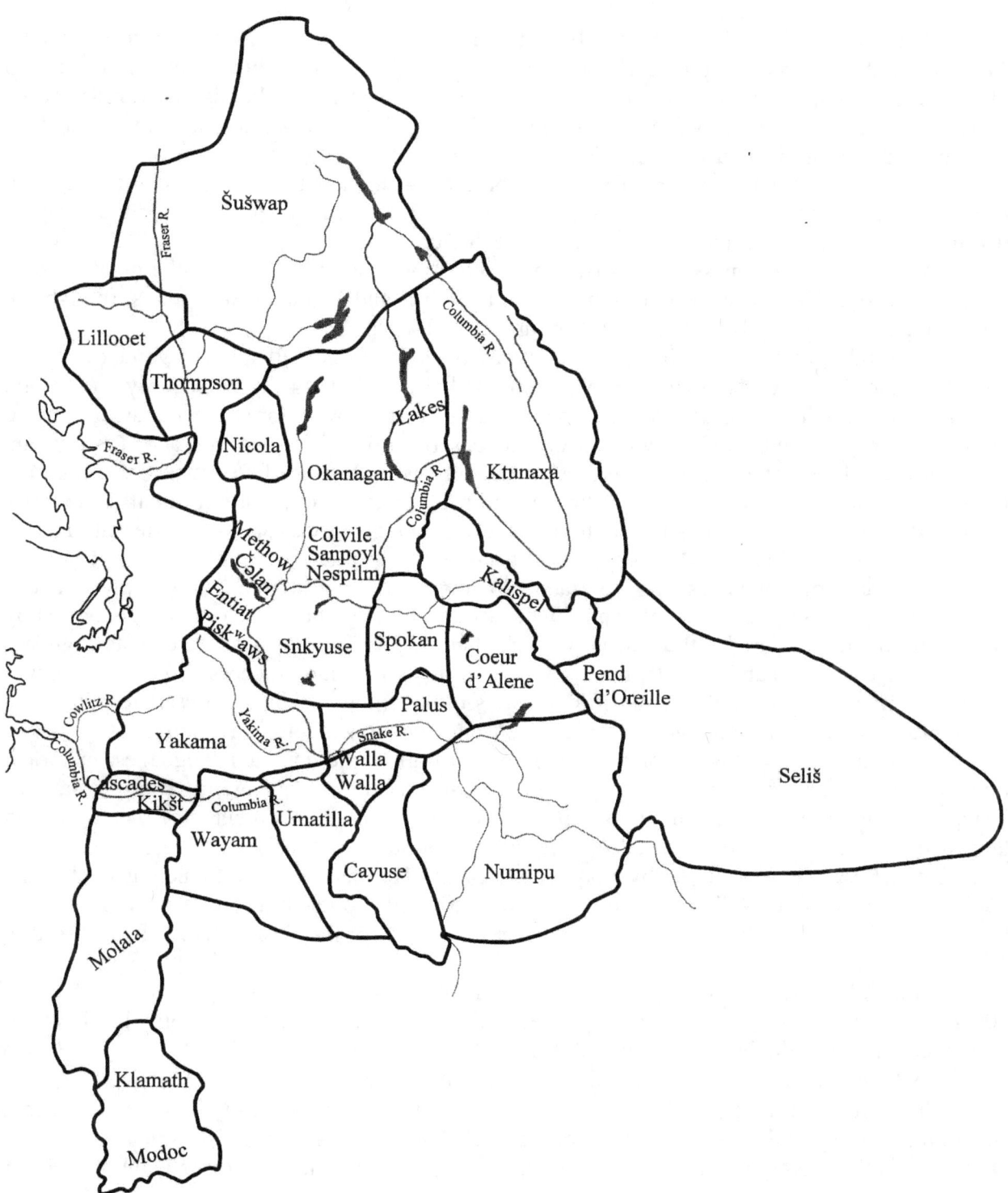

Vic Kucera & J

PLATEAU

The Plateau is the most recently defined "culture area" of Native North America, advanced in the 1930s during the early career of Verne Ray (see all), a pioneering graduate of U of Washington with a PhD from Yale for a dissertation that confirmed the distinct validity of the separate Plateau. Of note, Ray financed his Yale schooling by reading construction manuals then building and selling two houses in Seattle.

Recognized for over a century as a subregion – studied by Franz Boas, James Teit, Harlan Smith, and others who noted its salmon, roots (camas, bitterroot, *lomatium*), and rivers (Columbia, Fraser), its linguistic diversity once included upriver Chinookans (Kikst) on the lower Columbia and Athapaskans (Carrier and Sekani), whose lands included the great bend of the Fraser. Today's Plateau was trimmed back to Salish and Penutian Sahaptians, though the tiny Athapaskan Nicola also live within its boundaries.

Culturally, Plateau's distinctive cultural passivism, contra the Plains, and gender equality, contra the Northwest Coast, continue to be espoused (Ray 1939: 145). Its ecology and terrain encouraged diversity, adapting to "Alpine peaks and meadows, forest lowlands, grassland prairies, deeply eroded river canyons, scorched desert landscapes" (Collins and Tushingham 2014: 30) and biodiversity at the interface of the linguistic duality of Penutian Sahaptian and Interior Salishan language families. Within the midColumbia region, many residents, especially leaders, were fluently bi~multi~lingual, though these languages stocks are very different in terms of their Distribution, Density, Diversity, and Difficulties.

The past of languages can be traced by their a) distribution, with kindred speech communities in close proximity until split by the arrival of other languages or dispersed, often by conditions of nature; b) by their density, such that long residence in a place fosters greater internal concentrations and complexities; c) by their diversity, since successive generations will develop variant dialects, and d) by difficulties, as mountainous, island, or desert terrain, often leading to isolation that limits intercommunication and encourages linguistic uniqueness.

By comparing words for plants and animals in all of the daughter languages, historical linguists are able to reconstruct the original habitat of their proto-language, revealing locations, dispersals, migrations, and populations shifts in the past. Thus, the homeland of the Algonkian language stock has been traced 2000 years ago to Georgian Bay on the southeast side of Lake Huron, which was later occupied by Iroquoian-speaking Hurons when the French arrived in the 1600s. Similarly, proto-Salish included terms for marine life so its homeland was on or near the Pacific coast, probably along Boundary Bay near the mouths of the Fraser River, as discussed in concluding remarks.

A fifth language family, tiny offshoots of the huge Athapaskan family driven south by an 800 AD volcano's eruption in central Alaska, settled in the hills above the Columbia River in British Columbia as the Nicola and in the Willapa Hills of southwest Washington as *Swaal*, also known by their Chinook names of Kwaliokwa and Clatskanie.

In terms of time depth, Proto-Penutian[77] seems to have favored the Willamette Valley, becoming an early widespread family, ranging from Mexico to Alaska's Tsimshian (*Tsmsyan*). Oregon Penutian diverged and spread into Chinookans living along the lower Columbia River

---

[77] If there was a language stock there before Penutian, it was most likely Hokan, which is widely scattered across the West and South, with suggestive links into the East.

and Sahaptians upriver and inland.

Penutian later gave ground to Proto-Salishans and Wakashans. Classic Salishan probably spread from the Boundary Bay region on the BC ~ US border, with the Coast branch moving north and south and the Interior branch moving east up the Fraser River before expanding on the Plateau (popularly known as the Inland Empire). The expansion of fir forests about 5500 years ago has been suggested as the habitat or ecological context for this Salishan diaspora (Suttles and Elmendorf 1962, Swadesh 1954). Kootenay, now considered an isolate, may have been the forerunner of this Proto-Salishan move into the interior. Nuuxalk (Bella Coola), though now the farthest north on the coast, has vocabulary that indicates time in the interior (in the Chilcotin-Cariboo), and represents a third major division along with Coast and Interior Salishans.

Eventually, the Salishan Language Family spread from the Pacific shore into western Montana, branching into 23 interlinked languages of Coast (16 daughter members) and Interior (7 members) Salish, separated by the Cascade Mountains. Such distribution, density, and diversity bespeaks great age. Salish is localized only in the Northwest, with no obvious links with the dozen or so major linguistic stocks (Algic, Siouian, Caddoan, Iroquoian, Uto-Aztecan, for example) across the continent. Kuipers (2002), testifying to the probing depth of concentrated scholarship, lists roots and suffixes reconstructed for Proto Salish, Proto Coast Salish, and Proto Interior Salish.

Coast Salishan branches, from the north, are Nuuxalk (Bella Coola), Central, Tsamosan, and Tillamook. Central Coast Salishan includes Comox, Sechelt, Pentlatch, Squamish, Nooksak, Halkomelem (including Chilliwack, Musqueam, Cowichan), Straits (including intergrading Sooke, Saanich, Songhees, Lummi, Samish, Semiahmoo, and, more apart, S'Klallam), Twana, and Lushootseed. Tsamosan, once called Olympic, includes Cowlitz, Upper (including Satsop) and Lower Chehalis, and Quinault. Localized adaptations encouraged subgroupings of the Salishan family, such as Tsamosan which distinctively adapted to abundant prairies and Straits Salish on island homelands which were ideal for the deployment of reef nets during ocean runs of salmon.

Salishan languages use dozens of complex sounds, and their grammars feature aspect, transitivity, control ~ care, voice, person, and causation, mostly expressed through suffixes. Tense and number are optional, and gender is absent from Interior Salish languages, but present in all others. Reduplication ~ redoubling serves to express diminutive, distributive, and out of control ~ careless (Kinkade 1998: 53).

Key to understanding complex coastal prehistory is the role of the "Salishan Funnel" along the route carved down the Chehalis River by the outflows of the glacier that covered Puget Sound 17,000 years ago. Tillamook was the first down the Funnel, settling along the coast until split off to the south by the spread of Chinookan.

The Lushootseed subgroup has northern and southern dialect chains (interlinked speech communities) around Puget Sound. To the north (with ~ indicating alternatives, equivalences, synonyms, and - links in a dialect chain) are Skagit (including Sauk-Suiattle), Swdabsh (*sx^{w}ədaš* ~ aboriginal Swinomish, including *dx^{w}ə'ha* ~ Nuwa'ha), Stillaguamish, and Snohomish (*stəhobš*, including Skykomish); while south of Whidbey Island, dialects were Snoqualmi, Duwamish, Puyallup, Nisqually, and Sahewamish at the south, together with Suquamish on the west side. Lushootseed is characterized by an ancient reworking of the two sets of transitive person markers, regularization of the suffix system, and an elaboration of prefixes.

Over a century ago, a shift away from nasals (M > B, N > D) by Lushootseeds, Twana, Chimakum, and southern Nootkans (Makah and Ditidat, though still called Nitinat in English) may have been a counter-response to territorial aggression by nasal-using Straits Salish speakers such as Lummi, Klallam, and Samish (Duwaha, Nuwaha, dx^{w}a'ha). Thus, any snowcapped mountain is now called *taq^{w}oba*, which is the source for what the settlers applied as *takoma* (Tacoma) to Mt. Rainier and a nearby city.

Interior Salishan branches consist, from the north, of St'at'imcets ~ Lillooet, of Nlakapamuxcin ~ Thompson and of Sexwepemxcin ~ Shuswap, and of Mid-Columbia "upriver" (Methow - Okanogan - Nespelem - Sanpoil - Colvile - Lakes) and "downriver" (Chelan - Entiat - Psk^{w}aws ~ Wenatchi – Columbian ~ Snkyuse), of Kalispel - Spokan - Selish ~ Flathead, and of Coeur d'Alene, which has little internal diversity.

Current understanding, then, is that Kootenay and Proto-Salish split early from a common *ursprach*, then Proto-Salish branched into Coast, Interior, and Nuuxalk, with the last shifting from the interior to the coast at a later time and borrowing Wakashan terms for sea foods. This language famously relies on only three vowels, with many words formed only of consonants.

Archaeologists David Burley and Owen Beattie provide the most comprehensive assessment of the Salishan timeframe, using dated components to indicate a new population arriving on the coast 2400 CE as the Baldwin ~ Locano Beach phase making a break with the preceding Marpole (Burley and Beattie 1987). In all, the sequence for the lower British Columbia core of the Salish Sea is Charles at 4500-17 00 BC, Locarno Beach at 12-1400 BC, Marpole at 400BC-400AD, and Strait of Georgia at 400-1800AD. Charles is a later Pebble Tool tradition, which Roy Carlson links to Coast Salish, though the preponderance of evidence suggests that they were replaced by the *ursprach* of the Salish, which came out of the Baldwin phase inside the Fraser Valley (Mitchell 1990: 349).

The sequence for the lower Fraser Canyon is Charles at 4500-1700 BC, Baldwin at 1700-500 BC, Skamel at 500BC-500AD, and Canyon at 500-1800AD. "Baldwin was distinguished from the others by the presence of microblade technology and labrets, rings, earspools, numbers of beads, and other small products of a soft stone carving industry" (Mitchell 1990: 348).

In all, four lithic traditions with deep roots in the Northwest overlap in their spatial distributions with the four major language stocks ~ phyla ~macro-families: stemmed point with Macro Penutian, foliate biface with Salish-Wakashan, microblade with NaDiné, and fluted with Hokan if not scattered isolates. Penutians (derived from shared words for "5" ~ "2") range from Oregon to California, including Chinook, Sahaptians, Alsea, Kalapuya, Wintu, Maidu, Miwok, Yokut. NaDiné fill Alaska and western Canada as Eyak ~ Tlingit ~ Athapaskans. Hokan (shared "2" words) forms an arc across the edges of southern California, through Baja – including Shasta, Pomo, Yana, Washo, Yuma, Seri – to the Texas Gulf coast – Coahuiltecan – and on to Honduras and Nicaragua; with questioned links to Siouians of the East as "the most diverse and most dispersed of the superstocks and therefore ... the oldest grouping in North America" (Foster 1996: 85).

Along the mid-Columbia, Downriver Sahaptian, as a language family split on either side of the Cayuse linguistic isolate, is easier to deal with because it has two branches: *Nimiipu* ~ Nez Perce and *Ichishkiin* ~ Sahaptin dialects spoken on the stem and tributaries, such as the Yakima, of the Columbia. (Sahaptian's final "a" means it includes both branches.) *Nimiipu* has two (eastern ~ upper, western ~ lower) subdialects, while Ichishkiin ~ Sahaptin has two northern (NW, NE) and one southern (Columbia stem) subdialects. Northwest includes Klikitat, Yakama, Taitnapam, and Mishalpam, the last two west of the Cascades on the upper Cowlitz and upper Nisqually. Northeast (Walla Walla, Naxiyampam, Palus, Wanapum) occurs on the Columbia from Wallula Gap to Priest Rapid and on the Snake east of the mouth of the Palouse. Columbia

River dialects stretch east of the Dalles and include Tygh, Tenino, Celilo (Wayampam), John Day, Rock Creek, and Umatilla.

Sahaptin features complex phonology of 40 sounds, and grammar noted for case marking (like Latin), dual number, and verbs inflected for mood, aspect, directionality, and tense. The dozen cases in *Ichishkiin*, with (=) its diagnostic suffixes translated (~) as English prepositions, are genitive = -*nmi* ~ of, benefactive = -*(y)ay* ~ for, dative = -*yaw* ~ to, allative = -*kan* ~ to, ablative = -*knik* ~ from, locative = -*pa* ~ on, and instrumental = -*ki* ~ by, along with more subject - object marking nominative, absolutive, accusative = -*nan*, inverse ergative = -*nim*, and obviative ergative = -*in* in sentences (Beavert and Hargus 2009: xxxv-lxviii). Sahaptin's northern edge overlapped with Interior Salish, especially along the mid Columbia River.

Dynamic multilingualism of Sahaptin and Salishan speakers, especially leaders, enhanced a vast trade in a local jade, ranging from waxy white to black – most especially bright pale green – tapped into continental networks. Lush pasturage encouraged large animal herds, and the quick adoption of livestock. Larger groups on horseback – venturing into the Plains to hunt bison though opposed by resident tribes – needed more protection and hence more centralized leadership. These Salishans "through disease and wars [became] mere remnants of what was once the largest of tribes ... and commanded the Snoqualmie, Yakima, and all the principal passes through the Cascades, including those to the Cowlitz country ... the first horse seen by the Coast tribes ... was brought over by Wenatchi" (Teit 1928: 95, 97, 121). Thus, horses, pasture, and an easier communication route joined at Kittitas to aid the founding of two powerful alliances.

First, it was the homeland of Wiyawiikt ~ Weowitch, the founder of the Yakama confederation. Second, along the Columbia's Big Bend just to the east was the homeland of Split Sun ~ *sə́q̓taɫk̕ʷúsm* ~ Suktalkosum, founder of the Columbian Confederacy eventually headed for decades by his younger son, best known as Moses, also holding this hereditary Split ~ Half Sun name-title.

Snkyuse Columbian Salish were "the only major pastoralists not in contact with a hostile area, seem to have played a stabilizing role in maintaining peaceful relations in the Plateau" (Anastasio 1975: 146). Their family of leaders, who led bison hunts into the Plains once horses were adopted, peaked with the famous Chief Moses (1829-99), who carried the dynastic name of "Split Sun". Named for an 1800 eclipse, his father *sə́q̓taɫk̕ʷúsm* ~ Split Sun ~ Half Sun ~ Eclipse ~ Sulktalthscosum led hundreds into the northern plains to hunt bison, dry the meat, and bring it back to the Columbia for winter meals. He was killed and dismembered by Blackfeet, resentful of his encroachment into their hunting territory. His short-lived sons Patshewyah and Louis Quiltenenock succeeded him, then the title was inherited by Moses, whose boyhood name was Loolowkin ~ headband and adult name was Quetalican ~ One Blue Horn (Ray 1960, Ruby and Brown 1965, Teit 1928, Spier 1938).

In the 1800s, the Upper Yakama chiefly line at Kittitas included eight sons of Wiyawiikt, of whom the best known are brothers *tiyayaš* ~ Teias (elder), *awxay* ~ Owhi, and *shawaway* ~ Showaway.[78] Teias's daughter was wife of Kamayakin, whose own brothers were Ice ~

---

[78] Richard Scheuerman and Michael Finley, *Finding Chief Kamaiakin ~ The Life and Legacy of a Northwest Patriot* 2008. Erroneously, Anastasio (1975: 198) refers to a "failed" unification by We-ow-wicht of Kittitas when leadership passed to his eight sons about 1800, instead broadening its alliances via many dynastic intermarriages. Indeed, Anastasio's

Showaway (named for the uncle), and youngest Shkluum ~ Skloom. These were leaders of the Lower Yakamas. Owhi and his son Qualchan, related as cousin to Leschi in Puget Sound, were killed by the US Army during the Treaty War, precipitated when Indian Agent AJ Bolon was killed and cremated by *mušiil* ~ Mosheel, son of the younger Showaway, and others. In 1858, Qualchan was hanged without trial on 24 September and Owhi shot 3 October.

Moses, chief of the Salish-speaking Snkyuse,[79] was married to Owhi's daughters, Quomolah and Sanclow ~ Mary. He famously had other wives and children among allied tribes (Flathead, Wanapum, Nez Perce). The family of Pat Kanim, pro-US leader of Lower Snoqualmies during the Treaty War with many brothers, also came from this area. From the north around Nespelem, by way of Snohomish, came the family of the Skagit Prophet, whose daughter and granddaughter rose to prominence in northern Puget Sound and intermarried into local leading families. Somewhere in this mix was mid-1800s Upper Snoqualmie leader Saniwa, baptized as Aeneas, with ties to Psk^{w}aws ~ Wenatchi. He is buried at Cashmere, along highway 2, with his wife and others.

Wanapums long lived at P'na ~ Priest Rapids, and claim perpetual residence there (Longenecker, Stapp, and Buck 2002), led by the prophet Smohalla ~ *smoxala* (c1815-95) and the Sohappy families, adding a religious dimension to the region. Smohalla was born 1815-20 at Wallula, the large village at the mouth of the Walla Walla River on the opposite side of the Columbia River. His mother was Wanapum from P'na. Rivalry at Wallula from Homlai, nephew of murdered leader *piupiumoksmoks* ~ Peopeomoxmox ~ Yellow Swan (Stern 1993: 268), led him to relocate about 1855 to P'na and draw in followers. Wanapums have vibrant tradition of religious leaders, with several known in the historic record (Relander 1956, Ruby and Brown 1989, Rigsby and Finley 2009):

For the interface at Vantage (Miller 1998), in terms of rivalry and cooperation by these communities, we have the report of Abbot Gerald Desmond (1952: 34, 35), in his study of Yakama gambling:

> "Chief" Moses of the Sinkaquai'ius band of the Columbia was considered not only a great athlete but also a "great race horse man" who was willing to pay almost any price for a race horse he wanted. Smoxa'la of Ghost Dance fame, the most prominent man among the Wanapam, was also considered a professional gambler on horse racing who, in a race between his champion and a white man's horse, bet ten horses, and he and his followers added a hundred dollars to the wagers on this single race.

In addition to these obvious language differences, Anastasio and Brunton have specified cultural distinctions:

> activity was properly conducted as directed by the salmon chief [Salmon tyee] ... quite uniformly for all the Salish groups.... among the Sahaptin, the ritual control of salmon fishing was less important than it was among the Salish (Anastasio 1975: 176).

---

affinity diagrams consistently undervalue the vital nexus of the Kittitas.

[79] Bruce Rigsby (Beavert and Hargus 2009: xxix) derives the name "Yakama" from the midColumbia Salish place name for the Kittitas Valley, further emphasizing its crucial importance across the languages, traditions, and dynesties.

The events themselves differ in expressed orientation from one congregation to the other, the Interior Salish congregation typically having pow-wow or encampment type gatherings while the Sahaptian one typically has the feast type. The notable exceptions to this were the Nez Perce encampment at Mud Springs and the Yakima encampment at White Swan Long House (Brunton 1968: 17).

Spiritual traditions also continue to contrast, with men and women always sitting separately. At winter ceremonies, Salishans look outward into the cosmos, with each visionary grasping a central pole while singing a power song. Sahaptins focus inward, seeking the wellbeing of each member in turn during a *Waashat* service. "Wanapum … seem to be inward-facing … yet they produced Smohalla, who had a wide effect in the Plateau with his religious doctrine" (Anastasio 1975: 186).

The language of the earliest humans in the Americas remains unknown, but given its vast dispersement, Penutian is longstanding and somehow linked to Chimakuan isolated on the Olympic Peninsula, where Quileute remains. Oregon Penutian emerged along the Columbia, spreading upriver as Sahaptians and downriver as Chinookans, who split a continuum of Salish languages along the coast, with Tsamosan to the north and Tillamook to the south of the Columbia. Wakashan spread from the tip of Vancouver Island, where there were known ice-free pockets during the Ice Age of 12-13,000 years ago.

Salish has the most complicated history, beginning in the lower Fraser and nearby bays of the Salish Sea. Kootenay moved west, leaving Proto-Salish, which branched into Nuuxalk, Coastal, and Interior chains, as forests advanced during changed climate conditions. Cooler temperatures encouraged more salmon upstream migrations, fueling human ones.

With regard to climate and region, correlated with drier Hypsithermal about 8000 years ago, Penutian arose in semidesert Basin, Wakashan on the coast, and Salish in "riverine and forested valley environments" until their present distributions were achieved during the wetter Medithermal about 3000 years ago (Suttles and Elmendorf 1963: 49).

The Kittitas emerged as a major contact point, pivotal in the trade of local lithic materials, especially a bright pale green jade (like Granny Smith apples) and the exchange of Coastal and Plateau products. Its lush meadows fed large game herds, and fostered the early adoption of livestock, especially horses. Increasingly mobile, leading families went and married far and wide, founding dynasties with lasting impacts today.

The result was a region of complex linguistics, across two culture areas and along major rivers. In addition, leading families were multilingual and married into vast, resourceful kinship networks. For simple barter, exchange, and trading there was also a set of words and simple grammar, such as Chinuk Wawa in historic times, that fostered "skin trade" transactions. Indeed, the study of trade, exchanges, and gifting in the archaeological and ethnographic record should be able to trace the rise of dynastic families throughout the region, as well as material shifts due to prophetic movements. The Columbia, especially the holy land of the Kittitas Valley, has a mixture of ancient occupants and subsequent language complexities which bespeaks eons in terms of this mosaic of distributions, densities, diversities, and difficulties.

RESEARCHES

The Wilkes Expedition, a US exploring and scientific expedition sent around the world by the American government, spent considerable time in the Northwest. Lt Johnson of the *Porpoise* reached Ft Okanogan on 8 June 1841 and Ft Colvile on 15-19 June 1841. He marveled that when the Kettle Falls basket trap was raised three times a day, each haul filled with 300 huge salmon, which were shared among all. He also approved of the 200 acres of level land nearby and the large herds of livestock. Horatio Hale, expedition philologist, disembarked in Oregon and went home across the country. He visited the Whitman Mission, Walker Prairie, and Ft Colvile, collecting a set of native Salish month names from the dynastic founder Split Sun himself (Wilkes 1845 IV: 433-45, 441-474).

In August of 1883, in his last year as Commander of the US Army, William Tecumseh Sherman toured the West. While camping at Osoyoos Lake (on the US border), he sent 1st Lts George Benjamin Backus and George Washington Goethals into the Methow to search for a pass across the Cascades, probably following up on rumors of Hartz Pass. They included six men, six saddle horses, four pack mules, and a hound dog. Careful to leave blaze marks on trees, their efforts lead to a deadend, and they missed any of the passes, while raving at the abundance of game and rich soil.

Franz Boas, having met James Teit, a transplanted Scot married to a Thompson woman in British Columbia and active in First Nations rights, he secured funds (from sportsmen he guided) for him to survey Salishans through 1900-10, with 1908 spent among Snkyuse and Psk^{w}aws at Colville. Later he surveyed the Okanagan. His transcriptions are flawed but often identifiable to native speakers, relying on his findings as published at UW (Teit 1928).

In 1930, a field school for graduate students, mostly from Ivy League universities, concentrated on the locale, and produced a monograph eight years later, edited by Leslie Spier (1938), the professor in charge.

       This ethnographic study was made during July and August, 1930, by a group of graduate students participating in a field training course of the Laboratory of Anthropology (Santa Fe, New Mexico) under my direction. The party comprised Miss Rachel S Commons (of the University of Chicago), Miss May Mandelbaum (Columbia University), Emanuel Gonick (University of California), Walter Cline and Richard H. Post (Harvard University), who were joined by Miss LVW [Lucy Velpha] Walters, financed by the University of Washington. A collection was made for the Washington State Museum (University of Washington {Burke}), which has been used as the source of illustrations for this paper. [3]

       As a field for investigation for the group I hit on the Southern Okanogon {Okanogan}. The cultures of the southern Plateau in eastern Washington, Idaho, and western Montana have been neglected. It was, and is, my contention that the more typical forms of Plateau culture are to be found in the southern part of that area rather than in the north. Further, the solitary general ethnographic report published at the time, JH Spinden's "The Nez Perce Indians," tends to over-emphasize Plains elements, although these are demonstrably recent and superficial.

       After a choice of tribe to be studied had been made, I received through the kindness of Dr Franz Boas, a proof copy of James A Teit's "The Salishan Tribes of the Western Plateaus," which contains an account of the Okanogon. Since it appeared, however, that Teit's account was brief and that he had not obtained information from the Okanagon bands in Washington, it seemed wise to proceed with our plan. The results appear to justify the decision, for the culture of the American Okanagon was found appreciably different from that of the Canadian bands.

Since I felt that the training would be incomplete unless it included the preparation of a printable manuscript, each member of the party was requested to prepare a section of the general ethnographic account. This despite our awareness of the insufficiency of the data. Before we disbanded we discussed a suitable division of the material and reached an agreement on the manner of treatment. Actually, when it came to writing these sections, the authors saw fit to depart quite widely from the agreed form.

The several sections were allocated partly in accordance with preferences, partly by lot. All the field notes were then collected so that I might sort them by topics and dispatch them to the authors. It proved impracticable to send the whole set of notes or the finished manuscript to each in turn. Hence it fell to my lot as editor to scrutinize [4] the full set of notes to see that nothing was missed. The whole procedure was awkward, and without doubt valuable details and interrelations of phases of culture have been lost in the process.

It must be distinctly understood that each author is responsible only for the presentation of his topic, not for the content with all its inconsistencies and gaps. I, too, must share this responsibility: I have added, deleted, and otherwise changed these manuscripts to a considerable extent, for the most part without consulting the authors or initialling my contributions. This is especially true of the sections Material Culture and the Individual Life Cycle.

It is unanimously our feeling that this ethnographic account is incomplete and inaccurate. Local differences is culture seem to have been marked: informants had quite diverse backgrounds. These, plus the inevitable contradictions of informants, caused confusions which were never resolved. It is our feeling that the culture of the Sinkaietk should be restudied by one who will use these data as merely provisional.

The Southern Okanagon now live on and about the western part of the Colville Indian Reservation. They now number about 250-500. The group is much mixed, both by intermarriage with other peoples for generations and by the inclusion of many individuals of neighboring tribes. Add to this a high mobility, such that most or all of our informants had resided at one time or another with other peoples. Mixture and intergradation of bands and tribes in this area is clearly ancient and only accelerated by the concentration of interior Washington tribes on the Colville Reservation in the middle of the last century. The upshot is that the ascription of various items of culture to particular bands and tribes is exceptionally difficult.

The aboriginal culture is now largely a thing of the past. Older people maintain some aspects of their former economic life and material culture. There is some fishing at weirs; some gathering of berries and roots; some casual hunting. A few tipis and sweat lodges are in use; baskets and bark buckets are still made; occasionally a cradle board prepared and hides tanned in the old manner. The simple social structure has been adapted to reservation purposes, but is now nearly functionless. Shamanistic procedures, the winter dance, the Dream cult, and other organized religious activities of the ancient type are gone.[80] Yet, while many are at least nominal Catholics, the old religious outlook, with its emphasis on guardian spirits, prevails to a surprising degree.

The language is still functioning ... they are about as much deculturated as the Klamath or Walapai {where Spier researched tribes suffering oppressive conditions}.

The following notes on some of the informants and interpreters were prepared by the members of the party.

Michel Brooks, Southern Okanagon, aged 55, was born of a Canadian mother (Northern Okanagan ?). He remembers the old life as a little boy. His father and grandfather told him much of the old ways. [4b]

Cecile Brooks, about 58 years old, was born at the time of the great earthquake (1872 ?). Wife of Michel Brooks by the levirate. (Her first husband had been a cousin of Michel's and a son of Lucy Joe's.) Kalispel by birth, but married into the Kartar branch of the Okanagon at a rather early age (about fourteen). There got rather full technological training as well as some insight into the functioning of the social and religious order, and traditions about the tabus of menstruation and so forth, which were for the most part no longer practised. Very able and intelligent. Distinguished very carefully between customs of the Okanagon and those she knew of the Kalispel.

Lucy Joe, Kartar, aunt of Michel, was more than 70 years old. She first married at the time of the earthquake, or somewhat before: her oldest child died at the time of the Nez Perce war (1877). Remembered days before the establishment of the mission. Herself able and intelligent, she was respected and somewhat feared by the others, particularly as she had a reputation as an important shaman. She did not admit this power openly during the five days we [M.M. and R.S.C.] talked with her, but hinted at it. This may have colored her material on religion somewhat, but her disavowal of Catholicism was frank and clear enough. Had been strongly influenced by the Indian preachings of the local advocate of the Dream dance. Had travelled, particularly to the Thompson country. Intelligent and well-informed on economics and theoretical, social arrangements, ceremonies, and so forth.

Julie Josephine, also Kartar, probably about 80, but only a little older than Lucy Joe. These two are cousins: Lucy Joe calls Julie Josephine "older sister," since the father of the former was first cousin of Julie Josephine's mother (or more distantly related ?). This informant was good at specific details, such as relationships between actual individuals in a particular village. Time too short to get very much information.

Suszen Timentwa, 46 years old, present chief of the Kartar band, was born at Okanogan town. Ancestry is mixed Moses-Columbia and Kartar on his mother's side for several generations, father a Chelan. Intelligent person with mystical tendencies,

---

[80] Wrong. This fieldschool lasted a summer month, during the economic not religious season.

prone to formalise everything as a cosmic scheme centering around his religious ideas.[81]

Mary Carden, about 78 years old, member of the Tukoratum band. Her ancestry is Tukoratum and Chelan. Very shrewd, excellent memory, no scruples about divulging the past, and no pet philosophy to uphold.

Josephine Marchand, 59 years old, Mary's daughter. Her father was white. Considers [5] herself a Tukoratum. Excellent Interpreter; interest was not in the past but in financial returns. Annie Marchand, aged 16, her daughter, furnished a tale.

Chilowhist Jim was born at Entiat about sixty-five years ago. He came to Malott as a boy of eight or younger. His mother lived at Malott, his father at Entiat. He has been on the Methow River a great deal and still goes there often.

Old Harry is also from the southern end of the Okanogan River. He married at twenty-six; had twelve children by two successive wives; his youngest son is now forty; hence Old Harry must be about ninety.

Billie Joe was an unsatisfactory informant whose views were undoubtedly colored by wide contacts with other tribes: his father a Wenatchi; his mother Northern Okanagon from Penticton; his stepmother Wenatchi; and his wife a Wenatchi shaman.

Johnnie Louie, aged 49, served both as interpreter and informant. His affiliations seem to be mostly among the central and northern bands, but one or more of his grandparents were Colville, and there is a question how far be Identified himself with the Colville. Much of our Colville information was supplied by him. He is shrewd, intelligent, well-informed, and was active in furthering our enterprise.

Emma Louie, his wife, aged about 25, was also interpreter. She is Colville by birth, marriage, and normal residence. Nine years of mission school education. Adequate knowledge of languages; fairly intelligent, completely naive. Translations fairly accurate, as far as could be judged, and unbiased, but not always full enough.

Andrew Tillson, aged 78, affiliated with the northern bands and with the Northern Okanagon. Difficult to work with because of Johnnie's resentment of his deafness, and his character. Material seems to have been trustworthy whenever

---

[81] CB Suszen (1853-1949), at the death of Charlie Swimkim, was elected Okanogan chief during Easter rites of 25-27 April 1919. His native name was Kinemilt, though his mother endeared him as Susoonia "little one", which he later spelled as Suszun once his brothers and primers (not schooling) taught him to read and write. His typewrite incongruously is now at the University of Utah library. His wife was Lucy Jim, daughter of Chillowhist Jim, and they had six children; the oldest, George, killed in an Oregon racetrack stampede in 1936. CB laborious hand copied, later typed, government documents, and sent letters to DC. His large library was lost in a house fire, his Bible unfinished (Hart 2008; OCHS files).

certainly checked as his own.

Tom Martin, about 60 years old, member of the Inkamip band, Northern Okanagon. He gave reliable information, but there were many things about the past that he did not

Since this was written we learned of the untimely death of Rachel S Commons. In her we have lost an ethnographer of promise and a companion whose charm meant so much to our life in the Okanagon country.

Yale University September 1933

At Seattle's University of Washington, two local students, Verne Ray and Viola Garfield, earned early MAs and went East for their PhDs, Ray to Yale and Garfield to Columbia, with Boas focusing on Tsimshian where she had taught in a village school to earn money to finish college. Limited to Seattle and UW by her marriage and family, Garfield, the first UW MA, did not have other career options.

Home-grown, male, and mobile, Ray's career is especially instructive, dedicated to defining the Plateau Culture Area as we now know it. Growing up in Spokane, he attended UW (1924-28), studying mostly with Leslie Spier, and went on to UC Berkeley (1929-30). After Melville Jacobs joined UW in 1928, Ray returned for his MA, publishing his classic *Sanpoil ~ Nespelem* (1933) in the UW series. For his PhD, he followed Spier to Yale (1936-37), financed by the building of two Seattle houses using carpentry skills learned from self-help books. His definitive PhD on Plateau Cultural Relations (1939) moved him up the UW faculty ranks, then becoming a graduate school dean (1948-54, with time off at Yale) before resigning in 1966 to become expert witness for native land claims in court, based in DC. He retired to Port Townsend, and died in 2003 at the age of 98, outliving his family. His library and papers are at Gonzaga University in Spokane, notably not at UW.

Archaeology

A Methow survey [72] was authorized by Project 2 of the Division of Mines and Geology, Department of Conservation, State of Washington, Marshall Hutting, supervisor. It was set in motion by the Research Committee of the State College of Washington, Dr Richard Daugherty. The fieldwork (by Mr & Mrs Claude Warren, Matt Hill, Christopher Hulse, John Rice, Swanson family) was conducted in July and August, 1957, in conjunction with excavations at the old Astor trading post, Fort Okanogan.... A number of sites were unquestionably destroyed by the catastrophic 1938 flood, which tore out great sections of the floodplain as well as older terraces. At its mouth, the Methow deposited that year over 20 feet of coarse sand. Copies of report went to Olympia, Pullman, and Idaho State Museum, Pocatello. {Of note, publication was in *Tebiwa* 2 (1): 72-82, the journal of the Idaho State Museum, founded by UW anthro refugees} In addition, UW grad student, Robert Theodoratus began ethnographic study of the Methow with parents and grandparents of the 1980s generation.

In his summary, Swanson notes their findings:

Types of Sites

Talus Pits: Four excavated, two others seen, and two reported by an amateur. These are similar to talus pits elsewhere in eastern Washington: circles of dry-laid masonry, 7-10 feet in diameter (though sometimes oval), situated on rock slides. The pits of the Methow contain thick deposits of wood ash, charred pine cones and wood, and layers of rock, suggesting that these are a modified form of earth oven. No bone was found. Such a use would set these apart from talus pits elsewhere in the Plateau.3

Burials: Two "cemeteries" located (45OK36, -44). In both locations, burials are marked by rock circles about two feet in diameter, with at least 100 of these present at 36. That site also contains large rock cairns which may represent burials. An extended interment was turned up accidentally at 45OK39 by farm work, but no other data are available. Two burials were excavated on a hill above Winthrop in which the interred individuals were in a "sitting" position. This may have indicated tight flexure rather than upright position, though it was not possible to interview the amateurs {looters!} responsible.

Rockshelters: 45OK33, -45, -47. The last of these contained an unusual pictograph (Fig. 2), but deposits were scanty, and had possibly been removed by road construction in front. Shelter 45 was tested, with negligible results. 45OK34 is of prime importance. It contains pictographs of several ages, some of which are Northwest Coast in character (See Figs. 2, 3, 4). The sequence is uncertain, but it seems that the masks are more recent than the paintings in Group 5, while Group 7 is probably most recent of all, judging from the horse and rider and from the fresher condition of the paint in a more exposed location. Trenching beneath the overhang evidenced a hearth, a mano {hand grinder} of rectangular shape, and a few flakes.

Housepits: 45OK-30, -33, -35, -37, -40, -41, -42. Sites -40, -41 need testing for verification. Circular depressions, 20-28 feet in diameter, up to 2½ feet deep, were identified at sites 35 and 37 for a total of five. One of these at site 35 contains the stump of a 300 year old ponderosa pine, cut some 20 years ago, thus providing a <u>terminus post quem</u> of c.1640 A.D. Square depressions, up to 30 feet across, as much as 3 feet deep, were recorded at sites 30, 33, 35, and 42, for a total of four. Three rectangular depressions were recorded at site 33, so that at least three different ground plans are present in the Methow River valley. Two houses were excavated at 45OK30, two tested at 35.

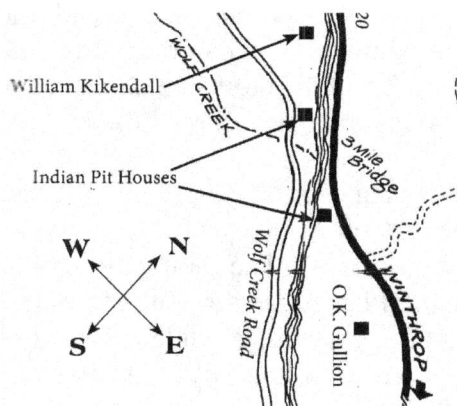

Sweathouses: 45OK-35, -37. Small circular structure and a pile of fire-cracked rock being eroded away by Methow River at site 35. One described for site 37 has been completely destroyed.

Historic Data: Three sites (45OK-37, -42, -46) are known to have been used by Methow Indians within the last 60 years. Mr Kikendall, of Winthrop, witnessed a burial at site 37 in 1909. His comments are of interest since this location also possesses house depressions. In 1909 the Indians were mounted on horses, used a travois, and lived in tipis, spending only a portion of the summer in the upper valley. Similar accounts were given by other people [74] in the upper valley concerning a large campground below Twisp, now intensively farmed. This site (42) was one where "large numbers" of Indians died around the turn of the century from complications associated with measles. The complications apparently developed in connection with sweat baths which were followed by plunges into the icy Methow River! Mr Lloyd Williams, of the town of Methow, informed us that 45OK46 was used for fishing in 1908. A mat blind, however, was used rather than a platform. A rock causeway one mile below Twisp, used by Indians for fishing, was destroyed in 1948, but a wooden platform still survives at site 30, near the mouth of the river. Both were used until "a few years ago." An old Methow Indian still comes in the autumn to the Kikendall Ranch above Winthrop, for the purpose of spearing salmon. Mr Kikendall described the spears to us as being either three or four-tined, barbed, and of two pieces of wood glued and bound together. Mr Williams said that the spears used in 1908 at 45OK46 were of variable length, four-fined, and barbed. Below the platform at 45OK30, a three-tined, barbed, two-piece arrow was retrieved from brush along the river's edge. Neither Mr Kikendall nor Mr Williams recalled the use of arrows. During the excavations at Fort Okanogan, however, a broken wooden pole with three freely moving gang hooks was recovered from the surface near the Okanogan River. Thus, whether the technique used at the Kikendall Ranch by that solitary figure out of the past represents the survival of a once-common custom is not clear. Certainly it will not be carried on much longer.

All local white in the valley old enough to remember told of an upriver occupation by Indians in the last 50-60 years during the summer months. Winters were spent along the Columbia, though no one seemed to remember the type of winter dwelling in use.

Artifacts: These are few in number, even where excavation took place. See Tables I and III. Private collections revealed polished "jadeite" adzes and chisels from the entire length of the valley. They conform to finds elsewhere in north central Washington. Unadorned pestles were common all over, while two elaborately carved specimens came from the Twisp-Winthrop area. The finds from 45OK30 are considered below.

Pictographs: No petroglyphs {pecked stone} were observed, which fits with Cain's observation that they were lacking in the northern part of the Plateau. The pictograph {painted stone} at 4OK47 (Fig. 2) seems to be an abstract form of an animal referred to as a "water monster" and found at five locations in Central Washington.

The large number of pictographs at 45OK34 (Figs. 2, 3, 4) presents a variety of styles and paint colors. Some were organized into groups, definable by their arrangement and the proximity of the figures, and by similarities and differences in paint used. Paints ranged from a very light orange in Group 5 (Fig. 3) to a very dark red in Group 1 (though badly faded). Because of the variable exposures, differences in weathering offer no reliable clue to the relative chronology of the groups.

The two figures in Group 1 bear similarities to several human figures described by Cain. One is a phallic male, to use Cain's term, but is paired with another figure ("Brothers") which may, however, represent a female. The male figure exhibits X-Ray ribs. The mountain goat in Group 2 and the [75] deer in Group5 are found elsewhere in the Plateau, as are the concentric circles in Group 5, and the "tally mark" series in the same group. The spread-eagle appearance of the one human figure in Group 3 is found along almost the entire Columbia River, and was associated with an uncertain quadruped, a category which in the Plateau has a more restricted north-south distribution than the human figure of spread-eagle type. According to Cain, the lizard form in Group 7 is also a common Plateau feature.

The rather large face to the left of Group 1, in dark red (Fig. 2) is, however, unusual, and the faces shown in Figure 4 are not Plateau in style.[82] They are definitely reminiscent of Northwest Coast masks in style, and one of them resembles a Kwakiutl death mask in the Bossom Collection at the Canadian National Museum. Apart from these, the pictographs are predominantly Plateau in style and probably, therefore, in

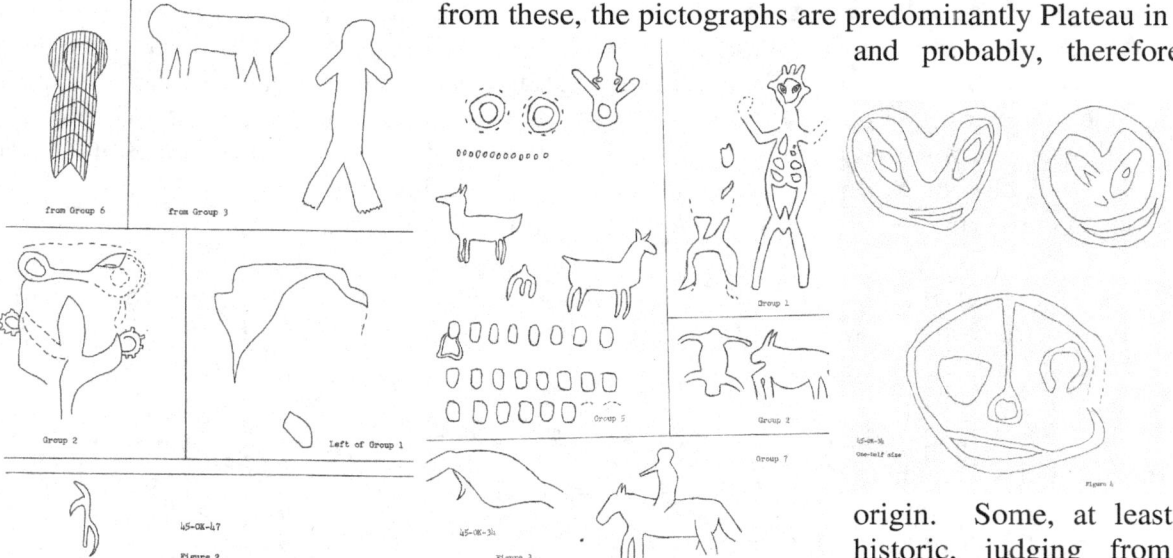

origin. Some, at least, are historic, judging from the mounted horseman. Most are probably prehistoric. The diversity at this site is unusual in the Plateau.

Excavations at 45OK30: This site, near the mouth of the Methow River, was subject to testing. Two houses were visible in profile (see Fig. la for one of them) and a later, square house depression was visible on the surface. This is the second instance of superimposed houses in the Central Plateau,[83] and these in turn are above a layer containing artifacts but no structural features. Tabulations of artifacts and non-artifact material are shown in Tables I and II. The stratigraphy was the same in each house, and both are similar in size and profile. From the limited testing we could not determine the plan of either house. Both have deep depressions in the center, possibly old hearths, or even earth ovens. House A yielded most of the material recovered, and the most notable change is in non-artifacts. Level 8 at House A, which is the camp layer beneath the earliest floor of the house, provided mammal bone only. In the layers associated with the use of the house, fish bone becomes of equal importance, quantitatively, and mussel shell is present in small quantities in the latest level (7-8) at House B. Some change in food sources appears to have taken place. The most distinctive implements are shown in Figure la. The bi-pronged object is similar to specimens further south, as is the round scraper (knife?). Both date from the Cayuse phases or post-1300 A.D, in the Vantage region. The steep scraper

---

[82] These three faces are vertical on the rockshelter wall, with the blinking eye one (upper right) in three dimensions since it painted on both sides of a rocky protrusion.

[83] The correlation of survey sites with state registry is MV 1 = 45OK 30, MV 2 = -32, MV 3 = -31, MV 4 = -34, MV 5 = -33, MV 6 = -35.

illustrated is a degenerate form of the steep scraper found through a great span of time in the Vantage region, and which went through a fairly well defined series of changes. The specimen found in level 3 at House A appears to be the tag end of the typological series and, therefore, quite late in time.

Levels 15 and 16 in House B, and levels 3, 5, 7, 8 in House A are beneath a fossil A horizon from an old soil. Level 7 in House B represents a later floor cut down into the A horizon at a time when it was still forming, so that once the house was abandoned and began to fill, the sediments developed the characteristics of the A horizon. This in fact suggests that occupation of level 7, House B, was brief. This is an interesting phenomenon mainly because this soil horizon is found elsewhere in the Plateau, and at Vantage it is clear that at least the Cayuse I-II phases follow the termination of soil formation. If the fossil soil at this site is comparable to that at Vantage and elsewhere, then it suggests that the development represented by the Cayuse phases began earlier in northern portions of the [76] Columbia Plateau.

Figure 1 – A: Profile of House B, 450K30 [83]. Level 5 is clayey silt, 6 is fine gravel, 8 is gray to dark brown find sand, 9 light yellow sand, 10 very dark brown, 11, a light tan sand, 14 is extremely compact, very chalky colored clay (?); level 15 is fine sand, yellow to red with evidence of burned particles included; 16 is coarse gray sand, 17 light yellow-tan, horizontally bedded, and darker yellow at base. Definite evidence of two floors with one occupation preceding building of the house. The dip in the first floor may represent a fireplace exposed tangentially.

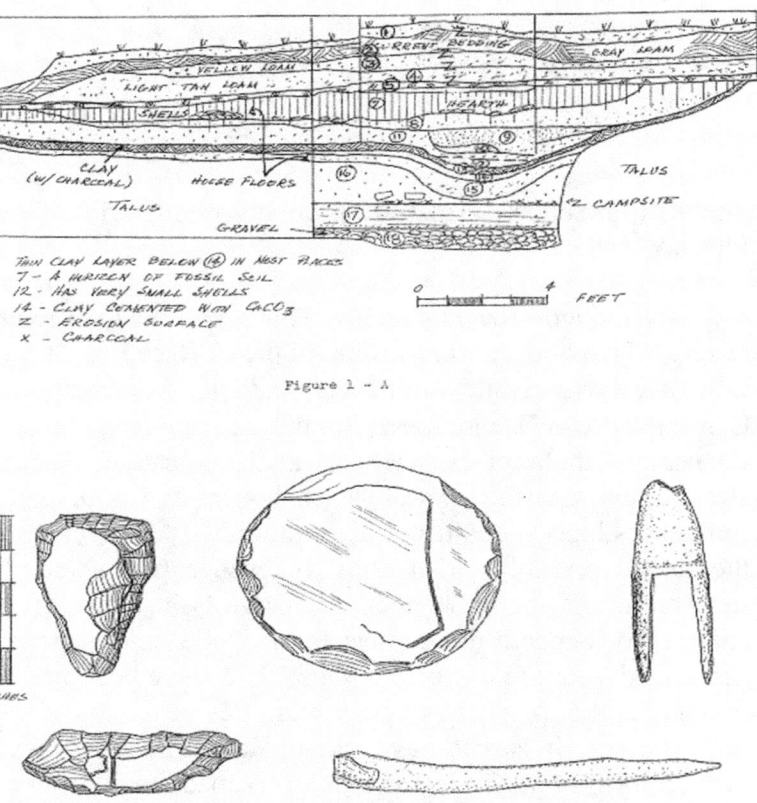

Figure 1 – B: Artifacts from 45OK30. Left to right: steep scraper of chalcedony (2½ x 1¼ x 3/8 in.), a round knife of quartzite (2-7/8 in. diameter x 5/8 in.), bipronged object (2¼ x 3/4 x ½ in,), a curved scraper of chert (2¼ x 7/8 x 5/16 in.), and fibula bone awl (4 x 7/16 x ¼ in.)

Images on Rock

Methow traditions provide insightful understanding into the profoundly cultural and spiritual importance of rock writing beyond, actually primordially before, human dimensions usually assumed to provide their meanings. After reviewing work specific to the Methow, discussion expands to include reports from the Amero-Canadian Plateau, especially by James Teit, and ends with wider considerations. While rock images[84] are usually assumed to be colored or pecked markers made by humans, they are long preceded by primordial signs left by a creator to instruct life forms – humans, other species, sentients – yet to appear. In addition, there are special flash point spots marked in white at the moment that the world transformed ~ capsized into that of today, at the instigation, good and bad, of Coyote.

Cain

In July and August of 1945, (Harvey) Thomas Cain undertook a full time study of midColumbia rock art, now called rock writing, by car, boat, horse, afoot, given WW II time travel restrictions and man-power shortages. Most especially, he relied on amateur recorders, such as Howard Cundy.[85] Cain's key contribution was rigorous identifying of motifs and plotting distributions after a preliminary reconnaissance that took place in the Winter and Spring before low water in the Fall made access more available.

---

[84] Mark DeLeon – archaeologist for Okanogan National Forest in Omak, Bureau of Reclamation in Yakima, Grant County PUD – worked closely with Plateau tribal representatives for many years, noting Colvilles prefer the term "rock images" for these features, some of which are "messages" that native specialists could read (pc 3/24/16).

[85] Cain's booklet (1950) is problematic, as noted by William Layman, rock art devotee and scribe of the upper Columbia. Overall Cain ignores scale and general layout in favor of aesthetically rearranged figures, though he usefully tallied motifs and charted distributions. At Sentinal Gap, he misidentifies petroglyphs as pictographs, while at Selah Canyon he provided good records. Working during WWII, with rationed gas and film so scarce he took few if any photographs, Cain and others, such as Doug Osborne at UW, well knew that dams would soon flood many of these sites. Funded by Washington State (now Burke) Museum and sponsored by Erna Gunther, advice came from UW, Bureau of Reclamation, Smithsonian's Columbia River Basin Survey, EB Sayles of Arizona State Museum, and Emil Haury of University of Arizona Anthropology, which awarded Cain a Masters. UW published his thesis as a booklet on 1 November 1950, when he was at Harvard. In 1953, Cain became the first salaried staff, later director, of the famous Heard Museum in Phoenix, where he spent an enthusiastic career.

Cain's main guide and source, briefly thanked, for many of these sites was Harold J Cundy, a Wenatchee regional salesman for Centennial Flour, Peach Blossom Brand, who produced his own meticulous pen and ink drawings of MidColumbia rock writings with layouts and contexts, along with carefully detailed notations, some from Mourning Dove ~ Christine Quintasket. His notes and a memoir are at Wenatchee and his report is at Washington State Historical Society in Tacoma.

The Methow sites were:

WINTHROP (Fig. 12) SITE 12 [14] Pictographs: It is possible to be certain of the outlines of only five figures at this site. Faint traces of color show in many places, but weathering and  lichen growth preclude anything else in the way of definite figures. The group is found on a large granite boulder two miles north of the Eight Mile Ranger Station (situated northeast of the town of Winthrop). The boulder is 100 feet above the bed of Chewak Creek. An overhang on the east side of the rock forms a small natural shelter that is of sufficient size to hold the body of one person. This crevice is well smoke-blackened and was probably used as a shelter as well as a fireplace. The elongated "rake" design is shown in *d, e.*

METHOW VALLEY (Fig. 13) SITE 13 Pictographs: These are located eight miles north of 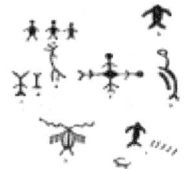 Winthrop, across the road and the creek from an abandoned sawmill. The figures are painted on a large single boulder about 100 feet above the Methow River on the east side. The figures are on the west surface of the rock and are badly weather stained and difficult to follow. There is no evidence of a camp site or any reason for a trail to have been used on the bare rock of this steep hillside. Many ideal camp sites are to be found along the river flats, and there are remains of a pit house about one mile north of the pictographic site. No other pictographs were found in the vicinity. Figure *e* has been classed as a conventionalized bird. Whether g should be classed as the same is open to question. Another unusual treatment of the "brothers" is shown in *f.*

PATEROS RAPIDS (Fig. 15) SITE 15 Petroglyphs: This is the only site with  petroglyphs north of Wenatchee. They are carved on the north surface of a large granite boulder about 50 yards above the river (at low water stage) on the east bank of the Columbia, one-half mile south of Pateros. The rock is quite difficult to find. The carvings are very badly weathered for they are covered during the high water stages. The carving averages one-sixteenth of an inch in depth.

Resurveys in the Methow recorded the same sites in better detail and layout, though still lacking any native cultural interpretations. William Layman provided comparisons (→) for one of the most complex arrays, at OK82, the 82nd site recorded in Okanogan County, Washington State.

45OK82
Featherston, 1993

45OK82
Cain, 1945-6

45OK82
Cundy, 1936

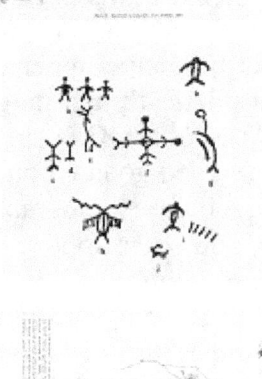

Human

In the apt phrase of Thompson elder Annie York, *They Write Their Dreams on the Rock Forever* as a way to retain some of the vital energy gained from a spirit during a successful vision quest. This emphasis on human effort derives from reports by James Teit – a transplanted Shetlander whose wife Lucy Artko was Thompson – recruited, trained, and funded by Franz Boas to survey Plateau Interior Salish tribes. Teit was already fluent in Thompson and familiar with neighboring Salishan languages when he met Boas in 1896, as well as a strong advocate for native rights, fueled by his own Scots background. Waxtko, a Thompson matron, described her interpretation of rock images marking a girl's puberty site.[86]

In the interior of British Columbia numerous rock paintings are found, most of which are laid on in red ochre. Many of these have the appearance of having been made quite recently. Mr James Teit has had the good fortune to find one near Spence's Bridge, BC, which the Indians were able to explain in detail.

According to the custom of the Thompson River Indians, who form a branch of the Salishan family, girls on reaching maturity must retire to the hills where they undergo a long ceremony of purification and make offerings to secure good luck. At the end of this period they record their offerings and the ceremonies that they have performed on a boulder. The subjects of these records are therefore identical in many cases, and all the women of the tribe are able to interpret their meaning. Mr Teit found a boulder of this sort near Skaitok,[87]1 about one mile northeast of Spence's Bridge. It is partly imbedded in the ground and faces northward and southward. The paintings are all on the south side. The size of the boulder is about six feet square, and it rises to a height of four feet above the ground. The paintings occupy a space about 5 feet by 4 feet in size.

The explanations were given by Waxtko,[88]2 an old woman living at Spence's Bridge. In giving her explanations she stated that she had made paintings of the same character when undergoing the ceremonial of purification at the time when she reached maturity, and that she was perfectly familiar with the meanings of all the designs. According to her statement the paintings were made by various girls at the time when they reached maturity. This is borne out by the appearance of the paintings, some of which are quite fresh, while others appear old and indistinct. [228]

In order to facilitate description I have numbered the paintings, and where it seemed desirable, separated the individual figures by broken lines.

FIG. 1. - The crossing of two trails. At such places girls used to bury part of the food they were given after having fasted four days at the beginning of the period of purification.

---

[86] Bulletin American Museum of Natural History, Volume VIII: 227-30, Edited, from Notes of the Collector, by Franz Boas: A Rock Painting of the Thompson River Indians, British Columbia by James Teit, 1896. {Of note, these images link women and plants.}

[87] #1 o = o in German *voll*. {as a guide to pronouncing this sound}

[88] #2 x = aspirate guttural, like *ch* in Scotch *loch*.

ROCK PAINTING, THOMPSON RIVER INDIANS, B. C.

FIG. 2. - Crossing of trails; see Fig. 1.

FIG. 3. - Four fir branches, such as the girl had to deposit at the entrance of her lodge, which was built of three or four fir branches. The horizontal line connecting the three branches at the left hand side indicates that they were placed near each other.

FIG. 4. - A fir branch, the needles of which have been plucked off; used as an offering. The girls pluck the needles one by one, that their fingers may become nimble, and that they may not grow tired by the work that will be her share in life.

FIG. 5. - A girl's lodge, made of fir branches. The lower portion of the figure up to the dotted line represents fir branches that hang down from the roof of the lodge. The girl plucks the needles from these one by one. The top of the figure represents the roof of the lodge, or the fir branches placed in front of the entrance, like Fig. 3.

FIGS. 6, 7, 8. - Crossing of trails; see Fig. 1.

FIG. 9. - A fir branch; see Fig. 3.

FIG. 10. - The explainer was in doubt if this figure was a poor representation of a fir branch-it will be noticed that the short central line at the base is missing-or if it meant a trench with a fir branch at each end. Girls used to dig trenches in order to attain skill and endurance in digging roots and doing hard work of all kinds.

FIG. 11. - The cross line on top of this figure and the two downward lines to the right represent the roof of a fir lodge. The long line with the short diverging lines at its lower end represent a fir branch which is suspended from the roof of the lodge, the needles of which have been plucked off; see Fig. 5.

FIG. 12. - A snake, which had probably formed the subject of one of the girl's dreams.

FIG. 13. - The two long lines [230] which cross at right angles represent the crossing of trails. The four short lines which run downward from the horizontal line represent four sticks that are placed at the crossing as an offering. The longer line to the right with its two diverging branches represents a fir branch that is also placed at the crossing.

FIG. 14. - The unfinished edge of a mat or of some other kind of basketry work. Girls had to make, during the period of isolation, small mats and baskets in order to become expert in this line of work. The painting represents work of this kind that the girl has done.

FIG. 15. - Crossing of trails; see Fig. 1.

FIG. 16. - Either two trenches (see Fig. 10), or two sticks given as an offering, or simply the numeral two (2) having reference to the snake (Fig. 12), or to another of the surrounding figures.

FIG. 17. - A fir branch; see Fig. 3.

FIG. 18. - The unfinished edge of a mat; see Fig. 14.

FIG. 19. - An animal, probably a dog, which had formed the subject of one of the girls' dreams.

FIG. 20. - A fir branch; see Fig. 3.

FIG. 21. - A fir branch; see Fig. 3.

FIG. 22. - An animal, probably a dog, which had formed the subject of one of the girls' dreams.

FIG. 23. - The unfinished edge of a mat; see Fig. 14.

FIG. 24. - A fir branch; see Fig. 3.

FIG. 25. - The upper part of this figure represents the crossing of trails. The branches farther down represent fir branches set up as offerings at the crossing.

FIG. 26. - The unfinished edge of a mat; see Fig. 14.

FIG. 27. - A fir branch; see Fig. 3.

FIG. 28. - Either a fir branch or an imperfect representation of a fir lodge.

More generally, during his survey of US tribes, Teit[89] describes wider applications of these images on a variety of artifacts and places, as portals or sources for residual *puwha*.

---

[89] Salishan Tribes of the Western Plateaus [Okanagan, Flathead, Coeur d'Alene] 1927: 23-396.

Coeur d'Alene [194] Men painted images or representations or symbols of their guardian spirits and pictures of their most important dreams on their clothes, robes, shields, and weapons.

Pictographs of battles, and of important events or experiences in a person's life, were also painted on robes, which in consequence were treated with great care. Pictures and symbols of guardian spirits were also often painted or tattooed on the body. It was believed that these pictures had offensive or defensive power derived directly from the guardian spirit. (See p169) Thus a man who had an arrow tattooed or painted on his arm, if the arrow was [194] one of his guardians, believed that his arm was made more efficient for shooting. In the same way a mountain tattooed or painted on the arm rendered it strong provided the mountain was a guardian of the person. Likewise the reproduction of a bear or deer on the arm gave the person skill in bear und deer hunting, provided these animals were the guardians of the hunter. Most of the painted designs on shields had a protective meaning. Some of the common figures were mountains, arrows, sun, eagle, hawk, and owl. War horses were often painted with representations of guardians and dreams, and the horse itself was a guardian of some men. Tents also were painted with pictures and symbols of guardians and dreams, or with geometrical designs.

ROCK PAINTINGS — Rock paintings were common in some parts of the country, but I did not hear of any petroglyphs. The nearest rock paintings to the present location of the Coeur d'Alene are said to be at Chatcolat. There was no belief that spirits or "land mysteries" made certain rock paintings. All were made by people. Besides being records of dreams, objects seen in dreams, guardian spirits, battles, and exploits, they were supposed to transmit power from the object depicted to the person making the pictures. Young men during their puberty ceremonials made rock paintings, but girls very seldom did. From time to time older men also painted dreams on cliffs.

IMAGES OF GUARDIAN SPIRITS — Men formerly carved images of their guardian spirit. These were generally stone figures of animals, birds, and men, or parts of them. Usually they were small and kept in the medicine bag. Occasionally they were kept in view in the lodge. Most figures were of human form, not because the men who made them had guardians of human form, but because almost all guardian spirits could assume human form; and most men preferred to represent them in manlike form. Sometimes a guardian spirit would appear in dreams to his protegé in human form only and, were not he himself to reveal his identity, his protegé would not know what he was and what his name. He might say, "I am the coyote," "I am the grizzly bear that runs." "I am the grizzly bear that walks," and so on. Sometimes he might say, "I am the one who helps you," and then add some description of himself as an animal, so that his protegé knew him.

Some stone images did not resemble any known animals, because they were representations of beings, or of parts of beings, seen in dreams. Some resembled mythical beings, "mysteries," and animals, which Indians had never seen alive, but only in dreams and visions. [?? 332] Compare also war dress (p. 118). [195]

Some were even of a composite character, such as half animal and half human. Human figures were made full size; arms and legs, also busts, consisting of head and neck, or head and upper part of body. Most figures were made in an erect posture, but some in other attitudes. Many were made nude, and some were carved clothed. Others, not made this why, were clothed by painting and by adding decorations such as feathers. Usually the image was made to correspond to the figure and dress of the guardian spirit as he usually appeared. These stone images were regarded with considerable reverence, and were thought to possess a mystic power beneficial to the owner, but sometimes injurious to others. Therefore these figures were never bought or sold, or treated as mere ornaments or works of art. In fact, they were seldom or never handled except by the owner, and when he died they were placed in his grave or deposited near by. They were inherited only in a few cases – for instance, when son and father had the same guardian. Then the image would be of some service to the son as he would "know " the guardian it represented. A long time ago these images were common. They were not generally carried around on hunting expeditions, but were left at home in the lodge.

Other images were made rather for ornament. They were generally set up in view in the lodge, and may have been house ornaments. It is doubtful, however, if this was their only purpose. It seems, at any rate, that they were not considered real images of guardian spirits, although some people thought they were connected with them. It is said that even they were considered "mystery and never sold. In rare instances some of them were given to friends who were not afraid of them. As a rule, they were larger than the images cf guardian spirits, perhaps about 12 or 15 cm. in height. No images of any kind were treated as family property; they were the sole property of the person who made them, in the same way as a medicine bag. If the owner died in a distant place without his medicine bag and without the image of his guardian, his relatives placed these objects in the forest or burned them. In a few cases the image was kept and placed in or by the grave of the next one of his family who died, even if it was a mere child. A few images of both kinds were carved of wood or antler, but most were stone.

Primordial ~ Archetypes

Yet before these human derived markings are images left by the Creator to instruct "people coming soon" via awakening consciousness. As CB Suszen Timentwa reinforced:

When they [spirits] woke each [tribe] up, they told the humans, "Here are roots; salmon to spear; berries to pick. This is food." They told them how to eat…. You look and see how you should do." God had put the pictures there. From then until now, people go there and look at pictures of salmon traps and bow and arrows. People make these just like the pictures. People still learn from the rock. (The pictures are red.)

Thus, these initial images show NOT a bow hunter of today, but a template for a bow to construct and use – along with weirs, surrounds, and utensils – at the beginning of human awareness of time. Indeed, this explanation has universal application since it also explains the placement of rock images in Nevada near game trails and ambush sites, not to mark current hunting blind locations but to continue them from very orderly beginnings. CB Suszen specifically identified these as red, obvious standouts from their context and background.

As Teit (1930a: 418-19) noted

"Red signified 'good' in a general sense. It also expressed life, existence, blood, heat, fire, light, day. Some say it also meant the earth. It appears also to have had the meaning self, friendship, success.
Black had a meaning opposite to that of red....
White had the meaning of a 'spirit' color, and stood for ghost, spirit world, dead people, skeleton, bones, sickness, coming from the dead".

Pictographs showing visionary experiences had figures with a rayed circle drawn around their heads. Grant (1967: 92) distinguishes this "balloon" as "a motif that is very often seen ... in the Columbia drainage – a semicircular shape with attached rays," showing emanations from within, an "aura". Teit (1930: 194) illustrates several anthropomorphs with auras, remarking that most guardian spirits were pictured in this human form. Similarly, near Nespelem a red pictograph called "salmon" marking the locale of First Salmon Ceremonies portrays a phallic figure with an aura because only men attended this rite, thanking the male chief of salmon.

Flash Points

Much of native literature teaches by negative examples of bad behavior, but when the land is the concern, concern is with anticipation ~ preparation for the age of humans "coming soon". At Creator's instigation, Coyote was responsible for many of these coming changes. When the Change did come, it was momentous and instantaneous, described like capsizing or a flashing burst. Remaining forever are special white markings, such as the dog named *mikmik* on a cliff at Lake Chelan and the standing salmon spear at Lost River. Elsewhere a foggy white haze surrounds rock images.

The world change ~ apocalypse was repeated in microcosm at the burial of a visionary in a talus slope. When he or she died, their vision spirit briefly also went into the grave, then, as it departed, left a white residue[90] on the stone cairn as a "consecration mark" of its transformation.

James Teit's classic study of body decoration among the Thompsons of British Columbia cites a shaman named Baptiste ~ Iron Stone, who died in 1902, reporting "White had the meaning of a 'spirit' color, and stood, for ghosts, spirit world, dead, people, skeleton, bones, sickness, coming from the dead" (1930a: 419). Among the Kootenay, shamans also wore white paint at all times (Turney-High 1941: 94). Further, rock images sometimes had shiny fixatives; Teit (same: 37, 218) specifically mentions a beaver tail rubbed over newly applied pigment by the Coeur d'Alene, while the Okanogan smeared cactus gum over paintings.

---

90 Shiny white lines along rock edges abound in talus, territorial markings left by generations of rodent urine, whose nitrites drain off to promote the growth of lichens in this arid climate as residues slowly build up into white precipitates. Sometimes gathered together on burial cairns, they indicate that indeed everything has a human purpose and meaning.

Signpost Messages on the Land

In summary, the world over, humans painted, pecked, and sculpted markings on smooth rock surfaces. Later people attribute them to powerful causes, sometimes spiritual, sometimes ancestral, sometimes both. No better example of human reverential relations with the land can be found than such "rock art writing," which is best described as a system of notation for showing special human relations with the land in all of its dimensions. When natives provide interpretations, they mention concentrations of vital energy (*puwha*) available to and for adepts.

Unlike graffiti, done anywhere by anyone, these markings required special privilege and blessings. In some native belief, after the world was made, a Changer (or a team of transformers) went through the landscape preparing the way for humans. Sometimes these changes were deliberate, and sometimes they were inadvertent or clumsy, depending on the characters involved. Two-way rivers and abundant foods were taken away so that humans would be motivated by not having life too easy. In other cases, brambles were provided with berries and trees impregnated with fire so that humans would later benefit.

In the process, the most dangerous inhabitants of the earth – variously called monsters, cannibals, dangers, and demons – were reformed, modified, or petrified. For example, whenever a Changer met monsters, he variously sent them into the earth under a hill (for DunneZa), dismembered the body to fling pieces in various directions (for Lushootseed), petrified the body on the spot (for Pueblo), or turned a giant into something harmless. Thus, Mosquito was once a huge blood-sucking killer until a Changer burned its body, with ashes becoming tiny bugs that continue to plague the world, reduced to nuisance rather than fatal menace (unless teamed with a lethal germ like malaria, yellow fever, or, now, West Nile virus).

To mark each of these sites of transformation, particularly to remind humans of acts done for their benefit, rock art appeared, usually at river rapids, springs, trails, and mountain peaks. Often, these markings indicate the type of being or *puwha* who is fixed there to become available as a spirit partner, as well as providing direct physical contact through touching the image. When a boy or girl had a successful encounter during a vigil, they marked clothing and other artifacts with a disguised sign of its source.

Shamans, however, did even more by marking details of their own visions on outcrops near the site where each happened.[91] Because shamans dealt with great reserves of *puwha*, their marks served to substantiate and harness these flowings. Using red iron oxide (ocher), black carbon, and, rarely, white glaze, the source and direction of the *puwha* was vaguely indicated, as a reminder to the shaman and others who came after him or her that vital *puwha* flowed from that spot. Yet the pictographic representations were never explicit because that would reveal too much and make the *puwha* both too accessible and too ordinary. The colors show what is otherwise unseen, and red ocher indicates that which is holy.

---

[91] Annie York, Richard Daly, and Chris Arnett, *They Write Their Dreams on the Rock Forever: Rock Writings of the Stein River Valley of British Columbia* 1993. Mallory (1972) surveys the world in 1893, Young (1988) is Zuni, and Williams (2001) is a Kwakwaka'wakw 1998 cliff face by Marianne Nicholson, with spray paint acrobatics by Val Fraser.

Like an icon painter in the Orthodox Church tradition, the shaman in trance became a channel for the flow of *puwha*. Thus, he or she could also apply marks to other locations to spread powerful influence. In this way, approaches to the town or camp where the shaman lived were marked with signs of his or her *puwha* as counter-protection against enemies or hostile thoughts. More than boundary markers, these images were warding-offs, warning signs, legal claims, and military challenges to any enemies venturing too near and intending harm.

In general, rock art research indicates a great disparity between cultural perspectives. While researchers, both amateur[92] and academic, have concentrated on the locale of these markings near springs and game trails, supposedly indicating likely hunting places (where life and death compete),[93] natives themselves emphasize that such markings – whether on rocks, debarked trees, or cave walls – really interlink these spirits, species, and humans at that place from its beginnings. Like a carved totem pole, which grew out of this same tradition, the marks were a "claim" ~ "deed" ~ "covenant" between place and people in all shapes and intelligences. More than "signs from the ancestors", rock art is a kind of aboriginal writing, a messaging signpost preserved at a revered place which was simultaneously a university, cathedral, library, and Eden. These seen designs instruct later generations of well-trained questers, who fast in proximity to such images to gain success for a career that benefitted themselves and their people – human and otherwise. They, like earth mounds, focus vitality through the ages.

Moreover, rock panels are rarely smooth surfaces to better show off figures drawn from visions. Many spots show forceful acts, especially in lava with petrified bends, twists, and arcs indicating violent times and upheavals and enhancing such overlaid images. Such primordial geologic turmoils fueled later pecked or painted images tapping into earthly energies. As conduits of power, therefore, images on rocks are doubly significant as both global and personal messages of active enduring informing powers.

Ballards

Mainstays of the Methow were Ballard brothers; miners, surveyors, guides, and engineers. The youngest, Arthur, remained at the family homestead south of Seattle, where he recorded and wrote important volumes about Puget Sound natives, their lives and stories. While his older brothers were also literate, they chronicled local history in lieu of native neighbors. They appear in this book both as an apt instance of a "near miss" for Methows but also in hope that they too left unknown records on natives in the family scholarly tradition.

Charles and Hazard, of the second set of siblings by their father Levi's third marriage, worked in mining and both settled in the Methow, with a prosperous mine in Harts, formerly Slate, Pass. Charles (1858 – 1934, wed Anna Elliott 1893) and Hazard Ira (1868 – 1938, wed Zora Mae Johnson 1901), were often joined by Leon (1870 – ? , wed Martha ?), who seems to have been a jack of all trades, from woodsman to miner to merchant.

---

[92] These amateurs had no scientific motives: Harold Cundy (1930s) was a curious local who later turned to James Churchward's "Lost Mu", Oluf Lauritzson Opsjohn (c1919) sought battle scenes between natives and Norse Vikings, and Debora Featherstone (1980s) was motivated by native family ties. The lasting value of their works lies in the accuracy of their images and layouts, not motivations.

[93] Robert Heizer and Martin Baumhoff, *Prehistoric Rock Art of Nevada and Eastern Cal* 1962.

Their life-long mining enterprises began with the opening of the Okanogan district. Because a treaty never was negotiated with most MidColumbia Interior Salish, after several false starts, Moses and his intertribal community was given lands in 1879 stretching to the British Canadian border, but, for national security, a 15 mile strip along the northern boundary was returned to public domain on 23 Feb 1883 and then entirely legal abolished, allowing mineral entry on 1 May 1886. Soon after arriving on horseback, Charles and Hazard successfully prospected at Ruby Hill, Salmon City, later renamed Conconully. Virtually the only profitable gold mines in the North Cascades, the Azurite and Gold Hill were found on opposite sides of the same ridge near Hart's Pass. Charles Ballard staked the Azurite in 1916 and Hazard Ballard claimed Gold Hill in 1917. Just after Charles died, Hazard sold his mine in 1935 and became manager of the Azurite.[94]

As a mining and civil engineer, Charles plated Okanogan towns of Ruby, Conconully (~Salmon City), Swansea, Oroville, Chelan (1889), and located Mammorth Mine near Barron (1895) before the Azurite (1916). He also served as probate judge. Charles and Anna moved to Twisp in 1917, both are buried in Washelli Cemetery, Seattle.

Hazard and Zora (1875 – 1956) married and bought a hotel at Robinson Creek in 1901, near her Wehmeyer family, before buying in 1916 the Mayfield homestead at Lost River, the same year they staked their Azurite claims. As a widow, Zora continued to run pack trains and sell famous boysenberries. They are buried in Johnsons Sullivan Cemetery at Winthrop.

Their youngest brother Arthur was born 18 October 1876 on the family homestead near Slaughter, a town platted in 1886 by his brother Charles on land homesteaded by his father Levi. He named it in honor of Lt William A Slaughter, who stood silhouetted by firelight when he and others were killed by hostiles on 4 December 1855 during the Treaty War. Later the name was changed to Auburn, less sanguinary and more genteel to its growing population in rural King County. As a child, Ballards had a native nanny, and Arthur learned to speak Lushootseed.

Levi (1858 – 1897) was born in New Hampshire, educated in public schools and Hancock Academy, and trained as an MD at Western Reserve Medical in Cleveland, Ohio. He was married thrice, widowed twice (Phebe 1844-50, Angeline 1850s, Mary Esther 1857), and had eight children, six living to become adults. From the first marriage were Irving and William Rankin (who developed the Ballard neighborhood of Seattle), and of the third were Charles, Hazard, Leon, and youngest Arthur. Another son (Edgar) and a daughter both died young.

After living in southern Oregon, Levi moved to Kent, then homesteaded what became Auburn, where they had a favorite Indien, "The color line was strictly drawn and there was no common basis for friendliness. Certain [native] families would attach themselves to certain white families. Old Nelson attached himself to our family."[95] Levi was a staunch Presbyterian, but his wife Mary was Methodist, so the four boys were strictly raised without dances or frolics. The Ballards were hard hit by the 1893 Panic, when the Auburn bank failed. Their home burned down in 1896.

Levi was very handy. For his family, he made all the brooms, tubs, buckets, handles, shoes, boots, and some of the furniture,[96] using only an ax, saw, and jack knife. As personal

---

[94] See JoAnn Roe, *The North Cascadians* 1980: 49, 154.

[95] Interview with Arthur Condit Ballard, by Ella Brannan Wollery, Washington Pioneers, White River Historical Society, Auburn.

[96] Charles H Ballard, Pioneer Experiences of the Ballard Family on White River, King Co,

challenges, he made a bathtub for a neighbor and a farm wagon. Since money was scarce, his older boys hunted with bow and arrows until they could buy guns.

Mary (?? – 1909) had a supply of colorful quilts that the family traded to natives who cleared off their land. Otherwise, the standard price was $10 and a sack of flour per acre. Levi bought a flock of sheep in Steilacoom to keep the ground cover from growing back. Shearing them provided wool for knits and padding. Potatoes were a cash crop, sent by native canoe to Seattle, which took a few days. The usual rate was 50 cents for a hundred pounds, while churned butter cost 50 cents a pound.

The Ballard home was near the ancient thoroughfare where the Green and White Rivers converged to join the Duwamish flowing into Puget Sound. Many of these native people had been settled on the Muckleshoot reservation, established by the treaty of Medicine Creek but on land ceded at Point Elliott. Nearby reservations were delayed by lengthy congressional reviews in the aftermath of the war.

Education and reading were important to the family. Nearby universities (Umpqua Academy in Oregon, Whitworth in Sumner, UW in Seattle) were always intended destinations for Ballard children. Charles and Arthur attended a local grammar school and went on to Whitworth College while it was still in Sumner (before moving to Tacoma, later to Spokane).

The brothers seem to have partnered in pairs, older and younger, first and second families. Of the first born, Irving (1845 – 1880), married to Lucinda with four sons and a daughter, apprenticed in law, practiced in Tacoma and Seattle, was elected prosecuting attorney as a Republican, and owned Seattle trolley cars and the packet steamer *Zephr*, which was captained by his brother William Rankin (1844 – 1929), married to Estelle. The other brothers, noted above, came to the Methow.

Arthur transferred from Whitworth and graduated in Classics from the University of Washington in 1899. He worked as school teacher, postman, and Auburn city clerk, as well as secretary of the Azurite Gold Company. He had a daughter and two sons, who became MDs.

Fearing ridicule by his white neighbors, Arthur hid his interest in native lore until he went to a lecture by JP Harrington, the first professional anthropologist at the University of Washington for 1910 summer session, who strongly encouraged this work. Inspired, Ballard took his first set of notes on 21 December 1911.[97] Later he worked closely with TT Waterman, the first resident UW anthropologist, on a study of place names and oral literature. In all is was a "near miss" that his three older brothers lived in the Methow but recorded nothing of its natives, while Arthur devoted his live to recording all that he could.

He would walk from his home uphill onto the Muckleshoot plateau to visit elders. His most successful interviews were with blind John Xot ~ Hote, who married into the family of Jerry Meeker's mother of the native town at Minter. Through his interest and contacts, he guided most of the early anthropologists working from Seattle, including John Peabody Harrington, Thomas Waterman, Herman Haeberlin, Erna Gunther, Marian Smith, Melville Jacobs, and Leon Metcalf, who made sound recordings of several speakers and one of Ballard himself. In addition to collecting variants of the same story, in fine scholarly style, Arthur was also careful to note genealogical information on family background of the storytellers and their own sources.

Wash 1914-15. Washington Pioneers, White River Historical Society, Auburn.
[97] National Archives, RG 279, Indian Claims Commission, Docket 109, Duwamish, Ballard Testimony of 18 June 1952, Box 1168, Folder 7, page 33.

Ballard lived alone after his wife Jane died in 1939, filling their huge house with artifacts and debris, probably as an obsessive-compulsive (OCD). Even as he remained very concerned with natives, despite some elder abuse, his heirs, finally, suppressed his life's work, *Listen My Nephew, Myth, Tradition, and History on Southern Puget Sound*, as it was at a Portland press.

Only one collection of Ballard's work can still be consulted, archived in London, because Marian Smith[98] gave him $25 for these pages. An important source was Charlie Ashue, who in 1929 and 1931 expressed the anti-Eells and pro-Stanup sentiments frequent among the Puyallups. Aschue insisted that $250,000 of native monies had been misappropriated to buy a dairy ranch and stock that later became Eells's wife's property. Investigators could find nothing wrong. When the agent decided to get rid of Rev Peter Stanup, he had soldiers get him drunk as a trap and then "hired someone to push him into the water".

Ashue also provided details on the execution, in graveyard between Sumner and Puyallup, of a "bad" doctor by Old Kitsap "when he could hardly see." Old McKai (*nakco'ya*), a Tulalip married to a young Puyallup wife, was suspected of having killed two of Kitsap's daughters and the young man then being buried. Kitsap's wife guided his hand so he could shoot to kill. Old Kitsap went into hiding, but he was so old the authorities decided to treat him leniently. There was no jail, so his son-in-law (Joe Taylor) settled him in the schoolhouse where Charlie was a pupil (about 1873) and Rev Mann the teacher. Kitsap sat by the stove and smoked his pipe. If he was thirsty, he would call out. The teacher would ask, "What does he want?" "Water." "All right, get him a drink".

The John Xot family is mentioned frequently. His father had been chief at the village on Clear Creek, which enters the Puyallup River on the south side about a mile from Cushman school. Chief Old Xot was stabbed and killed by his wife's brother over a misunderstood jest.

John had a brief first marriage. Offers by his family had been rejected by that of the girl. Later the father and two daughters were seen digging clams on the beach at Buenna, north of Tacoma. Xot allies approached them in a sealing canoe (which was very quiet) and seized the two girls. John married the one he had desired, and gave generous gifts to her family. But this wife was not industrious and John had to find a polite way to divorce her. While they lived with her family, John gathered only green cottonwood for the fire until all the smoke made his mother-in-law scold him and he could leave with dignity.

John Xot himself provided "Notes on Village Sites and People." At Allen on North Bay were the *skwa'ksdabc*. Chiefs there were *tca'auxc*, *ka'walac*, and *txA'pted*. *Ka'walac* died after the white people came. Jim Goudy said this community was the "First to come back after the flood." At Quartermaster Harbor was *sdAgwa'lut*, derived from *udA'k^u* 'enclosed', sheltering ducks and other game in winter time. Their chief named *^{xwut}xwi'tkeb* is mentioned in Edward Curtis' narrative of an expedition against the Cowichan people. He belonged to the *sxwoba'bc*, and died before white people came. His son *ko'yAlk^u*, also a chief, died before the War of the Treaties, and his grandson died about 1890. At Gig Harbor, *dxwa'ulkotl* was a village at the mouth of the bay. Another village was on the prairie back from there. At Wilatchet [Wollochet] Bay, the town was named *sxolo'tsiD* (mouth of *sxolo't*). At the head of Carr's Inlet were the *^{tux}sxo'tl'babc* [Eaters]. Their chief *wila'tcalt^{xu}* died before the War of the Treaties.

---

[98] Marian Wesley Smith, Microfilm Roll 4 (Reel A1739), British Columbia Archives, MSS 268:Box 8, Folder 4; Royal Anthropological Archives, MSS 2794.

At Long Branch Bay, the people were the *tksba'kebabc*. A chief there was *to'lskid*, who died after the war. He taught Michael Simmons's children the native language. They grew up to be interpreters. The beach had an abundance of clams and mussels, free from disease the year round. It was the oldest part of the Sound, *dokʷebaɬ* couldn't change that place [Devil's Head]. McNeil's Island was named *suxo'xted* (steam house) [sweatlodge]. Its north side was full of clams. The island belonged to the Steilacoom people. At South Bay were located a branch of the sxoba'bc known as the *ᵗᵘˣtce'tsaɬabc* (people of the bark sliver).

As city clerk and booster of Auburn, Arthur Ballard was easy to find and engage. He lived as a neighbor of several native communities and came to know informed elders well. Aside from his articles and the volumes of material in his court testimony, his book manuscript's suppression by his own family has meant that he is not as well known as he deserves to be because of his life-long dedication to "this vice" of scholarly study of traditional variations in dialects, folklore, and perception of nature.

All the Ballards knew and liked natives, in Puget Sound and the Methow, but only Arthur seems to have left a valuable detailed record for future generations.

Pottery

Although removed by several hundred miles from the nearest "pottery area," the Sanpoil manufactured and used a crude type of clay ware. The information was furnished by John Tom; he spoke for the Sanpoil and Nespelem only. He knew of no similar practices by "outside" peoples such as the Lakes, Columbia, Nez Perce, etc. Nor had he heard of the use of pottery by more remote tribes.

The first suggestion of the use of clay came in answer to a question regarding the material used for the core of the ring employed in one of the hoop and pole games. The game concerned was the variety in which a small ring is rolled along the ground and against a small log used as a buffer, the pole being thrown after it on the rebound. John Tom's first answer was that iron was used, since it was desirable to have a heavy ring. Questioned further as to what was used before iron became available he answered without hesitation: clay. Damp clay was molded into a small ring two or three inches in diameter and before completely dry was wrapped tightly with, damp or green rawhide in two or three layers. After the rawhide has dried and contracted the ring was tough and rigid and of sufficient weight due to the clay core.

John Tom revealed, upon further inquiry, that at least one type of clay pot, always supplied with an outer covering of fish skin, was made and utilized in former times. It was not used for cooking, but solely for carrying water. Firm white clay, easily available along the banks of the Columbia river, was dug for making pots. Other clays were also plentiful but proved inferior to the white mud for this purpose. Pots were always built up in a form. The ordinary method was to dig a small pit in the firm sands along the river bank conforming in shape and size to that desired for the pot. The clay, after being worked to the proper consistency by mixing with water, was smeared about inside the pit to the thickness of about three-quarters of an inch. After roughly applying the clay in this manner the inside was smoothed carefully with the hand. The vessel was then left to dry in the sun. A thorough drying was accomplished in a short time since the heat becomes quite intense along the river valley during the summer and the sands are correspondingly hot. When completely dry the pot was removed from [40] its place in the pit. The particles of sand adhering to the outside were scraped off with a sharp edged stick, leaving a fairly smooth outer surface. Unusual irregularities were corrected by moistening the uneven portions and smoothing with the hand. This completed the building of the pot proper. Firing was never practiced so far as John Tom's information went. He stated that pots would crack if allowed to get too hot. Hardening seems to have been satisfactorily done by sun's heat alone.

A cooking basket was occasionally substituted for the pit in the sand in which to form the pot, using one with a fairly smooth inner surface or it would be difficult to remove the pot. In addition, it had to be turned out before thoroughly dry to avoid sticking to the basket.

A pot was never complete without a covering of fish skin. This was added for strength, to prevent cracking and possibly to render the container more waterproof. The skin of the white or silver salmon, (*Oncorhynchus kisutch*) was utilized for this purpose. A green or dampened skin was carefully cut and sewn to fit closely around the vessel. Tightly rolled sinew from the leg of the deer served as thread. The covering extended over the upper edge and down on the inside for an inch or two. Near the top of the pot two or three small holes were made, extending through the outside covering, the clay, and the inside projection of the skin. Through these holes rawhide thongs were threaded and knotted on either side. These served to hold the covering in place; they were not used as places of attachment for a handle since such were never applied. Upon drying the skin tightened; the vessel was then completed and ready for use.

The commonest shape in which clay vessels were made was identical with that of the typical cooking basket: elliptical in cross section, tapering gradually from top to bottom. Such vessels were seldom built as large as cooking baskets … depth was often as little as eight inches.

As stated above, these vessels of clay were used exclusively for carrying water; they were always soon emptied for they were not capable of holding water over longer periods of time than twenty or thirty minutes without damage.

Clay pots of the type described were in common use at the time when John Tom was a boy. He learned the details of their manufacture from his mother who made such a vessel and used it for some time during his youth. They gradually fell into disuse while he was in his teens, at which time metal buckets were introduced by the Hudson's Bay Company.

Clay was also used for making the heads of children's dolls. These were rudely molded and attached to bodies of cattail tule, or later, cloth.

Pipes were made only of stone; clay was never utilized for this purpose.[99]

The preceding data were originally published in the American Anthropologist 34 (1): 127-133 under the title of Pottery on the Middle Columbia. In that paper the problem of accounting for the presence of pottery in this isolated region was considered, and the distribution of pottery-making peoples in the surrounding area was noted. The general conclusion was that the pottery of the Sanpoil might be assumed as historically linked with that of the Sarsi with the least possibility of error, if an assumption of linkage were to be made.

Subsequent to the writing of that paper I have received from Dr Franz Boas the information that he has unpublished data concerning the use of pottery by the Kutenai, a tribe much [41] nearer the Sanpoil than were the Sarsi. Two tribes, Lakes and Colville, occupy the intervening territory between the Sanpoil and the Kutenai. I have recently spent a few days with these peoples. An old Colville woman recalled that her people used vessels made of clay while she was very young, but could give me no concrete information. Mr Tardy, who is in charge of the subagency at Inchelium, in the old Colville territory, reported to me that while ploughing at

---

[99] Pipes were also carved of horn or hardwoods (Ray 1942: 188).

the agency he had unearthed a sherd of crude clay ware, but had thrown it away as worthless. (He had just been transferred from an agency in the Southwest, where pottery was plentiful.) My single Lakes informant disclaimed any knowledge of the use of pottery by his tribe.

examination[100] of the Kutenai, Sanpoil, and Sarci data is most convincing that they are all of the same tradition. ... It appears probable that we are dealing with an ancient Woodland style which was still active in the Northwest during the historic period. [28]

Okanogan and Similkameen Valleys. [28] During 1952 and 1953 Norman Lerman and Warren Caldwell, graduate students at the University of Washington, carried on ethnographic and archaeological survey work in the Okanogan River valley of north central Washington and adjacent British Columbia. The work was financed by an Agnes H Anderson grant, and supplementary funds furnished by the Department of Anthropology of the University. Lerman, the ethnographer, recorded several informant references to the practice of pottery making and its utilization. None of the informants appear to have had the first-hand experience that Ray's older informant had. Consequently details are lacking and are not as trustworthy. One informant stated that a [29] people they did not know well, called the *K'tkšin*, who lived in the Similkameen Valley, had clay pots; they did not know how they were made but the clay could be found anywhere in the valley. It was "mixed with something else." Another person stated that pottery was called *tlktčin* and was made from a pure white mud from the bottom of a lake. This was mixed with ordinary clay and baked by putting it in the hot ashes of a fire. Shaping was "by hand" (probably molded). A third informant, who also called the pottery *tlktčin*, stated that some 7½ miles south of Oroville, in the Okanogan River, are small mounds under water. Clay taken from these mounds was shaped by hand and dried hard. "When cooking in these pots, the pots were set directly on the fire." Still another informant stated that white clay from the Okanogan River was used to make pots which were shaped by hand. They dried by themselves but had to dry slowly. The vessels were used to hold water and sometimes they "used them as fingerbowls." One gathers from this that the more northern Okanogan used some form of pottery fairly widely, that it was probably molded, and that some of it may have been partly fired and used over a fire in cooking. Further work in the region would almost certainly increase our knowledge on these and other points. No pottery appears among the southern Okanogan (Post and Commons 1938: 64), hence it might well be that local ceramic arts, if they were recently diffused, may have come from northeast.

Archaeological references to Okanogan pottery are not entirely lacking. Caldwell, while surveying the area, was told that a pot had been found by some boys at his site C-O-2 (Caldwell 1953-4: 12, map). It lay about 50 feet east of the old bridge over the Okanogan River, on the north bank in the eastern part of the town of Oroville, Washington. The pot lay under the turf, embedded in the river bank; it was about 6 inches high and 5 to 6 inches in diameter. Its shape and situation jibe well with the ethnographic data available in Ray and recorded by Lerman. Unfortunately the item was found by school boys, given to another boy, and has never been located. We have no data as to whether it was fired or unfired.

---

[100] Douglas Osborne, Pottery in the Northwest, *American Antiquity* 23 (1): 28-34 July 1957. Nicola (**K'tkšin* ?) of the Similkameen spoke Pacific Athapaskan, a language family widely associated with pottery.

Cedar Cave. [29] Five items of sun-dried clay were found in amateur's backdirt in Cedar Cave, on the Columbia River north of Vantage, Washington. One rectangular item is 4 by 2.25 by 0.75 inches and carries a punctate decoration. Another fragmentary piece has a punctate and incised chevron decoration. Three other items, all fragmentary, have been interpreted as possibly phallic (Swanson 1956: 40, Fig. 12).

Summary [33] Certainly there is a more extensive distribution of clay artifacts in the Northwest, especially the Plateau, than previous evidence has suggested. Future workers in the area should be alert for information along these lines on both ethnographic and archaeologic levels. No doubt the use of stone mortars and bowls, and the prevalence of the earth oven and stone-boiling in baskets would have made the acceptance of pottery, at least for cooking, difficult or dubious in the region. If we continue to find evidence of the ceramic art it will presumably be in other categories, such as most of those described. It will probably not be explained on the levels of ethnographic diffusion but rather upon the bases of more deep-seated, old cultural relationships, presumably with representatives of the more ancient aspects of the Woodland pattern.

More recently, attention has turned to the Shoto ~ Lake River clay industry (Slocum and Matsen 1968, Stenger 2009), often figurines, in the Portland~Vancouver area of the Lower Columbia River, of 700 years ago, with a century range on either side. Given its age, locations, and contacts, it seems the most likely source for this upriver pottery of more recent time.

Dialect Shifts

Lewis and Clark coming from the east noticed the similarity among the Salishan languages, which are named for the native ethnonym of those also now known as Flathead. As noted, two closely related Interior Salish dialect chains are spoken by those living along the Mid Columbia River. Snkyuse ~ Columbian (*nxaʔamxcín* = 'the language of the people here') is the language of the downriver bands, the Snkyuse, Pskʷaws ~ Wenatchee, Entiat, and Chelan (Kinkade 1981). Okanagan (Okanagan-Colville; *nsiləxcín)* is spoken upriver by the Methow, Southern Okanogan, Nespelem, Sanpoil, Lakes, and 'true' Colviles (Mattina 1973, 1987). Okanagan is also the language of the peoples immediately to the north in British Columbia along Lake Okanagan, with a vibrant native community of speakers, writers, and teachers.

The phonemes of Columbian Salish are

p t c ç k kʷ q qʷ ʔ   (voiceless stops & affricates)

p' t' c' ƛ̓ k' k'ʷ q' q'ʷ   (glottalized stops & affricates)

s ṣ ł x xʷ x̱ x̱ʷ ḥ ḥʷ h   (voiceless fricatives)

m n r y l ḷ w ʕ   (resonants)

m' n' r' y' l' ḷ' ẃ ʕ̓ ʕ̓ʷ   (glottalized resonants)

i a ə u   (vowels)

i̱ a̱ ə̱ u̱   (retracted vowels)   (Kinkade 1981, 1991)

Raised and now buried in the area, Dale Kinkade was the master of Salishan languages, especially of Chehalis on the coast and Snkyuse in the Plateau. Anthony Mattina, raised in Sicily, is the master of Okanagan dialects, especially in British Columbia where there are more viable speakers than in the <u>English only</u> United States. Both were intrigued that Methows speak the upriver Okanagan (Ok) version, though there were indications, especially in local place names that in earlier times the downriver Columbian (Cm) dialect was used. Dale marshaled the linguistic evidence in 1967, less aware of the history and ethnography about epidemic devastations and dislocations that strongly influenced the more recent conditions.

3.2. But place-names in the Methow Valley [196] nearly always have morphemes in their Cm form when they contain morphemes that differ in the two languages.

Seven place-names occur with the suffix for water (-átk^w): nmitxawátk^w = *Methow River* (from mit$\underline{x}$aw = *Methow*, at least one Methow speaker says nmit$\underline{x}$awitk^w, however), nẃřà•kátk^w = *Squaw Creek* (from wářk = *frog*), n$\underline{x}$a$\underline{x}$sátk^w = a place in the Methow River north of the community of Methow (possibly derived from $\underline{x}$əst = *good*), ncəcəṅátk^w = a place upriver from the town of Winthrop, nəxt'átk^w = *Patterson Lake*, and ntřqxənátk^w = a small lake near Patterson Lake (from stříqxən? = *mudhen*). The seventh occurrence is a counterexample, for it has the Ok form of the suffix: ṅm'ənəkítk^w = a swampy area near Twin Lakes (from mənək = *excrement*).

Between (-áẃs) occurs on five forms: t$\underline{x}$^{w}íy$\underline{x}$^{w}iya?páẃsxən = a place south of Twisp, sx^wəráẃs = a place between Twisp and Patterson Lake, kàlà•páẃs = *Twin Lakes*, klq'^{w}áẃs = *Poplar Flats* (meaning *open*), and kɬq'^{w}áẃs = a place upstream from Early Winters Creek (meaning *drape over*, from iɬəq^{w}ən = *put away, cache*).

Stone (-á?st) occurs on four forms: npspísa?stən = *Gold Creek* (possibly meaning *flat rock*), q^{w}əy'apá?st = *Camp Gilbert* (meaning *blue rock*, from q^{w}íy = *blue*), ?aslíp$\underline{x}$^{w}à?stəm = *Lehman's Butte* (from ?aclip$\underline{x}$^{w} = a type of rock formation), and na$\underline{x}$^{w}íq^{w}a?stən = *Frazer Creek*.

Side (-ánk) and *earth* (-úłux^w) occur on three forms each: nwə$\underline{x}$táltánk = a place upstream from the community of Carlton (from wa$\underline{x}$tált *infant, youngest child*), nləq'^{w}pánk = a red bluff upstream from Carlton (meaning *rock wall broken off*, from ləq'^{w}p = *broken rock, ice, glass*), nk^{w}a?ɬtánk = a place below Lost River, p'əƛ̓múłux^w = *Methow Valley* (from sp'əƛ̓əm *bitterroot*; an alternative name to mít$\underline{x}$aw), and p'əƛ̓mkənúłux^w = a place near McFarland Creek. The third name with the earth suffix has it in its Ok form: yəřk'^{w}úla?x^w = a place below the community of Mazama (from yəřk'^{w} = *bend*).

The *plant* suffix (-áłp) occurs only in $\underline{x}$a$\underline{x}$iyáłp = a place downstream from Methow (meaning *thornberry bush*), and *ear* (-ána?) occurs only in kcuẃcuẁxána? = *Black Canyon Creek* (meaning *streams coming into the main creek*, from cwáx = *creek*). *Leg* (-xən) occurs twice, but neither form could be properly classified as definitely either Cm or Ok on the basis of this suffix since it is unstressed (and therefore the same in the two languages) in both names. The lack of stress is probably due to the presence of other suffixes which are normally stressed in preference to other suffixes, although this would be relevant only if the forms were Ok; as it happens, these two stressed suffixes are useful for classifying the forms, and they have already been treated above: tx̌ʷíyx̌ʷiyaʔpáẃsxən = a place south of Twisp, and ntřqxənátkʷ = a small lake near Patterson Lake. -ált *child* occurs in nwəxtáltánk (cited above), and possibly in nqʷłqʷłáltəm = *Libby Creek* (from snqʷłaltən = *a sloped bank for drying berries*).

4. Since these names were provided by both Cm and Methow informants using Cm morphemes, a Cm origin is indicated, in spite of the fact that the Methows now speak Ok. There are three possible explanations of this. One involves the direction of the sound shift that partly distinguishes these two languages. This would assume that the Cm forms were originally common to both languages, and that Ok then shifted the relevant sounds, but the Methow Valley names remained in the original unshifted form. Such a retention is not unreasonable, since place-names are known to be conservative as to change, and in any case, even a change of language by the Methows assumes this retention of earlier forms. But a residue from a pro-sound shift period is not tenable; one would expect place-names in other Ok speaking areas to retain 'earlier' forms as well, and they do not. The reverse, incidentally – that Cm shifted from earlier Ok forms – is not feasible; this would imply that Methow Valley place names underwent [197] this sound shift, but the rest of the language did not.

A second possibility is that this was originally Cm territory which was taken by the Ok in warfare. But the Indians of these two groups were traditionally peaceful and on good terms with one another, and did not fight unless attacked. Territorial gain was never a reason for fighting. The third, and most likely, explanation of these Cm names in Ok territory is that the Methows changed languages, for what reason I do not know (perhaps through intermarriage with the Ok, perhaps for political reasons, etc.) I believe there is evidence for such a change both in these Cm names and in the comments of the early explorers and ethnographers who say the Methows and Cm are the same people and speak the same language.

Native Place Names

The place names which follow were collected from JT (native names = *šix^wimtk^w* from her grandmother, *sʔayyal'qs* from her mother) and TBC in July of 1979.[101] JT said large native settlements were on the east side of Black Canyon at *intataʔham* (the biggest), Lost River, Early Winters, and Twisp (at the modern saw mill).

Addition terms were provided to Dale Kinkade by Jerome Miller (JM) of Desautel whose ancestors were Methow, where his son's family has a native homestead. Suzanne Michel Morgan (SSM) and Sue Matt (SM), Jerome's sister in law, also had Methow ancestors, whom Morgan described as short, stocky, and very independent; never having to leave the Methow valley because they had everything they would ever need.

While the Methows (*mitxaw*) were a distinct group of Interior Salishans, each of the major tributaries was occupied by a separate band. Smallpox and other diseases, however, devastated [3] Methows in the early 1800s and survivors of these internal divisions joined together to forge a new community.

John Abraham, a Chelan, told SSM that a sickness, probably cholera, decimated the ancient Methows. Toward spring everyone was dead except a sister and brother, who were so young that they could not make fire. They lived by snaring game and heating it on a flat rock in the sunshine. Meadowlarks were their most steady food. Finally, a visiting family found them and took them in. Then other families moved into the Methow. Some families wintered across the Cascades toward the coast, where food was always available.

Once, a famous native doctor named *təmənway* foresaw a famine in the Methow (SSM). He had a daughter and five sons. The mother and sons went to the coast, but the daughter and father stayed in the valley. The daughter had children and a baby so she did not want to travel far away. When famine did come to the Methow, they soon ran out of food. The daughter cut up her beautiful buckskin dress and boiled it for food. The father refused to eat and died. Eventually, rabbits and other food came back to the Methow and the daughter and her children survived to repopulate part of this region.

---

[101] During July 1979, the Methow became a focus of research because of the interest of TBC in recording its place names and stories. He had typed up a list of such names given by JT, but these terms were spelled impressionistically rather than linguistically.

Through the office of Colville Tribal Historian, Adeline Sam Fredin, arrangements were made with the Okanogan National Forest to drive a van through the Methow to visit and record these places. The van, driven by Sandy (Lionel Gaylord) Sandberg, carried TBC, JT, BC, Larry Fredin, Jay Miller, and tribal trainee, George Abrahamson.

Driving through the lower valley, JT and TBC emotionally remarked how sad they felt at seeing the region so overgrown and neglected. When natives lived in the valley it was park like and beautiful, largely because the valley was burned over every fall to clear out the undergrowth brambles and provide ashes to nourish fresh growth in the spring.

On August 2, TBC, SC, and Jay Miller toured Twisp to record memories.

Specific names and incidents provided by a speaker are indicated by their initials:

     JT   TBC   JM   SC

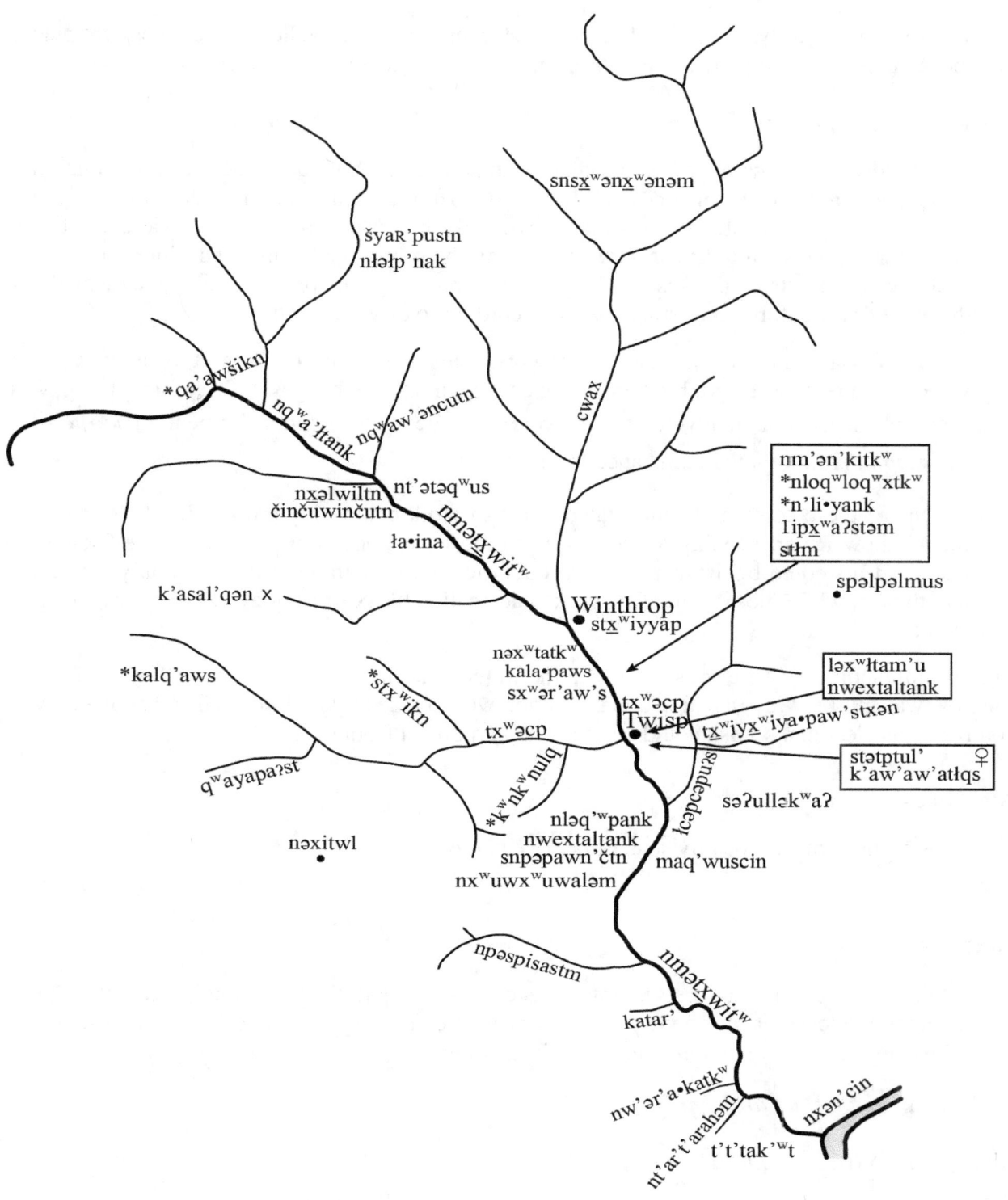

Vic Kucera & J

145

More importantly, various holy places occur throughout the valley. Often these are places of exposed rock that, even now, stand out from the glacial gravels and deposits.

Methow River = *nmətx̱wit*[w]

The lower ~ downriver ~ south dialect chain such as Snkyuse ~ Moses Columbian use the cognate *nmətx̱wat*[w] {**a** for **i**} or apply a descriptive term *špiƛmatk nmətx̱wit*[w] = "bitter root place" to indicate the distinct flavor of that root crop in this valley. Exact characterizations of this flavor vary. Some say the roots were sparse and bitter; others that roots were abundant and tasty. In part, different digging places may be indicated, or different times before or after settlers, or according to diverse palettes.

In Salishan mythology, before the world changed to become as it is now, Coyote wandered the world and by happenstance began these changes. Once something was accomplished, often inadvertently, Coyote then decreed a commandment (*sk̓(ə)tċəṙaṙ*, *skċəṙṙipla?*) to fix that circumstance for ever more.

One of these commandments stated that fisherfolk could only probe with their spears in the Methow River, keeping a firm grasp on the leister or fishing spear. In the Okanogan River, spears could be thrown. Once brought to shore, Methow salmon can only [5] be cut lengthwise, while those of the Chewack (once called the North Fork of the Methow) can be cut across the flanks.

These commandments were consistent with the water conditions of each of these flows. The Methow was murky with glacial debris so salmon were located by probing. The Okanogan, by contrast, was clear and so fish could be seen and harpooned from overlooks.

Alta Lake = *t't'tak*[w]*t*

A horned spirit, probably snake-like, lived here.

Pateros = *nxəńcin*

Town at the mouth of the Methow at its confluence with the Columbia. It was the site of a major winter village where people from upstream congregated to host and visit other Salishans also dwelling along the Columbia for the winter.

Black Canyon = *nt'aṙt'arahəm*

Black Canyon Creek = *nt'əṙt'ərahəm* (JM)

JT's mother died here.

Squaw Creek = *nẇ(ə)ṙa•katk*[w]

Where JT's grandparents fished for salmon and her grandmother died. She translated the name as = "frog in the water"

MacFarland Creek = *ɫataɬ*

Gold Creek = *npəspisa'stm npəspisa'stn* (JM)

Libby Creek = *nxʷuwx̣ʷuwaləm*

Specifically the South Fork of Gold Creek (JM)

Carlton = *maq'wu'scin*

JT translated this name as "big lump." A famous battle with the Spokans occurred here.

Silver = *sċalləqʷaʔ səʔulləkʷaʔ* (JM)

Earliest white town, founded by Jim Byrnes in 1890 after he bought out the squatters rights of John Chickamin Stone[102] for a red shirt and a bottle of whiskey; the town was destroyed by a flood in 1894.

McClure Mountain = *nləq́ʷpank*

Locus of guardian spirit helpers. A particularly important place was a large outcrop of exposed rock called *mxlilt* = "baby board" or, more fully, *nwextaltank*. Adjacent rolling side hills = *snəpawn̓čtn*

Beaver Creek = *ɫcəpcəpuʔs*

Several camp sites clustered here. A fishery was located at the confluence with Fraser Creek and called **yəlkʷ* = basket because of its shape. A path along the creek led to Buck Mountain = *spəlpəlmus*. After leaving these fall camps, people moved to the banks of the Columbia for the winter.

Fraser Creek = *tx̣ʷiyx̣ʷiya•paẃstxən tx̣ʷiyx̣iyaʔpaẃsxən* (JM)

Michel Charlie (native name = *skʷahəm'qən*) and Ed Walsh (native names = *wanaqa, q'əmmənula'xʷ*) had a fall hunting camp along this creek, now seen as a hallow on Route 20 below mile marker 211. The rigorous commandments relating to fall hunting are detailed in *Mourning Dove* (1990: 114-122). [7]

Twisp = *txʷəcp* JT translated the term as "broken tail", by others as "yellowjacket" who has this attribute.

Term for both the town and the tributary. Local landmarks include an oval track = *snkʷk̓ʷɫakn* for horse races, on the east side of Route 153 south of town, and a salmon trap before landfill created the city park on the site.

Nearby rocky hills figured in local legends. A low mound since removed by construction

---

[102] Chickamin is the term for 'money' in Chinuk WaWa jargon, which combines stripped down words from Nootkan, Chinookan, and, over time, Spanish, French, English, or other languages to enable simple "skin" trades to take place throughout the Northwest.

was called *stⱡm* = "boat" because it was the remains of a canoe used by two sisters from the Big Bend Country who came to court a handsome man who lived here. The mound was located where Route 20 meets Route 153.

At the World Change, the man became a rocky hill half a mile north of Twisp. Called *1ipx̱ʷaʔstəm*, its rough surface was due the man pulling his fur robe over his head when he rejected the women. Since the robe was shaggy when he turned his back on Twisp, the rock face became rugged.

Double hills half a mile south of Twisp are called *stətptul'* and *k'aẁaẁatⱡqs* (~ *k'aẁaẁatⱡqs*), the names of the sisters from the Columbia Big Bend who changed into these reddish hills.

Somewhere near Twisp was *ləx̌ʷⱡtamu* (*ləx̌ʷⱡtam'u*), perhaps a fishery at City Park. In ancient times, during salmon season, many Big Foot ~ Sasquatches ~ *sc'wanaytm* fished along the banks of the Twisp River.

At Twisp, during an eclipse, everyone knelt and prayed [8] until it was over.

Poorman Creek = *$k^w nk^w nulq$

A good area for berries. Steve Cleveland's mother put up her tent where the present road meets the Twisp River. Jim Libby had a cabin nearby.

Little Bridge Creek = *$stx^w ikn$

Good for hunting grizzly bears. A grizzly once attacked Paul, step father of Sam Miller, from Pateros. Further up on Midnight Mountain a famous 12 point buck named Little Alex roamed, sought to no avail by men from the 1930s CCC camp.

Buttermilk Creek = ??

Good for deer hunting, salmon, and bitterroot. Once horses were acquired, nearby pasture was valued. A campsite = *$ntq^w ləks$* was on the west side. Another camp in the brush at the end of the largest point was massacred by "Blackfeet".[103] During another threat,

---

[103] References to Blackfeet raiders might be generic. Battles were fought between Coastal and Interior peoples, although the central Plateau espoused pacifism. Outer Plateau peoples, however, had to contend with hostile neighbors, both from the Plains and from the Fraser River of Canada. Once the horse entered the Plateau, however, local people moved more widely. An intertribal Columbian confederacy was formed by members of the dialect chain under the leadership of the chiefly family from Vantage, transmitted through the name of Split Sun. Chief Moses, a younger son, inherited the name and commanded respect from natives and federal officials during the late 1800. Granted the 1879 reservation from the Okanogan River to the Cascade crest that included the entire Methow, he relinquished it in 1884 for annual payments and moved to the Colville Reservation near Grand Coulee.

Since horsemen of this Columbian confederacy hunted bison in Blackfeet territory during the early 1800s, it is possible that mounted Blackfeet did undertake retaliatory raids into Salishan [63] territory with reckless courage, but, on the whole, neighboring peoples with

a young girl was painted, elaborately dressed, and sent to Winthrop to say that a Blackfeet attack was imminent.

Two other place names once existed, but are now forgotten. At one spot, a man pointed up to a hill where he saw Blackfeet scouts. When they, in turn, saw him, he cleverly confused them by standing still with his arm out for hours, looking like a tree stump. The locale where the scouts were sighted had its own name. [9]

Eagle Creek = ??

A campsite was 4 miles upstream, serving as the first stage of a route up Eagle Creek to Snowshoe Ridge, along Sawtooth Ridge, and into the upper reach of Lake Chelan.[104] Blackfeet also attacked this camp, carrying off the daughter of the chief. Her brothers followed and rescued her.

Another route went up Eagle Creek to Duckbill Mountain, famous for huge billy goats and special plant medicines.

War Creek = *qʷayapaʔs qʷaẏapaʔst* (JM)

Several small fall campsites featured for fishing, berrying, and hunting.

Poplar Flat = **kalq'aws*

A fine horse pasture

Abernathy Ridge = ??

A long tunnel through the rock, 2 miles south of Gardiner Mountain, probably once had spiritual significance.

5 miles north of Twisp, a sharp bend in the Methow = **ńli•yank*

Oval Creek and Mountain

The abode of a giant shape-shifting supernatural being = **nəxitwl* often with a grizzly body and eagle head and wings. A hunter who had seen it told the famous native doctor *spoxay* that its wings stretched across the valley. In 1909, when he was 9, Steve Cleveland was sent to the top of the mountain on an errand, certainly in the hope that the creature would gift him with power. Forceful winds kept him [10] from reaching the top. In ancient times, someone went to the top and returned with *ṗəṗcast* = stone turds to prove it existed.

In the fieldnotes by graduate students supervised by Leslie Spier[7][105] this being is mentioned without a location:

---

whom Methows are now friendly were likely culprits.

[104] At the upper end of this lake is a pass into the Skagit River. The name Chelan itself derives from an ancient Salishan word for 'lake', aiding reconstruction of the proto-languages.

[105] Walter Cline mentions this Bird being in Religion and World View (Spier 1938: 171).

"Nhithitwulh was a large bird about the size of a condor. No one ever saw it, but the trees rang with the great noise which it made, and when people heard it they became numb and did not feel right till it had flown {by} overhead. It could transform itself into any large bird, such as an eagle, or into a deer, etc."

5½ miles north of Twisp = *nm'əṅkitk*^{w} *ṅm'əṅəkitk*^{w} (JM)

A good place to get wild cherries.

Twin Lakes = *kala•paws*

Campsites for gathering wild potatoes and bitterroot.

Patterson Lake and Mountain *nəx*^{w}*tatk*^{w}

On a hill on the other side from the lake is a place called *x*^{w}*əṙaẃs*, *sx*^{w}*əraẃs* (JM)

Winthrop = *stx̲*^{w}*iyyap*

An important ancient campsite.[106] A famous leader there was named *ksalkn*. Hundreds of years ago, another chief there was named *sawe'ax̲n*, who became famous because he had warrior powers from lightning, thunder, and a small bird. On the other side of the hill above camp was a special reserved place called nλknax = "dance in the lake" where spirit [11] dances were held.

A salmon trap located 3-4 miles below Winthrop was called **nloq*^{w}*loq*^{w}*xtk*^{w}

Chewack Creek == *cwax* "any creek"

Noted for its tea color.

Mount Gardiner and Wolf Creek = *k'a'sal̓qən*

A primary camp was located a few miles up Wolf Creek at the coldest water in the canyon. Those in quest of spirit help bathed in that water to give them strength. A path along Wolf Creek led to Mt Gardiner, the highest peak and most powerful source of spiritual power in the entire drainage. Many people got some of this power, but only one man, *syolm*, ever received access to all of it. He lived at Olima, where a placed called *sməlqnapsaɬx*^{w} = "golden eaglets house" was located near the old store. During a trance, his spirit took him inside Mt Gardiner where he sang for ten days while several grey-haired man-like spirits taught him the uses of this power. His spirit said that he had to sacrifice a

---

[106] Methow Valley is also the birthplace of smokejumping into remote forest fires, after initial trials in fall 1939 from a SR-10 Stinson, the first Forest Service plane, led to two 1940 bases at Ninemile Camp, near Missoula, and at the Winthrop airport north of Twist. Francis Lufkin, a first jumper who led the Methow base until 1972, and Glen Smith made the first Northwest wildfire jump 10 miles west of the North Cascade Smokejumper Base. Today the USFS and BLM have over 400 smokejumpers at nine primary locations in the western US and Alaska (http://www.northcascades smokejumperbase.com).

relative if he wanted out of the mountain. He called his daughter, a little girl playing with dolls, into the mountain. When she went inside, she went blind. Her father led her home and asked another doctor to treat her, but his power only slammed into the mountain side. It could not get in. Then a shaman from Pateros tried, he was so powerful that rocks danced beside him during his curing. But he [12] could not get inside either. Eventually, the girl died. For the next three years, *syolm* hosted winter dances to get to know this power. After three years, he could use it to cure, but it got weaker and left him as he got older. Some older doctors stole powers from youngsters, but *syolm* did not need to. Such bad doctors misused their powers. Once they had used it to kill, they could never cure anyone again. You needed to pay them for the cure so they would stay honest.

Rattlesnake Point = *łc•ina*

Liberty Bell Camp Ground = **ntətək'oš*

A campsite was across from the entrance to this facility.

Mazama = *nt'ətəq^wus*

Early Winters River = *nx̲əlwitn*

A cold spring nearby is called *činčuwinčutn*.

Goat Peak = *nq^waẁəncutn qəm'q̇^wəncutn* (JM)

Hunting camps for deer and goats.

Goat Wall = *nq^wa'łtank*

A small pond = *nq^wa'łtn* high up on the rock face had been an important source for spirit power. It was described as "mean" because it plays favorites. If it knew you and your family (if you were a local Methow), a rainbow appeared in the spray. If it did not know you, clouds and rain greeted your arrival. In the 1930s, the CCC built a wooden walkway to reach it. Offended by this profane access, the spirit [13] left and the pond dried up.

Geologically, a glacier gouged out a 1,500 feet deep valley, sheering this wall off the east side and filling the gap between two fault lines with melted debris.

Upper reach of the Methow = **qa'awšikn*

A good place to gather cedar roots for basketry, although pulling the thin tendrils took stamina and strength.

Billy Goat Mountain = *snsx̲^wənx̲^wənəm*

Lost River = *šyaʕpuɛtn šyaʕpusən* (JM)

Coyote left a spear here (*ntəłp'ina'k*) standing against a cliff so that, during the universal change, it became a vertical white mark ~ flash point indicating it is a good fish spearing station.

Interior Salish Tribal Totems

Placing story characters at a specific place in the Plateau has subtle totemic aspects that took some time to reach an academic understanding. Indeed, the initial report served only to outline the subject, which then gained insight as other stories set in other places joined the encounters. What began as an only child developed into a twin, based on commentary after the first draft was finished and reviewed with elders. In presenting both papers, original and revision, emphasis can be added to the familiar injunctions that the best analysis is that supported by new data; the best fieldwork involves recurrent visiting, and the best data comes from close and conscientious cooperation, with mutual trust and sensitivity, among researcher and native teacher-advisors over a long period.

The original paper started when a person gave information that no one else could duplicate, but took increasing form as comparative data supported this lone report, requiring a second version after other Salish elders added their own comments. The first was not so much wrong as it was incomplete, missing entirely one of the major dimensions of a culture: the spatial one linking humans with their land.

While working for the Colville Confederated Tribes of north-central Washington, comprised of Interior Salish who ranged both sides of the international border, information by a reliable source initially stood alone since other Interior Salish were unable to confirm or to deny it because they had never heard of it. While initially in doubt, further questioning her more closely revealed that she had learned it from a much more exalted person, one of the last hereditary chiefs. By its nature, this would have been public knowledge since it involved group identification, but it now appears that the historic disruption of the Intermontane Plateau peoples brought this system to an end over a century ago, making this story useless for modern transactions after everyone had congregated together on reservations and reserves. Comparative research from other areas of Native America, however, restored confidence in the data and led to more thorough discussion here.

Fragmentary though it is, the information does specify a link between a particular tribal group and a particular animal in such a way as to suggest strongly the use of totems by several Interior Salish groupings on the American side of the Plateau. Most of these tribes are now gathered on the Colville Reservation, established by executive order in 1872, near or upon their aboriginal homelands. Linguistically, these tribes formed a chain of Interior Salishan dialects with at least two divisions, as noted. In an intermediate position between these two divisions were the villages of the Methow drainage, which had a dialect which historically shifted between Chelan and Okanogan chains.

Accordingly, each of these tribes had a particularly close relationship with an animal. While all of these bonds were not remembered, some were. Among members of the Okanogan chain, the Nespelem animal was the turtle; the Sanpoil a bluish lizard; and the Colville a frog. The Snkyuse identified with the bear and people camped at the upper end of the Grand Coulee (who may have spoken a Snkyuse dialect) identified with Eagle. In and of themselves, these data are vague and problematic. Yet, when these bonds are compared with other regions of Native North America, they enhance a widespread pattern of place-based tribal totems.

Comparative Data

Fully realizing this bonding of tribe and animal was not idle speculation and our source was very sincere, more pondering lead to the Shuswap totems discussed by James Teit (1909: 373-381) until closer inspection proved that this was a different phenomenon. Briefly, Teit found important social differences between eastern and western bands of Shuswap of the Canadian Plateau. By 1850 the Canyon Band and north bands (Lake, Dog Creek, and Pavilion) on the Fraser River had social classes of nobles, commoners, and slaves like coastal tribes. The freeborn were divided into totemic groups such as Grizzly, Raven, Wolf, Eagle, and Bear inherited bilaterally. Initially, the founders of these groups trained and fasted to join one of them, with that membership then passing to heirs. This primary recruitment was handled much like a guardian spirit quest since the guardian spirit complex exists simultaneously with these crests. Of the two, the shamanic~guardian spirit complex was much the older.

Comparing the two lists of totems and spirits, Teit showed that these spirits were ecologically appropriate to the Shuswap territory, while the totemic crests pointed to the coastal tribes. The totems were listed above, while the list of possible spirits included Wolf-Dog, Cannibal, Corpse (mostly for shamans), Bear, Thunderbird, Frog, Wind, Rain, Arrow, Moose, Caribou, Elk, Deer, Buffalo, Snow (to aid hunters in tracking), and Serviceberry (for women).

Accordingly, Teit proposed three routes from coast to interior for such totemic crests:

1) Tsimshian to Carrier

2) Bella Coola to Chilcotin

3) Squamish to Lillooet

As neighbors of the Shuswap, these Interior Athapaskans (Carrier, Chilcotin) and Salishan (Lillooet) tribes interact with them through intermarriage, joint fishing, and ritual cooperation. Strengthening his argument for these routes is the greater elaboration of the crest system of the intervening tribes. This was not a wholesale adoption, however, since the Shuswap molded the new crests to their older cultural forms by making them conform to bilateral descent, rather than the matrilineality or ambilaterality of the coast.

In contrast to the Colville evidence, the Shuswap used the totems to establish internal distinctions within their tribe, rather than having a single totem expressing their tribal unity. Further, Goldman (1941) detailed the diffusion of crests from the Nuuxalk ~ Bella Coola to the Alkatcho Carrier, who treat them as bilateral honorifics, and Miller (1981b) explored a similar transmission among the Coast Tsimshian, Upriver Gitksan Tsimshian, and the Carrier, who adopted crests progressively and incrementally through trade, intermarriage, and the assumption of prestigious patterns of clothing styles, cremation, and potlatching. Most commonly, these borrowed crests were Grizzly, Wolf, Raven-Crow, Beaver, and Eagle, adding further confirmation to the argument that the similar Shuswap totemic groups also had a coast origin.

Looking much further afield, moreover, is a system more analogous to that of the Interior Salish, found among the tribal totems in the Northeastern Maritimes, where it functioned independently from a system of matri-clans named for animals among the Iroquois, and from the bilateral "demes" of the Wabanaki Algonkians, though these may have been more matrilineal aboriginally before struck by severe depopulation. Among the Wabanaki, these tribal totems function aside from personal guardian spirits and family nicknames tied to economic specialties.

The Wabanaki tribal emblems are scaled, in terms of the intensity of identification with each, from the highly explicit Passamaquoddy, whose tribal name means "those who pursue the

Pollock (a fish)", to a more vague but nonetheless profound pervasiveness. Among the Malecite (now spelled Malaseet) the associated animal is Muskrat, with the Micmac (now Miqmaq) having Deer, and the Penobscot Otter (Speck 1917: 13). Frank Speck interpreted these emblems as game totems, expressing the most important staple of each group. In hindsight, however, this claim is overly functional, aligned with the famous phrase of A.R. Radcliffe-Brown that animals are totems because they are "good to eat".

The work of Claude Levi-Strauss (1962, 1966) supplied a corrective to such gastric determinism by suggesting that totems are much "better to think" (or think with) than to consume; since humans living closely with nature utilize the full range of their ethological observations in their symbolism.

It, therefore, seems most appropriate to view these game totems as expressions of the land/water opposition so important in these cultures, with each member acting as an amphibious mediator within the system (recalling that deer are efficient swimmers and that pollack have a diverse salt water habitat since they "can be caught from breakwaters as well as out to sea" (Ursin 1977: 111)). In addition, perhaps indicating the beginnings of an overall inter-tribal integration for the various Wabanaki tribes, these mediators show an internal progression from usually aquatic to usually terrestrial species:

> pollack muskrat otter deer <

While the Wabanaki lack this national totem, the existence of such can be seen among the confederated tribes known as the Iroquois, where "Bald Eagle ... is the totemite of all the Iroquois. The eagle perches atop the great tree of peace which is symbolic of the Confederacy" (Fenton 1953: 117). The *gastowe*, the cap worn by *royaner* ~ federal league chiefs, are adorned with eagle feathers, with the number and positioning indicating a specific member tribe. There were other such tribal or national emblems in the Americas, but the Iroquois will serve to illustrate the type.

The development of this type can be seen among the historically created tribe called the Mohegan of Connecticut. According to Gladys Tantaquidgeon (1973), herself both a Mohegan and an anthropologist, after the defeat of the Pequot and the ascendancy of Uncas as the leader of the survivors, the native name of his own Bear clan became extended and rephrased into the tribal name Mohegan, with the Bear as their special emblem.

The evidence of such unifying symbols provides further insight into the character of tribalism in Native America. It is presently fashionable to presume that such tribes have been the historic creations of federal interference, of treaty making, and of catastrophic dislocations due to epidemics and warfare. Wherry (1979: 34) stated that tribes existed more in the heads of Europeans than in the interactions of natives, although "The inhabitants of various river systems may have been gradually distinct culturally and politically."

His observation accords well with other evidence that indicates that river drainages or watershed often coincided with linguistic, community, and ritual groupings (Miller 1981a). Certainly, this is the case for both the Wabanaki and for the Salish. Each of the Interior Salish "tribes" named above occupied a major tributary of the Columbia River. In the aboriginal period, which lasted until a century and a half ago, each drainage defined a tribe in that all of the camps and settlements shared a common language, territory, economy, and series of seasonal rituals. Moreover, the village nearest the confluence with the Columbia was invariably the largest and most dominant. Its chief and ritual leader were given the most deference and the name of this village was extended to include the entire drainage and the people dwelling along it.

While lacking coercive powers, save for ostracism of community offenders and the discipline of children with the approval of a council of distinguished citizens, the chief and priest lead by example, by marital alliances with other tribes, and by moral suasion mixed with generosity.

In practice, the chief and the Salmon *tyee* ~ priest acted as regulators for all or most of the interactions among the inhabitants, neighbors, and the environment. In the event of community disruption or of malfeasance in office, these leaders had only to move to another river valley to become distinguished citizens there without any obligation to assume a leadership role.

During much of the year, people scattered among seasonal camps located at resource areas, so the full ceremonial organization or congregation did not emerge until everyone (or almost everyone) returned with stored surplus foods to the winter village along the river.

More than anything else, the chiefs and priests served as the foci of and for the sentiments of each community congregation, serving to define the Salish as members of a moral community composed of all forms of life. In nightly council sessions and periodic First Foods Fêtes, these sentiments were given public expression. From moment to moment, however, they were acted out in terms of personal orientations to a series of overlapping foci. Among these were the chief, the priest, the sacred space of the council house and of ritual sites, cemeteries, geographical features important in mythology (like Moses Mountain), and, most of all, the water course that serves as the tribal lifeline.

The larger inter-tribal community was similarly defined by common residence along the Columbia and its tributaries, joint use of bountiful fisheries and attendance at the First Salmon Rites at the Dalles among the Wishram-Wasco Chinook and at Kettle Falls among the Colvile, and shared mythic sagas relating to the adventures of Coyote finishing off the creation of the world, especially bringing Salmon up the Columbia to the different fisheries or not.

Given the tremendous amount of tribal interaction through fishing, ritual, and marriage, it seems likely that some means was developed to express these different tribal memberships in some obvious way. The most ready answer, of course, would be the use of emblem based on a pseudo-speciation among humans like that among animal species. These distinctions were not based on economic considerations, however, but rather on the need to express wide-ranging symbolism among these tribal cultures.

Thus, while the original data came from only one source, comparative information and the inter-tribal milieu of the Plateau provides a context for accepting their creditability. More to the point, such information has been passed down through a chiefly family line where the decision to share it with outsiders could be readily made without greater consultation with other elders. In all, it suggests the on-going importance of focal chiefs and totems for regulating the continuity of the tribe as an inter-meshed moral community interacting with the members, environment, neighbors, and the greater society of sapient beings of the biotic community.

Moreover, after the previous argument was written in 1980, more information came from another source that serves to place everything in proper perspective.

While totemic identifications can be interpreted as an expression of social solidarity, with comparative evidence for similar cases across the continent to support this, a single sentence from a Snkyuse elder provided the missing piece to the puzzle. Of course, her meaning would not have been as readily understood without five prior years among Colvilles.

When directly asked if she had ever heard that Moses people ever had a special association with Grizzlies or the Bear, she flatly said "no." A few minutes later, she added "Those Ellensburg people were mixed up with Bears." Ellensburg is a town in central Washington, located in traditional Psk^{w}aws ~ Wenatchi land, but also frequented by Snkyuse now at Colville and by Sahaptians now on the Yakama reservation.

"Bears at Ellensburg" refers to the story of a Bear family who lived, in the Timeless Age, where the water tower now stands near Rodeo Grounds. The place name in Salish for that knoll is "Bear's House" and it called to mind several other places, especially hills, along the Columbia which are named as the abode ~ house of a particular animal. Among these are Otter's House at Orondo and Coyote's House near Bridgeport, although Coyote has more than this one house because he traveled so widely. While not all of the tribal totems have been positively linked with houses in those areas, the tradition does hold for the larger area.

The result of this additional data has not been the rejection of the past analysis, but rather a considerable amplification of it. Concerns with tribal solidarity and overlapping foci continue to hold true, but, instead, the reference to mythology provides a means to ground a tribe within its territory, to locate them in space with a charter from the Myth Age. While the animal emblem of the tribe does express its commonalities during inter-tribal gatherings, it more importantly links the tribe to its land, making the tribe a united membership, an interacting congregation by virtue of occupying the same area where a humanoid spirit-animal or family lived in the primordial period when all the rules for human conduct were instituted. The Myth Age was the timeless period of what some Salish call the Animal Kingdom, when distinctions were minimal and the inhabitants shimmered simultaneously between spirit, human, and biotic forms. When all was ready for humans, this previous age changed instantaneously into the present age, permitting human ancestors to establish special relations with characters and places of the Animal Kingdom for the benefit of local descendents. This is what happened at Ellensburg between a Psk^{w}aws ancestor and the Bear family.

The creditability of the earlier analysis, then, stands with modification provided by new data. Seldom is an analysis so fortunate as to have new evidence, or previously unconsidered data lend confirmation and amplification to a previous model. Such instances are particularly unusual in the human sciences like anthropology.

Moreover, this analysis goes considerably beyond professional considerations to underscore with great emphasis the vital role that land and territory play in the definition and orientation of Native American identity, on personal, community, and tribal levels. As a generalization of these findings, mythology maps people to their land, making it theirs from time immemorial, but, especially, it indicates, at least on the Plateau, that a house is a tribal home.

Language ~ Religion ~ Culture ~ Land

Culture and language evolved with the unique development of the human species. Both culture and language have a single origin ~ underlying system. As human beings have diversified, so too have cultures and languages, but each of these remains translatable into the others because of their shared origin.

That said, however, there remains the fascinating if perplexing problem of accounting for the range of variation among the cultural expressions of different human societies. Thus far, the best explanation is the interaction between a particular set of cultural preconceptions and a specific environment. It is in the intermeshing of people and land that different cultures develop and maintain themselves. Further, it is in this diversity that the species as a whole maintains a survival advantage. It is an interaction that takes place on a very human level because throughout the world among indigenous populations the land is considered alive. Land is not property or object; it is a both a being in its own right – with stones for bones and vegetation for hair – and populated by a vast assortment of beings having claim to particular localities – glens, valleys, streams, mountains, and so forth. It is a tradition very much part of the lives of European peasants to this day, yet in the lands colonized by their forefathers, the analogous native beliefs have been disregarded or condemned so that land as property could be usurped. These beliefs have persisted, nevertheless, among the local populations because they have continued to live in intimate association with their homelands.

The relations between humans and ancestral land, therefore, are phrased in terms of familiar access to spirits or beings who are immortal residents of a place. In native view, every prosperity and human endowment is somehow traced to the bounty of these spirits.

In fairness to these religious systems, it must be pointed out that, by and large, these references to numerous spirits cloak a fundamental belief in a single deity who is the source for the power apportioned among various immortals. In short, these many spiritual beings, under close examination, are aspects of a unifying belief in a first cause or High God (Miller 1980).

Generally, the complexity of all these relations between humans (as groups and as individuals) to the land base are represented in the mythology of that community. In these sagas, told with increasing detail among the more elite families, are specified the ways and means in which the world has come to be as it is and the proper manner in which immortal inhabitants are to be approached and petitioned. In this way, the religious system is instituted in terms of rituals, sacred places, and items of power such as medicine bundles or personal tokens-

Often, a tribal genesis specifies that when humans were created and scattered, the Creator reserved the best gift of all and the original language for the tribe giving the account. [2]

Hence, a bond between a culture, a language, a land, and a deity was formed, and is sufficiently common to be found in the Christian Bible, where a special relations is specified between God, the Jews, the Holy Land, and Hebrew. Even among the early Christians, Hebrew was believed to be the language of God. Other cultures hold analogous beliefs. Two recent anthropological studies provide case examples of this with particular relevance to Canadians.

Among the Navaho, Dené people of Arizona whose ancestors moved from western Canada a few centuries ago, some of their immortals moved south with them and others became familiar to the people after arrival. In his definitive study of the interrelations between culture, language, and art among the Navaho, Witherspoon (1977: 5) asserts "all cultures are constructed from and based on a single metaphysical premise which is axiomatic, unexplainable, and unproveable. A single premise can serve as the starting point for more than one conceptual scheme or ideological system. From this single premise a conceptual scheme develops by the positing of an opposition to it, from which it is them expanded into a more complex structure utilizing analogy, opposition, and synthesis as its tools of construction."

For Navaho culture, this axiom is motion/pause or active/static mediated by air, expressed as Holy Wind (1977: 48, 53). Similarly, Navaho and other Athapaskan languages place great grammatical emphasis on these same categories, suggesting that the axiom of the culture applies equally to the component social institutions such as language. [3]

By extension, motion is feminine and pause is masculine, which are also respectively outside and inside. "The symbolic action of ritual is the process by which the Holy People {immortals} are controlled and compelled ... The goal of the earth surface people {humans} is to die of old age after a long life of beauty, harmony, and happiness. The inner forms of the various natural phenomena are humanoid. They can hear the speech of ritual and can see the movements and prestations involved in the symbolic action of ritual. These inner forms (in-lying ones) of natural phenomena also have inner forms (in-standing wind souls). Just as with the earth surface people ... the nature or class of the in-standing wind soul ... determines [if a] particular Holy Person is benevolent, malevolent, or a combination" (same: 35-36).

For the Navaho, "This world was transformed from knowledge, organized in thought, patterned in language, and realized in speech (symbolic action). The symbol was not created as a means of representing reality; on the contrary, reality was created or transformed as a manifestation of symbolic form. In the Navajo view of the world, language is not a mirror of reality; reality is a mirror of language" (same: 34, emphasis deleted),

Witherspoon has provided the most sophisticated treatment of another philosophical system currently available for Native North America. He makes clear that the Navaho believe that the world was thought into being by immortals gathered together in a sweat lodge, creating to the accompaniment of a pulsating rhythm a series of inner and outer forms nested together to create and [4] populate their universe. These immortals provided language and land for the people, who keep in touch with them via religious rituals. In all, a seamless web was created of humans, immortals, language, and land woven tightly together.

Among the Mistassini Cree, the long academic controversy over the character of family hunting territories has been resolved by Tanner (1979) in terms of a mystical bond between a senior hunter and the resident spirits of the game animals, particularly the "boss" (or spirit ancestor) of the area. "A central attitude in the conduct of hunting is that game animals are persons and that they must be respected" (1979: 130).

"While membership in the hunting group may change from year to year there is continuity of leadership, and the leader is identified with the area used by the group in such a way that we may speak of the leader having overriding 'title'. However, in order to have this title generally recognized the leader must have a history of residence in the area, and a prestige built upon his demonstrated relationship with the animals, in the religious sense" (1979: 186).

"When the group abandons a campsite they must spend some time cleaning up, in order to avoid offence to the spirits, but this mainly involves seeing that the bones of game animals are properly disposed of. If the campsite is not left in a proper condition it is thought that the animals will not return to the area, a Rupert House man explained the same idea to me in a different way. He said that a short time after a group leaves a place where they have camped the 'spirit' of the hunting group leader flies over the site. If he finds everything left as it [5] should be he is pleased, and gives the group good luck in their future hunt trig- The hunting group leader's spirit cares about the condition of the land, and he can send the animals away if the land is not looked after" (1979: 74-75).

Here again, the basis of the relationship between humans and resources is expressed in terms of communication through a mystical or spiritual bond between humans and immortals who are at base equally human in their form and sentiments.

In terms of my own research, I have become increasingly aware of the close links among culture, language, religion, and land. As the late Martin Sampson, hereditary leader of the Swinomish Salish, often remarked "If you don't understand the land, you don't know anything. The land is your teacher."

By land, he meant the living entity; the spirit of the land, rather than mundane features of ecology, resources, or property. It was this living land that children were sent out to contact on spirit quests and that adults sought to influence in rituals. Its immortal inhabitants spoke to these petitioners by mind and by mouth, although telepathy was the preferred form.

Speech was an integral part of the quest because the person gifted with a vision then had to recite an account of the meeting and sing the song that conferred the power provided by the immortal. Since most children were~are sent out to quest in the same locales as their ancestors, they come back using the language of their home group. On rare occasions, however, someone not resident or native to an areas encounters an immortal and receives power. In this case, they sing and recite in the [7] language of that place, indicating the intensity of the bond between spirit, language, and locale (cf p144).

Two cases of this are reported. A boy from Puget Sound visiting in the Okanagan inadvertently acquired power and a song using Okanagan words from Rattlesnake. A white woman living around Ellensburg, Washington would sing in Wenatchi Interior Salish about her guardian spirit, although she was otherwise ignorant of this language. An Interior Salish man who gained power in Nez Perce territory and sang in that language.

It has taken tens of thousands of years for natives to adapt to the continent of North America and develop many distinctive ways of relating to this landscape. Since the arrival and settlement of Europeans, many aspects of their bond with the land have been shattered and gutted, nevertheless, its outlines persist in general native belief.

Schematically, the meshing of society and its institutions can be represented as follows:

t		
e	economy	l
c		a
h	polity	n
n		g
o	kinship	u
l		a
o	ritual	g
g		e
y	ideology	

To help explain such persistence, the distinction between culture and society needs to be introduced at this time. Culture, as we have seen, is the conceptual framework providing order and meaning to a distinctive lifeway as selectively derived from the canons of universal Human Culture. Society is its behavioral expression, heavily based on the biology of the species. Society consists of closely intermeshed institutions related as a system, such that a change in one produces changes in the others. Yet of them all, science is best able to plot the changes from the most tangible institutions like economy to the least tangible, such as ideology. Two institutions seem to crosscut the others, involving all of them. These are language [8] and technology. Language intrudes on the others because it supplies the order and the terminology for articulating them. Similarly, technology provides the means and representations of them, from the dibble of the farmer to the idol of the deity. Changes in the economy are most likely to have far reaching consequences for the other institutions, particularly language and technology. These are obvious, tangible changes, but they may be more apparent than real since they do not seem to influence the axiom of the culture itself.

Accordingly, changes in the economy effect the organization of the group and its leadership, often modifying the kinship system by changing the pattern of residence. All of these, of course, alter relations with the supernaturals, requiring new or modified rituals and explanations. The vocabulary and grammar of the language are changed or even replaced by another, often after a period when speakers are bilingual to some extent. Yet, as we are only now beginning to realize, the replacement of one language by another does not mean that fundamental relations are broken or [9] changed. In Australia where English has replaced some aboriginal languages, linguists are now aware that speakers are not using standard English, for they have turned English into an aboriginal language in terms of etiquette, intent, and meaning. The same can be said of the English that has replaced many native languages in the Americas.

The difficulty with all this change, of course, is that the society is never balanced or content. The system remains disharmonic while struggling for a new synthesis, vulnerable to outside and hostile pressure in ways that result in reactions that are more intense and severe than previously. Throughout this period when stability is sought, the rudder is provided by the on-going relations with the land and its innate inhabitants, who have provided the wisdom and council from ancient times. It is this sacred and eternal link of human to land that provides the surest hope and opportunity for continued existence and intelligent use of the planet.

Appendix A

To illustrated a typical native composition by unschooled writers along with the hard labor of editing a coherent version, here is the first page of Okanogan Name Day ~ genesis ~ creation as typed by CB Suszen Timentwa. The sheets are dark and the typing sometimes faint, but mostly legible. To spare a reader, to the verbatim page have been added a space after any punctuations. To the edited version are added paragraphs, subject ~ verb ~ plural agreement, treatment of "if" as indicating a conditional, past tense changed to present tense, capitol letters put on proper names and first word of a sentence, and all important quotation marks placed around dialog concerned with verbal directions, eternal laws, and names.

IN THE FIRST BENNING {BEGINNING} OF THE WORLD[107]

There was God hold a Meeting amongs the creatures and told them that I am you be my God, Am God. I am going to appointed some of my own powerful laws for all you creatures, To remember until if I came back, Now I say to all creatures, And each of you have names, After this. Am God this is what I speak about the powerful laws that am appointed to all of you creatures. Now I say if who gets it the first name that I am going to gave away it would be the powerful creatures from all the creatures that upon the face of the earth, And if one of you creatures gets the last one name left it would be worthless and unpowerless creatures from all the other creatures to live upon the face of the earth, am God that I have said to all of you creatures, Behold, and remembered until if I came back next time, Now I say, if when I have names all you creatures and that I am going to created an huming {human} being for you creatures to let if he in charge of all you creatures that living upon the Earth, It would be looked a like that am with you creatures here to-day, And if what ever he says is all you creatures just have to followed him that what if he says to all you creatures that living upon the face of the earth, Now listen to me, This is only one law that I has appointed to all you creatures the day out it is two laws that have appointed to all you creatures to-day, Now again listen at me I am going to explained to all of you creatures this one law and became is two laws that has appointed to all you creatures , These is the way that if the would became two laws, Now that I among going to tell all you creatures please do not thinking with your own minds or your own ideas, until if I has named with all you creatures , I will blessed you for ever, And than if you would do your own thinking after that, But if who one of you creatures do theirs own thinkings that whiles a gone {while a go}, It would become lost the huming being that was going to be made for you creatures, I am God that I had spoke with you all creatures on the day, all you creatures that words has to behold to not forgeted until if I came back next time, and if you do forgetting that what I have tolds you this day you creatures hat suppose to taken care of you creatures that living upon the face of the Earth, it would be huming being less you are for year with out huming being with you for years and years, Now I am gone, Good day to you all, way God he went, and the creatures did not see which way God went, and all the creatures said good day to you all of you creatures , every one said that words, way the acartared {they scattered} everywhere, in twelve months one whole

---

[107] OCHS 703610.012, formerly # GO 873.005.

year around, And then all the creatures every where just remembered all at once with their own minds Oh yes we going to meet God to-morrow at that certain place to hold a big meeting with all the other creatures and we going to have names to us all and every one so if the had their own name after this, and so that we going to have huming being to taken care us all creatures that upon the face of the Earth for ever which nevertheless and so everlasting life, And at the same time that one of the creature turned off and part from which Gods own words and he do that his own thinking with theirs own ideas, he began thought if I could get the first name on me if I would be powerful creature from all a king myself for-ever, and also that if I would be very smart from all the other creatures that live upon the face of the Earth, But that he don't know that what he got to do that if he could get the first name that he wished for it, And God known him that he was thinking with his own ideas now and would image him to let he has some more smarter, Now he began thought Oh yes its easy for me now [2]

This only his nickname Coyoty,
but his right name Infinite Life Creature

VERY BEGINNING OF THE WORLD

There was God, about to hold a Meeting among the creatures and tell them, "I am your my God. I'm God. I am going to appoint some of my own powerful laws for all you creatures to follow, to remember until I come back. Now I say to all creatures, and each of you will have names after this. I'm God, this is what I speak about, the powerful laws that I am appointing for all of you creatures. Now I say that the one who gets the first name that I am going to give away would be the most powerful creature of all the creatures upon the face of the earth.

"And when one of you creatures gets the last name left, it will be a worthless and unpowerless creature from all the other creatures living upon the face of the earth. I'm God that I have said to all of you creatures, Behold, and remember until I come back next time.

"Now I say, If and when I have names for all you creatures, then I'm going to create a human being to be in charge of all you creatures that are living upon the Earth. It will look like what I am {seen} with you creatures here to-day. And whatever he says, all you creatures just have to follow him; What{ever} he says to all you creatures that are living upon the face of the earth. Now listen to me, This is only one law that I have appointed to all you creatures today. It is two laws that have appointed to all you creatures today. Now again, listen at me, I am going to explain to all of you creatures this one law that became two laws that have been appointed to all you creatures. This is the way that it became two laws.

"Now that I'm among you I'm going to tell all you creatures, 'Please do not be thinking with your own minds or your own ideas, until after I have named all of you creatures. Then I will bless you all forever. And then you could do your own thinking after that. But if anyone of you creatures do their own thinking {all} that will be gone. All would become lost, no human being that was going to be made for you creatures. I am God that I spoke with you all creatures on the day, all you creatures that speak words have to hold fast and not forget until if I come back next time, And if you do forget what I have told you this day, you creatures that are supposed to be taken care of, that are living upon the face of the Earth, by the human being, are less{ened} for a year without the human being who will hereafter be with you for years and years. Now I am gone. Good day to you all. Away God went, and the creatures did not see which way God went, and all the creatures said Good Day to you all of you creatures." Everyone said those words, as away they scattered everywhere.

In twelve months, one whole year around, then all the creatures everywhere just remembered suddenly all at once, with their own minds, "Oh, yes, we are going to meet God tomorrow at that certain place to hold a big meeting with all the other creatures and we going to have names given to us all and everyone, so if they had their own name after this, and so that we are going to have a human being to take care of us, all creatures that live upon the face of the Earth forever, nevertheless for everlasting life.

And at that same time, one of the creatures turned off and apart from God's own words. He did his own thinking with his own ideas. He began to think if I could get the first name put on me than I would be the most powerful creature from all; a king myself forever, smartest of all the other creatures that ever lived upon the face of the Earth. But he don't know what he had to do if he could get the first name that he wished for. And God knew that he was thinking with his own ideas now and could imagine himself to be so much more smart. Now he began to think, "Oh yes it's easy for me now …

His nickname is Coyote,
his true native name translates as
Immortal
Infinite Life Creature

Appendix B

Homesteads

Willy Harry   kam'əl'ə<u>x</u>aqa'st (#87) = across Okanogan River from TB's
Mary Carden   sc'ə<u>x</u>^wc'i•x^wálx^w (#86) = between Monse & Columbia River
Syolum's   nək'nik'ptn (#69) = Big Wilson, "muddy" dugout homes below Olima, GF Christine
    Stanislas
Billy Tom   kat(ə)tə<u>x</u>^wtə^{xw} (# 3, 83) = at Pateros
Loup Loup Jim   nləq̓^wwús (# 67) = on bluff near TB's
McKinley   nc'aáłt (# 63) = Camer Lake, near Dooley Lake, towards Timentwa Flats
Millie Simons   kələłk(^w)us (# 62) = across Okanogan, 8 miles from TB's
Mackey-Cain   sƛ̓əm'aqs (# 68) = near cemetery
Lucy Walls   yar'k'^wúla'x^w (# 35) = point on east side of Okanogan River
Agnes King   klə<u>x</u>^wqín (# 53)
Julianne's mother   k'əłłál (# 47) = near TB's
Little Dick   k'^wələła•pus (# 4) = near Pateros, FF of Mary Moses

Appendix C

Fishing

Plateau waterways abounded in fish, especially the staple seasonal salmon runs (Hewes 1998). As in other activities, success derived from access to certain spirits and powers gained by quests and family heritage. Foremost among these was Salmon spirit who empowered a Salmon Tyee to manage an important fishery. The Methow River originally supported large runs of Chinook[108] and silver[109] salmon, as well as steelhead trout[110]. The neighboring Entiat and Wenatchee Rivers to the south hosted these fish, too, but the latter river also had a sizeable run of sockeye[111] salmon. To the north of Methow territory, the Okanogan River provided Chinook, steelhead and sockeye (Bryant and Zell 1950, Fulton 1968, 1970). Runs of chum[112] salmon apparently also visited this area of the Columbia in the fall (Ray 1933: 57)[113]. Humpback or pink[114] salmon, however, were not plentiful according to Ray (1933). Their historic distribution is usually confined to the lower Columbia River.

Along with these smaller rivers, the Columbia itself conveyed anadromous fish (salmon, steelhead, and lampreys) upstream for hundreds of miles and native fishers could locally partake of these migrants as well[115]. On July 6, 1811, David Thompson encountered the tribe and village of Smeathhowe on the bank of the Columbia from which he and his companions obtained "three well roasted Salmon" (Tyrell 1916).

Methows shared net and spear platforms at major sockeye salmon fisheries at Wenatchee ~ Psk^{w}aws[116] and at the mouth of the Okanogan, in addition to benefiting from local fish, such as

---

[108] Appendix C is based on Kurt Reidinger 2016 November review. *Oncorhynchus tshawytscha* (Walbaum). Fish scientific names from Wydoski and Whitney (2003), which also contains keys, descriptions, and life history information.

[109] *O kisutch* (Walbaum).

[110] *O mykiss* (Richardson).

[111] *O nerka* (Walbaum).

[112] *O keta* (Walbaum).

[113] Fisheries literature on historic salmon distribution in the Columbia typically confines chum to the lower river and its tributaries. Perhaps because Celilo Falls was a complex of falls and channels through basalt rock (Schoning and others 1951), this species could migrate upstream to the middle reaches. Salo (1991: 239) notes that chum salmon are strong swimmers but not leapers and usually reluctant to enter long-span fish ladders. By implication, species survival in the Columbia middle reaches was impacted by early ladders built at Rock Island and Bonneville dams. Some chum stocks, however, migrate long distances, such as Yukon River fall spawns in Yukon Territory (Buklis and Barton 1984).

[114] *O gorbuscha* (Walbaum).

[115] Scholz and others (1985) summarize historical references for the presence of salmon in the headwater lakes of the Columbia River in Canada. Confederated Tribes (2011) records lamprey fishing sites as far upstream as Kettle Falls.

[116] Wenatchipam Fishery was set aside in the Yakama Treaty, then sold by Yakamas – not its Psk^{w}aws Salish managers – to DC, long contested in federal court until a recent decision allows Salish Colvilles to return for a share. Its thirty-six square miles was so often

whitefish[117], Northern[118], chub[119], and other minnows[120], sturgeon[121], suckers[122], burbot[123], and lamprey[124].Crayfish[125] and mussels[126] were taken, too. A few also attended the massive fishery directed by a Salmon Tyee at Kettle Falls, where an estimated 600,000 pounds of salmon were processed in 1841 (Craig and Hacker 1940). Whether Methow also visited the important salmon fisheries at the junction of the Similkameen and Okanogan Rivers near present Oroville (Spier et. al. 1938, Bouchard and Kennedy 1984) is uncertain.

In past times, a Methow consumed more than a pound of salmon a day, suggesting that 450 pounds were dried and stored for each family member (Hewes 1998). Along the Methow, weirs, traps, nets, tridents, and spears were deployed, according to rules specifically established by Coyote for that place and time, cf commandments on p146, Lost River site p151). Weirs were built of tripods set along firm bottoms, with walkways along the top to empty traps, box or funnel, set underwater or at its surface. Everyone present shared equally in each salmon haul, even if fish had to be cut up to get enough pieces. Family spearing stations, used one at a time as each got a fish and was replaced, stood beside side channels dug along waterways, with white quartz gravels, gathered by children, spread along the bottom to aid visibility. Psk^waws used fish

---

misplaced by surveys and DC documents that one elder ironically noted "Does the Great Father in Washington think a salmon is an eagle that lives on top of a mountain, or does he think a salmon is a deer that lives in the woods and hills, or does he think a salmon is a mountain goat that lives among the rocks of the snow-covered mountains." Hart (2000) gives a detailed account of the bureaucratic and legal wrangling over this reservation.

[117] *Prosopium williamsoni* (Girard) ~ mountain whitefish are most common, but pygmy whitefish, *Prosopium coulteri* (Eigenmann and Eigenmann), occur in Lakes Chelan and Osoyoos; a Buffalo Lake population was extirpated.

[118] *Ptychocheilus oregonensis* (Richardson).

[119] Possibly lake chub ~ *Couesius plumbeus* (Agassiz); Tui chub ~ *Gila bicolor* (Girard) may have been native to lower Crab Creek.

[120] Candidates: chiselmouth ~ *Acrocheilus alutaceus* Agassiz and Pickering, peamouth ~ *Mylocheilus caurinus* (Richardson), longnose dace ~ *Rhinichthys cataractae* (Valenciennes), leopard dace ~ *Rhinichthys falcatus* (Eigenmann and Eigenmann), Umatilla dace ~ *Rhinichthys umatilla* (Gilbert and Evermann), speckled dace ~ *Rhinichthys osculus* (Girard), and redside shiner ~ *Richardsonius balteatus* (Richardson).

[121] White sturgeon ~ *Acipenser transmontanus* Richardson.

[122] Longnose sucker ~ *Catostomous catostomous* (Forster), bridgelip sucker ~ *Catostomous columbianus* (Eigenmann and Eigenmann), and largescale sucker ~ *Catostomous macrocheilus* (Girard). Possibly mountain sucker ~ *Catostomous platyrhynchus* (Cope), although this species has only been found as far north as the Wenatchee River.

[123] *Lota lota* (Linnaeus).

[124] Pacific lamprey ~ *Entosphenus tridentatus* (Gairdner) is probably most sought after but river lamprey ~ *Lampetra ayresi* (Gunther) and western brook lamprey ~ *Lampetra richardsoni* Vladykov and Follett, also inhabit the area.

[125] Probably native signal crayfish ~ *Pacifastacus leniusculus* (Washington Department of Fish and Wildlife 2016)

[126] Perhaps western pearlshell ~ *Margaritifera falcata* (Gould 1850), a long-lived species now imperiled (Helmstetler and Cowles 2008).

poison to harvest trout, and the Methow probably did too. Hook and line provided snacks and quick meals. Many lakes provided burbot (aka ling or freshwater cod) and whitefish, often by torchlight in canoes. Waterfalls, cascades, and rapids encouraged deployment of various traps, woven of willow with open mouths, recalling how Coyote brought Salmon up the Columbia, bestowing fish on each community depending on their willingness to provide a "wife" for him.

Lake Chelan with its huge waterfall testifies to their haughty denial of Coyote's request. Nelson (2012), in a review of salmonid fish introductions to the lake, noted that bull trout[127] and westslope cutthroat trout[128] were originally present in Lake Chelan. The former, a relatively large predatory fish, spawned in the Stehekin River and other tributaries, so were vulnerable to harvest on their spawning migrations as well as in the lake. Along with burbot, whitefish, suckers, and minnows, they had probably inhabited the lake since the glaciers retreated. The original fish fauna, however, has been impacted profoundly in modern times.

A more personal traditional fishing account appears in an undated letter to Mable Gavin[129] from Cecelia Julian Brooks:

Aunt Lucy and Mother Sally's uncle Soyakin, of the Methow Tribe, had a salmon trap right down on the Okanogan River … at Chillowhist Creek…. He died July 4th, 1915. Soyakin {also} had a salmon trap at the mouth of Twisp River and on the Methow River too. Later Willie Harry and his father Harry Kulpinkikin put a salmon trap at this same place … Every year they did this … In 1923 Louie Timentwa had put a salmon trap on the {Okanogan} river right down where we live now. In 1925 I married Louie Timentwa's son Alex Timentwa. That same year he put his salmon trap on the river again, by the Island. We put his salmon trap half way across the river, not clear across. That's when {August 1927} the game warden started to become strict!

Louis Timentwa, Long Jim, Billy Bob, Jack Carden went up to Sand Point and cut pine trees – not too big but just heavy enough to haul on team. They drove up on a wagon, cut them down and took them to the place to stand them in the river. They had a chance to build it just half way across the river. (This half was Reservation and the other half was the White Side.)

First they had to get three poles, tie the three together at the top with willow bark. Three or four men helped to take it into the river and stand it up – near the shore. They cleared the rocks around the pole, [5] and let it go when it stood solid! Then they placed another and another, until they had four or five poles. Then one pole is laid clear across or as far out as they build. They tied it with willow bark, not wire. Then they gathered young willow and weaved two or three rows on the butt end (of willow twigs) and stretched it on the pole that they'd laid across. Tied them on with willow bark, or

---

[127] *Salvelinus confluentus* (Suckley).

[128] *Oncorhynchus clarki lewisi* (Girard).

[129] Also: On Okanogan River ~ Long-Braids Attend Early-Day Fish Trap, *Wenatchee Daily World* 10/2/66 summarizes this letter and adds that "Chief Louie {Timentwa}, broad-shouldered leader of the fish trap and master of ceremonies" was salmon tyee. Gavin was postmistress at Malott; her own clippings file is at Okanogan Historical Society, where Barry George and Gary Mundinger date this article to 10 February 1966, noting "Mabel wrote it on 2/7/66 and submitted it 2/8/66; She died in 1967".

young willow. They put rocks on the bottom to be sure the salmon won't go through. They made a place where they could sit down two or three places, depending on how many were going out to catch fish.... Women made a net out of Indian rope {for them}. They caught the salmon in the night time, sitting there all night.

After the first night the leader of the salmon trap would cook the first catch on the camp fire, and cook it only by roasting it over the fire. They would all eat first, in ceremony. After that he would give fish away to whoever got there. I remember lots of people came to Louie's from Kartar, Omak, Nespelem. When Louie caught plenty he passed them around. I remember we built a big camp down by the river. Every one came as they pleased. One morning Louie came to the camp and said, "I have so much I don't know what to do." He told some women to help him bring the fish to shore. You see the salmon in the hatcheries. The salmon was as thick then as it is now in the hatchery. Long ago no one planted salmon in the river, they plant themselves and hatch. There seemed to be millions and millions in the streams and rivers, no one planted them then. ... They used to get forty, sometimes sixty a night! ...

The old game warden, he really gave Louie trouble the second and third year {1927}. They really fought the fourth year. They finally had to blast his trap {14 August 1925}. He tried again. The Law became very strict and so he gave up. Felt very bad. Now, they're all dead and gone.

Specific fishery-related impacts to the Methow River by American settlement are mentioned in Bryant and Parkhurst (1950). Settlers appropriated Methow lands beginning in the 19th century and introduced intensive agriculture which required copious amounts of water for the semi-arid landscape. Open unscreened water diversions lead downstream migrating juveniles to their death in irrigation ditches. The diversion dams and reduced flows also hampered upstream migration of spawning adult fish.

Despite these and other early problems, Washington State tried to offset resource decline and determined the Methow was worthy of a hatchery to propagate coho salmon (*Oncorhychus kisutch*) at the mouth of the Twisp River around 1899-1900 (Washington 1901). But the hatchery experienced difficulties with competing native weirs and fisheries, loss of juveniles to downstream diversions, and adults spawning in the river downstream before they reached the hatchery weir. Construction of a dam a short distance upstream of Pateros probably sealed the Twisp Hatchery's fate (Moses 2009). All these factors led to abandonment of the facility in favor of a newer hatchery closer to the mouth of the river at Pateros (Washington 1917). Washington State, however, completely abandoned their salmon hatchery efforts in the Methow in 1935 (Moses 2009).

Methow and other native fishers experienced difficulties in the Okanogan River as well, where for centuries they employed weirs and other techniques to capture salmon.[130] Early 20th century newspaper reports adopted a somewhat neutral tone when describing native weirs (*Okanogan Independent* 1911, *Omak Chronicle* 1915). But by the 1920's, overt hostility arose as Washington State and local officials sought to stop traditional weirs (with dynamite; *Quad City Herald* 1925, *Okanogan Independent* 1925a b), and those caught spear fishing for salmon in

---

[130] Frank Matsura photographed a rectangular fish corral walled by outward slanting interlaced poles, and maybe the weir at Twisp (Hewes 1998: 627 Figure 6 b & c), on 13 August 1911.

the Okanogan were arrested and fined (*Omak Chronicle* 1927a b). *The Okanogan Independent* reported (Tuesday 18 August 1925a):

Salmon Dam Removed by State Inspectors
Dynamite Used to Open River Above
Monse so Fish Could Proceed to Spawning Grounds

A fish dam and trap in the Okanogan river at the Timentwa allotment above Monse was partially destroyed Friday afternoon at the instance of R A Spence and J W Mack, inspectors of the state department of game and fish. Three charges of dynamite were placed by T J Murray to open the center portion of the dam and permit the passage of salmon and other fish to spawn in the waters of the upper Okanogan.

The dam had been constructed by the Indians at considerable expenditure of time and money. It was about 175 feet long. Tripods of pine poles were placed about a rod apart in the river and connected with horizontal bars. The dam was built with a down river slope, so that fish would find themselves under a roof and not be tempted to jump the dam.

Woven wire netting was placed across the pole framework. Reeds and willow switches were used to weave long mats, which were put in place over the wire netting and the passage of fish {w}as effectively prevented.

The state inspectors, with Sheriff Eli Wilson and Prosecuting Attorney O'Connor, made a trip to the dam Friday morning and held a parley with the Indians, headed by Long Jim. Ed Walsh acted as interpreter.

The Indians declined to remove the dam, apparently determined that they would force the inspectors to take such actions as they desired and report the matter to the Indian department at Washington. Friday afternoon a second trip was made with dynamite.

So securely had the dam been built and anchored that it would have required a score of shots to completely remove it, and the officials satisfied themselves with making a substantial opening in the stream.

The Indian interpreter, loathe to witness the destruction of the dam, voiced his disapproval of the white man's laws. Who had put the fish in the river in the first place, he inquired, and asserted that the Indians had three dams across the river to catch salmon before the coming of the whites. Capt Spence replied that in early days there were plenty of fish and game for all, but as the number of people increased it became necessary to make laws to protect them so that all would not be destroyed.

Walsh, Big Wilson and other Indians, after talking the situation over in a friendly manner with the officers, retired to the east {reservation} bank of the river and watched the destruction of the dam. It was an impressive sight when each shot hurled water and debris sixty feet or more in the air and the wind carried the spray for {far} down stream.

The Indians had three smoke houses and had gathered a large number of salmon. It was reported that 175 were taken one night.

The Okanogan River originates in British Columbia (spelled Okanagan there), flowing from Okanagan, Skaha, and Vaseux Lakes to Lake Osoyoos on the US-Canada border. Anadromous fish reportedly used the watershed up through Okanagan Lake prior to European arrival (COSEWIC 2006). Beginning in the early 20th century, dam building and habitat degradation (e.g., channelization) has helped diminish the quality and quantity of fish habitat (Symonds 2000, Walsh and Long 2005). Consequently the anadromous runs originating in this part of the watershed and available to Methows and other native fishers farther downstream have also been reduced. The impacts to Chinook have been so severe that the population (the only remnant Columbia River Chinook run in Canada) has been designated as *Threatened*, and could be listed under the Canadian *Species At Risk Act* (SARA; COSEWIC 2006, CDFO 2009).

Undoubtedly, impacts to native fishing were not only confined to the Methow and Okanogan; as local natives also fished the nearby Columbia River with anadromous runs spawning locally and upstream. The upstream fishery resource was largely destroyed by Grand Coulee, Chief Joseph, Spokane River, and Canadian hydroelectric projects. There was an attempt to mitigate the destruction of upstream fish stocks just before completion of the Grand Coulee project by trapping fish at Rock Island Dam and attempting to re-establish runs through adult transfers to various river along with hatchery programs in the Wenatchee, Entiat, and Methow Rivers. A fourth hatchery in the Okanogan River system was never built due to lack of a suitable location. The Winthrop National Fish Hatchery was located on the Methow River about 45 miles upstream from the Columbia and raised spring and fall steelhead, spring and summer Chinook, sockeye salmon, and small numbers of coho salmon (Fish and Hanavan 1948). Sockeye typically require a lake environment to be successful and this part of the program was eventually discontinued as there is not a suitable lake in the Methow drainage. But a consequence of this project was the creation of a small, but persistent sockeye run that spawns in the Methow to this day (NOAA 1997).

Scholz and others (1985) estimate the magnitude of these upriver dam-related losses, but the total losses reported in their study might be unreliable because they can't accurately estimate impacts caused by the offshore fisheries in both the U.S. and Canada (e.g., troll fisheries in SE Alaska and coastal British Columbia) that harvested Upper Columbia River fish. Results of juvenile tagging studies with remnant Columbia River Chinook stocks in later years reveal such far distant migration patterns. Offshore fisheries have been exploiting Columbia River fish for quite some time, starting in the early 1900's when trolling first expand along the Pacific Coast (Damron 1975). These offshore fisheries, along with lower river net and trap fisheries, surely diminished the salmon supply to the Methows and other native upstream fishers.

Finally, Wells Dam, located on the Columbia River a few miles downstream of the Methow was completed by Douglas County PUD in 1967. In addition to providing another hurdle for both upstream and downstream migrating fish, it likely flooded the village sites of the Smeathhowe tribe who greeted David Thompson in 1811, and further diminished mainstem riverine spawning areas. Douglas County PUD has funded a hatchery program for spring Chinook and summer steelhead in the Methow basin as part of its mitigation responsibilities connected with the Wells Dam project. Hatcheries and acclimation ponds are mainly operated by the Washington Department of Fish and Wildlife.

Among positive developments, Colville Confederated Tribes recently completed (2013) Chief Joseph Hatchery on the main Columbia, one of four mitigation hatcheries for the Grand Coulee Project (with Leavenworth, Entiat, and Winthrop). Their hatchery program is designed to produce spring and summer/fall Chinook. The CCT has an active Fish and Wildlife program also engaged in extensive monitoring and acquisition of sensitive properties to protect habitat. In a somewhat ironic reversal of earlier restrictions on fishing weirs, they installed a modern resistance board weir, reminiscent of earlier native ones, across the Okanogan River near the town of Malott. This allows them to catch upstream bound salmon for use as broodstock in their hatchery program. Selective net fishing (i.e., retaining only sockeye and hatchery Chinook) at the mouth of the Okanogan River was revived in 2014 (CCT 2014, Mapes 2014).

The Yakama Nation has long-term plan to re-establish coho salmon runs in mid-Columbia tributaries, including the Methow and Wenatchee Rivers. They are also attempting to enhance habitat in the Twisp River for existing populations of Chinook, steelhead, and bull trout as well as removing invasive brook trout (*Salvelinus fontinalis*).

A consortium of US and Canadian tribes, called Upper Columbia United Tribes and author of *Fish Passage and Reintroduction into the US and Canadian Upper Columbia Basin*, lobbies for restoring anadromous fish runs above Chief Joseph Dam, where Colvilles doggedly maintain a TCP tribal fishery. Federal agencies responsible for running 14 dams through the Columbia River System Operations announced in 2016 that they are preparing a NEPA EIS (as a result of the Court's rejection of the NOAA 2014 BiOp). Whether these efforts turn out beneficial to native fishers and aquatic resources remains to be seen.

Appendix D

Engendered Leadership

Mary Carden noted that all four bands of the Sinkaietk, as well as the Methow and Chelan tribes, have chieftainesses (skū'malt, woman of great authority),[131] who serve in an advisory capacity (Spier 1938: 95-96). A chieftainess is officially elected. She receives formal appointment at a council meeting just as the chief does. Apparently this office is hereditary through the male line; these women are always related to the chief, and at death, the office passes to another female relative {niece, cousin}, and in no recorded case from mother to daughter, suggesting a node of sibling~cousins as the basis of allied male and female leadership in each succeeding generation.

Apparently, the status of such women varied in the several bands. In the Tukoratum band, whereas the chief served as the group manager, the woman skū'malt was a consulting adviser only in cases of murder, revenge or emergencies. If her decision differed from that of the chief, the people were free to follow either. Amity might be advised but could not be enforced. CB Suszen Timentwa, who has lived among Konkonelp and Kartar people, pictures these women chieftainesses as {female} group managers, serving as sole chief of the band from their appointment to office until death. It is doubtful if this was ever the case in either band; for the male hereditary chiefs are remembered for five generations back in both bands, and contemporary women skū'malt are recorded for the Konkonelp band. Kartar informants declare that women never had a voice in council and that there were no women chieftainesses. In consideration of their close social affiliation with the Nespelem tribe, this is intelligible, since the Nespelem never vested authority in women, except for Karneecher ~ Eller Runnels.

Such recognition among the Sinkaietk of the equality of women was noted historically. Ross Cox, at the beginning of the nineteenth century, comments upon the independence of the women of the lower Columbia, "where their exertions in collecting Wappitoo {wapato} roots" gave an "air of liberty and independence … unknown among the upper natives" such as Kutenai, Flathead, Spokan, though "elder women, equally with the men, are consulted".

The skū'malt had chief-like qualities such as being "good, intelligent, sagacious, and liberal … better dressed than any other woman of the band, and always wears a shell through her pierced septum, a sign of wealth" (Spier 1938: 96)

As much as possible, and much more than typical, Plateau genders were balanced. Hence, though men labored to build and maintain a weir, the 1¼ inch wide bindings that held its tripods together were provided by women, who closely guarded the nature of their raw material and sources (Ackerman 203: 71). Since it was likely willow bark, and willows were deliberately transplanted and nurtured, women probably managed special stands of willow for this purpose.

The greatest chief of the Lakes was a woman, identified as Gregory's mother, followed by Gregory, his cousin *arpaxən* ~ Orpahken ~ Arapaghan, then James Bernard, also a tribal policeman (Ray 2016: 154, Miller 1990: 235).

---

[131] Proper spelling is sk̓ʷúmalt, with thanks to Tony Mattina by email 11/27/16.

Bibliography

Ackerman, Lillian 2003 *A Necessary Balance ~ Gender and Power among Indians of the Columbia Plateau.* Norman: University of Oklahoma Press.

Alford, Thomas Wildcat 1979 *Civilization and the Story of the Absentee Shawnees.* Norman: University of Oklahoma Press. [1936]

Anastasio, Angelo 1972 The Southern Plateau ~ An Ecological Analysis of Intergroup Relations. *Northwest Anthropological Research Notes* 6 (2): 109-229.

Beavert, Virginia, and Sharon Hargus 2009 *Ichishkiin Sinwit ~ Yakama / Yakima ~ Sahaptin Dictionary.* Seattle: University of Washington Press.

Boas, Franz, ed. 1917 Folk-Tales of Salishan and Sahaptian Tribes. *American Folklore Society, Memoirs* 11: 1-201.

Borg, Chuck 2015 *First on the Land ~* The Native Americans and their land in the Middle Columbia and Lower Methow Valley region following the arrival of white settlers.

Bouchard, Randy, and Dorothy Kennedy 1984 Indian history and knowledge of the Lower Similkameen River – Palmer Lake Area. Victoria, British Columbia: British Columbia Indian Language Project.

Bower, John Wenatchipam Fishery Documents. Olympia.

Boyd, Robert, ed 1999 *Indians, Fire, and the Land in the Pacific Northwest.* Corvallis: Oregon State University Press.

Brunton, Bill 1968 Ceremonial Integration in the Plateau of Northwestern North America. *Northwest Anthropological Research Notes* 2 (1): 1-28.

Bryant, F.G. and Z.E. Parkhurst 1950 Survey of the Columbia River and its Tributaries - Part IV. Special Scientific Report: *Fisheries* # 37. US Department of the Interior, Fish and Wildlife Service.

Buklis, LS and LH Barton 1984 Yukon River fall chum biology and stock status. Juneau, AK: Alaska Dept of Fish and Game Informational Leaflet # 239.

Butler, B Robert 1978 Bison Hunting in the Desert West Before 1800: The Paleo-Ecological Potential & the Archaeological Reality. *Plains Anthropologist* 23-82, part 2: 106-112.

Byrd, Robert 1992 *Lake Chelan in the 1890s ~ Steamboats, Prospectors, and Sightseers. Stories of Lake Chelan and Stehekan Valley.* Wenatchee: Bird Song. [1972]

Cain, H Thomas 1950 Petroglyphs of Central Washington. Seattle: University of Washington

Press.

CDFO 2009 Potential socio-economic implications of listing Okanagan Chinook under the Species At Risk Act. Fisheries and Oceans Canada, Policy & Economic Analysis Branch, Pacific Region.

Chance, David, Jennifer Chance, and John Fagan 1977 *Kettle Falls: 1972*. University of Idaho: Laboratory of Anthropology, Manuscript Series 31.

Chance, David 1973 Influences of the Hudson's Bay Company on the Native Cultures of the Colvile District. *Northwest Anthropological Research Notes*, Memoir 2.
1986 *People of the Falls*. Colville, WA: Kettle Falls Historical Center.

Chicago Anthropology Exchange 1981 Native American Lands. Special Double Issue 14 (1-2): 1-218.

Collins, Mary B, and Shannon Tushingham 2014 Exploring the Future of Archaeology on the Plateau. The 2014 Washington State University Museum of Anthropology Plateau Conference. The SAA *Archaeological Record* November 2014: 30.

Columbia Basin Tribes and First Nations 2015 *Fish Passage and Reintroduction into the US and Canadian Upper Columbia Basin*. Spokane: Upper Columbia United Tribes.

CCT Colville Confederated Tribes 2011 Native American Place Name Along the Columbia River Above Grand Coulee Dam, North Central Washington and Traditional Cultural Property Overview Report for the Confederated Tribes of the Colville Reservation. Confederated Tribes of the Colville Reservation History/Archaeology Program. Bonneville Power Administration Contract # 35238.

2014 Fish & Wildlife Report (online document).

COSEWIC 2006 COSEWIC assessment and status report on the chinook salmon *Oncorhynchus tshawytscha* (Okanagan population) in Canada. Committee on the Status of Endangered Wildlife in Canada. Ottawa. vii + 41 pp. (www.sararegistry.gc.ca/status/status_e.cfm).

Craig, JA and RL Hacker 1940 The history and development of the fisheries of the Columbia River. US Fishery Bulletin 49 (32): 133-216.

Curtis, Edward 1911 The Yakima, The Klickitat, Salishan Tribes of the Interior, and the Kutenai. *The North American Indian*, Volume 7.

Damron, J E 1975 The emergence of salmon trolling on the American northwest coast: a maritime historical geography. Eugene: University of Oregon, PhD Thesis.

Devin, Doug 2008 *Mazama* ~ The Past 125 Years. Winthrop: Shafer Historical Museum.

Dibble, Dale Methow Valley Pioneers. Naples, Fla.

Doak, Ivy   1983   The 1908 Okanogan Word Lists of James Teit.   University of Montana, *Occasional Papers in Linguistics* 3.

Elmendorf, William   1951   System Change in Salish Kinship Terminologies. *Southwest Journal of Anthropology* 17 (4): 355-82.

1955 Linguistic and Geographical Relations in the Northern Plateau. *Southwest Journal of Anthropology* 21 (1): 53-78.

Featherston, Debra 1993 Pictographs of the Methow Valley. Passport in Time Field Study.

Fenton, William   1953   The Iroquois Eagle Dance ~ An Offshoot Of The Calumet Dance. Bureau of American Ethnology, *Bulletin* 156: 1-222.

Fish, FF and MG Hanavan   1948   A report upon the Grand Coulee fish maintenance project 1939-1947. US Fish and Wildlife Service, Special Scientific Report # 55.

Fulkerson, AC 1988 Predictive Locational Modeling of Aboriginal Sites in the Methow River Area: Deductive and Inductive Approaches. Pullman: WSU Anthropology MA.

Fulton, LA   1968   Spawning areas and abundance of Chinook salmon (*Oncorhynchus tshawytscha*) in the Columbia River Basin - past and present. US Fish and Wildlife Service, Special Scientific Report # 571.

Gibbs, George   1855   Indian Tribes of Washington Territory. *Reports of Explorations and Surveys* to Ascertain the Most Practical and Economic Route for a Railroad from the Mississippi River to the Pacific Ocean. Senate Executive Document 78: 400-449 in volume I, 33rd Congress, 2nd Session. {also Miller 2015a}

Galbreath, P.F., M.A. Bisbee Jr., D.W. Dompier, C.M. Kamphaus, and T.H. Newsome.
2014 Extirpation and Tribal Reintroduction of Coho Salmon to the Interior Columbia River Basin. Fisheries 39 (2): 77-87.

Gidley, Mick 1979 *With One Sky Above Us*: Life on an Indian Reservation at the Turn of the Century. NY: GP Putnam's Sons.

Goldman, Irving 1941 The Alkatcho Carrier: Historical Background of Crest Prerogatives. *American Anthropologist* 43: 396-418.

Gould, Marian 1917 Okanogan Tales and Sanpoil Tales, Boas 1917: 98-100, 101-113.

Gunther, Erna   1928   A Further Analysis of the First Salmon Ceremony.   University of Washington *Publications in Anthropology* 2 (5): 129-173.

Grant, Campbell 1967 *Rock Art of the American Indian*. New York: Promontory Press.

Hart, Richard 2000 The history of the Wenatchi Fishing Reservation. Western Legal History 13 (2): 163-200.

2008 CB Suzen Timentwa. *Okanogan County Heritage* Winter: 7-9.

The History of the Wenatchi Fishing Reservation. *Western Legal History* 13 (2): 163-200.

Heizer, Robert, and Martin Baumhoff 1962 *Prehistoric Rock Art of Nevada and Eastern California.* Berkeley: University of California Press.

Helmstetler, H, and DL Cowles 2008 Population characteristics of native freshwater mussels in the mid-Columbia and Clearwater Rivers, Washington state. Northwest Science 82 (3): 211-221.

Hewes, Gordon 1998 Fishing: 620-640. Handbook of North American Indians. William Sturtevant and Deward Walker, eds. Volume 12: *Plateau.* DC: Smithsonian Institution.

Hodge, Frederick 1907 Handbook of American Indians North of Mexico. DC: Bureau of American Ethnology, Bulletin 30 Part I.

1910 Handbook of American Indians North of Mexico. DC: Bureau of American Ethnology, Bulletin 30 Part II.

Keyser, James 1992 *Indian rock Art of the Columbia Plateau.* Seattle: University of Washington Press.

Kingston, C S 1932 Buffalo in the Pacific Northwest. *The Washington Historical Quarterly* 23 (3): 163-172.

Kinkade, M Dale 1967 On the Identification of the Methows (Salish). *International Journal of American Linguistics* 33 (3): 193-197.

Kinkade, M Dale, compiler 1981 Dictionary of the Moses-Columbia Language. Nespelem, WA: Colville Confederated Tribes.

Layman, William 1998 Drawing with Vision. *Columbia* 12 (1): 23-32.
2002 *Native River ~ The Columbia Remembered, Priest Rapids to the International Boundary.* Pullman: WSU press.

2006 *River of Memory ~ The Everlasting Columbia.* Seattle: UW Press.

Levi-Strauss, Claude 1962 *Totemism.* Boston: Beacon Press.

1966 *The Savage Mind.* University of Chicago Press.

Long, Albert 2001 Under the Guard of Ole Tyee ~ A Reflection of the Early Days in the Entiat Valley. Wenatchee.

Mallory, Garrick 1972 *Picture-Writing of the American Indians.* Dover [BAE AR 10 1893]

Mapes, Lynda 2014 <u>On Columbia, 'just add water' seems to be working</u>. *Seattle Times* 4 Aug.

Mattina, Anthony 1973 Colville Grammatical Structure. University of Hawaii, PhD Dissertation.

    1985 *The Golden Woman*: The Colville Narrative of Peter J Seymour. University of Arizona Press.

    1987 Colville-Okanoagan Dictionary. *University of Montana Occasional Papers in Linguistics* 5.

Miller, Jay 1977> Colville Interior Salishan Fieldnotes. In possession of author.

    1979 Delaware Language and Culture: 23-31. *Papers of the 1978 Mid-America Linguistic Conference*. Ralph Cooley and others, eds. Norman: University of Ok1ahom Press.

    1980 High Minded High Gods In Native North America. *Anthropos* 75: 916-919.

    1981a Go With The F1ow: Prehistoric Delaware Divisions in the Light of the Riverine Adaptation of the Middle Columbia Salishans. University of Oklahoma Anthropology Department Colloquium. March 27.

    1981b Tsimshian Moieties and Other Clarifications. *Northwest Anthropological Research Notes (NARN)* 16 (2): 148-164.

    1985 Salish Kinship: Why Decedence? Proceedings of the 20th International Conference on Salish and Neighboring Languages. August 15-17. Vancouver, BC.

    1989 Mourning Dove ~ The Author as Cultural Mediator: 160-82. *Being and Becoming Indian*: Biographical Studies of North American Frontiers. James Clifton, ed. Chicago: Dorsey Press.

    1998 Middle Columbia River Salishans: 253-270. Handbook of North American Indians. William Sturtevant and Deward Walker, eds. Volume 12: *Plateau*. DC: Smithsonian.

    2015 Another Plateau for Totemism: 240-245. *Pacific Plateau Portrayals ~ People, Places, Ponderings*. Amazon.

Miller, Jay, ed. 1990 *Mourning Dove* ~ A Salishan Autobiography. Lincoln: University of Nebraska Press.

    2015a *George Gibbs Northwest Array* ~ Full Reports, Place Names, Word List, Artifact Names, and Guide. Amazon.

    2015b *Pacific Plateau Portrayals* ~ People, Places, Ponderings. Amazon.

Mooney, James 1896 The Ghost Dance Religion and the Sioux Outbreak of 1890. DC: Bureau of American Ethnology, *Annual Report* 14: 641-1136.

Moses, P 2009 Okanogan County's fish hatcheries. *Okanogan County Heritage*, Spring: 9-13.

Moulton, Gary 1983+ *Journals of Lewis and Clark*. Lincoln: University of Nebraska Press.

Nelson, Charles M 1969 The Sunset Creek Site (45KT28) and Its Place in Plateau Prehistory. Washington State University: Laboratory of Anthropology, Report of Investigations 47.

1973 Prehistoric Culture Change in the Intermontane Plateau of Western North America: 371-90. *Explanations of Culture Change*: Models in Prehistory. Colin Renfrew, ed. London: Gerald Duckworth.

2015 http://www.chaz.org/Arch/45KT28/The_Sunset_Creek_Site.html

NOAA 1997 Status review of sockeye salmon from Washington and Oregon. NOAA Technical Memorandum NMFS-NWFSC-33.

OBrien, Michael 1966 Methow Dictionary.

Omak Chronicle 1915 Tersely Told Town Topics [re: large Indian salmon trap] 8 Sept 1915.
    1927a Oroville Indian Fined for spearing salmon 25 Aug.
    1927b Local people fined for spearing salmon 22 Sept.

Okanogan Independent 1911 Local and Personal [reporting Frank Matsura took photos of the Indian fish trap in the Okanogan River near the mouth of Chilliwist Creek] and Down at Mallot [describes traditional weir construction techniques] 18 Aug.

1925a Remove Indian fish dam below Wakefield: State deputy supervisors act to prevent curtailment of spawning run of salmon. Okanogan, Washington 15 Aug.

1925b Salmon dam removed by state inspectors: dynamite used to open river above Monse so fish could proceed to spawning grounds. Okanogan, Washington 18 Aug.

Portman, Sally 1993 *The Smiling Country ~ A History of the Methow Valley*. Winthrop, WA: Sun Mountain Resorts.

Powers, William 1975 *Oglala Religion*. Lincoln: University of Nebraska Press.

1984 *Yuwipi*: Vision and Experience in Oglala Ritual. Lincoln: University of Nebraska

Quad City Herald 1925 Inspect fish here. Brewster, Washington 14 Aug.

Rauffer, Sr Maria Ilma 1966 *Black Robes and Indians on the Last Frontier*. Milwaukee: Bruce Publishing.

Ray, Verne 1932. The Sanpoil and Nespelem ~ Salishan Peoples of Northeastern Washington. *University of Washington Publications in Anthropology* 5: 1-237.

1933 Sanpoil Folktales. *Journal of American Folklore* 46: 129-87.

1936a Native Villages and Groupings of the Columbia Basin. *Pacific Northwest Quarterly* 27: 99-152.

1936b The Kolaskin Cult: A Prophet Movement of 1870 in Northeastern Washington. *American Anthropologist* 38 (1): 67-75.

1939 *Cultural Relations in the Plateau of Northwestern America.* Publications of the Frederick Webb Hodge Anniversary Publication Fund 3. Los Angeles: Southwest Museum.

1941 Historic Backgrounds of the Conjuring Complex in the Plateau and the Plains: 204-216. *Language, Culture, and Personality.* Leslie Spier, A Irving Hallowell, and Stanley Newman, eds. Mensha, WI: Sapir Memorial Publication Fund.

1942 Culture Element Distributions: XXII Plateau. *Anthropological Records* 8 (2): 99-262.

1960 The Columbia Indian Confederacy: A League of Central Plateau Tribes: 177-89. *Culture in History*: Essays in Honor of Paul Radin. Stanley Diamond, ed. NY: Columbia University Press for Brandeis University.

2016 Aboriginal Economy and Polity of the Lakes (Senijextee) Indians. *Journal of Northwest Anthropology (JONA)* 50 (2): 145-166. 1947 draft, endnote by Madilane Perry.

Reichwein, Jeffrey 1990 Emergence of Native American Nationalism in the Columbia Plateau. The Evolution of North American Indians Series. Garland Publishing.

Ross, John Alan 2011 *The Spokan Indians.* Spokane: Michael J. Ross.

Ruby, Robert, and John Brown 1965 *Half-Sun on the Columbia*: A Biography of Chief Moses University of Oklahoma Press.

Salo, EO 1991 Life history of chum salmon (*Oncorhynchus keta*) in C Groot and L Margolis, eds. Pacific Salmon Life Histories. Vancouver: UBC Press.

Scheuerman, Richard, ed. 1982. *The Wenatchi Indians*: Guardians of the Valley. Fairfield, WA: Ye Galleon Press.

Scholz, A, K O'Laughlin, D Geist, J Uehara, D Peone, L Fields, T Kleist, I Zozaya, T Peone, and K Teesatuskie 1985 Compilation of Information on Salmon and Steelhead Total Run Size, Catch and Hydropower Related Losses in the Upper Columbia River Basin, Above Grand Coulee Dam. Eastern Washington University, Cheney: Upper Columbia United Tribes Fisheries *Technical Report #2.* .

Schoning, RW, TR Merrill, Jr, and DR Johnson 1951 The Indian Dip Net Fishery at Celilo Falls on the Columbia River. Portland: Oregon Fish Commission, Contribution # 17.

Schulting, Rick 1995 Mortuary Variability and Status Differentiation on the Columbia-Fraser Plateau. Simon Fraser University: Archaeology Press.

Schultz, John 1971 Acculturation and Religion on the Colville Indian Reservation. Washington State University, PhD Dissertation.

Slocum, Robert, and Kenneth Matsen 1968 *Shoto Clay* ~ Figurines and Forms from the Lower Columbia. Portland.

Speck, Frank   1917   Game Totems Among The Northeastern Algonkians. *American Anthropologist* 19 (1): 9-18.

Spier, Leslie 1936 Tribal Distribution in Washington. *General Series in Anthropology* 3.

Spier, Leslie, ed. 1938 The Sinkaietk or Southern Okanogan. *General Series in Anthropology* 6. with Walter Cline, Rachel S Commons, May Mandelbaum, Richard H Post, and Lucy Velpha Walters.

Sprague, Roderick 1998 Palouse: 352-359. Handbook of North American Indians. William Sturtevant and Deward Walker, eds. Volume 12: *Plateau.* DC: Smithsonian.

Stamper, Marcy 2006 High Hopes and Deep Snows ~ How Mining Spirred Development of the Methow Valley. Winthrop: Shafer Museum.

Stenger, Alison 2009 *A Vanished People ~ The Lake River Ceramic Makers.* Portland.

Swanson, Earl   1958   Archaeological Survey of the Methow Valley, Washington. NPS & *Washington Archaeological Society* 3 (1): 1, 1959; *Tebiwa* 2 (1): 72-82, 1958-9.

Symonds, BJ 2000 Background and History of Water Management of Okanagan Lake and River. Penticton, BC: Ministry of Environment, Lands and Parks.

Tanner, Adrian 1979 *Bringing Home Animals ~ Religious Ideology and Mode of Production of the Mistassini Cree Hunters.* London: C Hurst and Co.

Tantaquidgeon, Gladys 1973 Mohegan Persistence. Uncasville, CT.

Teit, James 1896 A Rock Painting of the Thompson River Indians, British Columbia. Edited, from Notes of the Collector James Teit, by Franz Boas. Bulletin American Museum of Natural History, Volume VIII: 227-30.

   1909 The Shuswap. American Museum of Natural History, Anthropological Papers, *Memoir* 4: 447-758.

   1928   The Middle Columbia Salish.   *University of Washington Publications in Anthropology* 2 (4): 83-128.

   1930 The Salishan Tribes of the Western Plateaus [Okanagan, Flathead, Coeur d'Alene]. Franz Boas, ed. BAE Annual Report 45 for 1927-28: 23-396.

   1930a Tattooing and Face and Body Painting of the Thompson River Indians of British Columbia. Franz Boas, ed. BAE Annual Report 45 for 1927-28: 397-440.

Theodoratus, Robert   1994   Shamanism in the Columbia-Fraser Plateau Region: 211-225. *Ancient Traditions ~ Shamanism in Central Asia and the Americas.* Gary Seaman and Jane Day, eds. Niwot: University Press of Colorado for Denver Museum of Natural History.

Thompson, Judy 2007 *Recording Their Story ~ James Teit and the Tahltan.* Vancouver: Douglas & McIntyre for Canadian Museum of Civilizations

Tobin, JH 1994 Construction and performance of a portable resistance board weir for counting migrating adult salmon in rivers. US Fish and Wildlife Service, Kenai Fishery Resource Office, Alaska Fisheries Technical Report # 22.

Turner, Nancy, Randy Bouchard, and Dorothy ID Kennedy 1980 *Ethnobotany of the Okanagan-Colville Indians of British Columbia and Washington.* Victoria, BC: British Columbia Provincial Museum.

Turner, Mark, and Ellen Kuhlmann 2014 Trees and shrubs of the Pacific Northwest. Portland: Timber Press.

Turney-High, Harry Holbert 1941 *Ethnography of the Kutenai.* Memoirs of the American Anthropological Association 56.

Tyrrell, JB, ed. 1916 *David Thompson's narrative of his explorations in western America, 1784-1812.* Toronto: The Champlain Society.

Ursin, Michael 1977 *A Guide To Fishes Of The Temperate Atlantic Coast.* New York: EP Dutton.

Van Vuren, D 1987 Bison West of the Rocky Mountains: An Alternative Explanation. *Northwest Science* 61 (2): 65-69.

Viola, Herman, and Carolyn Margolis 1985 *Magnificent Voyagers ~ The US Exploring Expedition, 1838-1842.* Smithsonian Institution Press.

Visalli, Dana 2000 The First People. *Methow Naturalist* 5 (4) Winter.

Walker, Deward 1998 Introduction: 1-7. Handbook of North American Indians. William Sturtevant and Deward Walker, eds. Volume 12: *Plateau.* DC: Smithsonian.

Walsh, M and K Long 2005 Survey of barriers to anadromous fish migration in the Canadian Okanagan sub basin. Westbank, BC: Okanagan Nation Alliance Fisheries Department.

Washington 1901 Tenth and eleventh annual reports of the State Fish Commissioner and Game Warden to the Governor of the State of Washington. AC Little, Commissioner and Warden, Tacoma 1899-1900. Olympia, WA.

Washington 1917 Twenty sixth and twenty seventh annual reports of the State Fish Commissioner and Game Warden to the Governor of the State of Washington. 1 April 1915 to 31 March 1917. Olympia, WA: AC Little, Commissioner and Warden.

Wherry, James   1979   Eastern Algonquian Relationships To "Proto-Algonquian" Social Organization. Halifax: Saint Mary's University, Occasional Papers in Anthropology 5.

Wilkes, Charles 1844 *Narrative of the United States Exploring Expedition During the Years 1838, 1839, 1840,1841, 1842.* 5 volumes. Philadelphia: C Sherman. [1845 IV: 433-45, 441-474 Lea and Blanchard.]

Williams, Judith 2001 *Two Wolves at the Dawn of Time ~ Kingcome Inlet Pictographs* 1893-1998. Vancouver: New Star Books.

Witherspoon, Gary 1977 *Language and Art in the Navajo Universe.* Ann Arbor: University of Michigan Press.

Wydoski, RS and RR Whitney   2003   *Inland fishes of Washington.* 2nd ed Bethesda, MD: American Fisheries Society.

Yanan, Eileen, ed 1971 Coyote and the Colville. Omak, WA: St. Marys Mission.

Young, M Jane 1988 *Signs from the Ancestors ~ Zuni Cultural Symbolism and Perceptions of Rock Art.* Albuquerque: University of New Mexico Press.

York, Annie, Richard Daly, and Chris Arnett   1993   *They Write Their Dreams on the Rock Forever: Rock Writings of the Stein River Valley of British Columbia.* BC: Talonbooks.

Index

#f = item on scattered pages before and after number
#0 = item scattered over ten pages after this decade number: 10 20 30 etc

Work in Progress

Forty Years On

Help banish typo-gnomes

Corrections Welcome

ACCULTURATING AMELIA ~ Round Valley 1937 California
ALASKA EDGE ISLAND ~ Siberian Yupiks of St Lawrence Island
ALLIED MOUNDS ~ Touching the Earth, Modeling the World, Reaching the Sky
ANIMAL PEOPLE ADVENTURES ~ Native North American Tribal Stories
AT BAY ~ Cultures Converging through Southwest Washington   > 5
BALLARD BULWARK ~
CHACO ECHOES ~ Pervasive Keresan Priesthoods
CHACOKIA ~ Chaco, Cahokia, Cities & Ceremonies ~ Bundles & Blood Lines Centuries Ago
CHINOOK CONCERNS ~ Emma Millett Luscier, Isabella Bertrand, Verne Ray
CIRCLING FOUR CORNERS ~ Re-Viewing Native American Indiens   > 10
CROSSING ~ LINES: An Educational Memoir of Native North America
DEL-AWARE ~ Lenape Legacies
DELAWARE INTEGRITY ~ Rituals, Removals, Reforms by Lenape Indiens
DISCLAIMING TREATIES I ~ Puget Tribes 1927 Testimonies
DISCLAIMING TREATIES II ~ Puget Tribes 1927 Testimonies   > 15
ELDERS' DIALOG ~ Ed Davis & Vi Hilbert Discuss Native Puget Sound Language, Culture, & Heritage
EVERGREEN ETHNOGRAPHIES ~ Hoh, Chehalis, Suquamish, and Snoqualmi of Western Washington
FEDERAL FISH FILES ~ Swindell 1942 Treaty Rights Report
GEORGE GIBBS NORTHWEST ARRAY ~ Full Reports, Place Names, Word List, Artifact Names, and Guide
GRASSROOTS JANET ~ Advancing Salish and Traditional Cultures   > 20
HERMAN HAEBERLIN REGAINED ~ Anthropology and Artifacts of Puget Sound 1916-17
HERSTORY NW ~ Women Upholding Native Traditions
INDIEN ~ ETHNOGRAPHY: Cultural Traditions of Native North America
INDIEN ~ ETHNOLOGY: Grounded, Gendered, Meaningful Cultural Traditions
LESCHI IN LOVE ~ A Novel of Native Puget Sound > x2   > 25
MARCO MUCK MASKS ~ Frank Cushing on Marshes and Mounds
MINTER BAY ~ Land, Lore, Loss, and Lucre in the South Salish Sea
NATIVE MET HOW ~ Improving Posterity
OLD LUKH ~ A Novel of Native Puget Sound Daily Life, Places, and Stories
OVER THE FALLS ~ Sdoqwalbixw Survivance Surrounding Seattle   > 30
PACIFIC PLATEAU PORTRAYALS ~ People Places Ponderings
RAY'S ARRAY ~ Raymond D Fogelson's Works
RIGHTING NATIVE PLACES ~ Adventures in Northwest Geography
SAHAPTINS STUDIES ~ Columbia River Plateau, Cora Du Bois, Homer Garner Barnett, Gerald Raymond Desmond
SDOQWALBIXW   > 35
SOUND SALISH STRAITS ~ Central Salish Sea Cultures
UNSETTLING SEATTLE ~ Arresting Local Talent and Academic Illiteracy
WRITING WORDS IN WARY WORLDS ~ World Wide Improved Spellings of Native America Languages

JONA Memoirs

RESCUES, RANTS, & RESEARCHES ~ A Re-View of Jay Miller's Writings on Northwest Indien Cultures ~ #9
TRIBAL TRIO of the Northwest Coast by Kenneth D Tollefson ~ #10   > 40
INTERWEAVING COAST SALISH CULTURAL SYSTEMS ~ Collected Works of Pamela Thorsen Amoss ~ #14

University of Nebraska Press

ANCESTRAL MOUNDS ~ Vitality and Volatility Crossing Native North America 2015
HONNE ~ The Spirit of the Chehalis 2015